IN THE WYOMING SPRUCE WOODS.

KNOCKING

ROUND THE ROCKIES

BY

ERNEST INGERSOLL

Illustrated

NEW YORK

HARPER & BROTHERS, PUBLISHERS

1883

Entered according to Act of Congress, in the year 1882, by

HARPER & BROTHERS,

In the Office of the Librarian of Congress, at Washington.

———

LIST OF ILLUSTRATIONS.

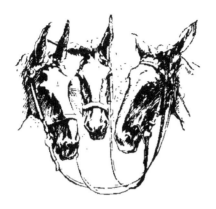

KNOCKING 'ROUND THE ROCKIES.

I.

IT was my good fortune, in 1874, to become attached to the United States Geological and Geographical Survey of the Territories, through the invitation of its chief. This led to my making a foot-and-saddle campaign through the southern part of the Rocky Mountains. It was so enjoyable and profitable a summer, that I have since availed myself of every opportunity to explore the fastnesses of those noble ranges, and I now propose to refresh pleasant recollections by recounting some experiences—none of which were startling, it may as well be said to start with.

If the reader should chance to recognize something he has read before, he should remember that I have dredged the material for these pages out of the deep sea of magazine* and newspaper† files where they sunk, years ago, after the briefest possible surface-existence.

---

* *Harper's Magazine, Scribner's Monthly, St. Nicholas,* and *Good Company.*
† *New York Tribune, New York Herald, Forest and Stream, The Country, The Congregationalist, Spirit of the Times, The Hour, Army and Navy Journal,* and others.

.

II.

THE initial point of all expeditions, large and small, into the mountains was, and remains, the city of Denver, the capital of Colorado, and a marvellous town.

That gold existed in the Rocky Mountains has been certainly known since the earliest exploration of them ; it is one of the most curious facts about the whole matter, indeed, that the utilization of this wealth did not begin sooner. About 1803, for instance, a Kentuckian named James Pursley, while travelling with a band of Indians "into the mountains which give birth to the La Platte, Arkansaw, etc., etc." (the locality seems to have been near Mount Lincoln), found gold there, and "carried some of the virgin mineral in his shot-pouch for months." Other wanderers reported it at various times, according to tradition, but no publicity was given to the fact, so that the real history of the mining excitement in the lofty mid-continent ranges, and the annals of Denver, their metropolis, begin with the summer of 1858, and are associated with the name of W. Green Russell.

This gentleman was a Georgian, who had learned the delights of gold-digging where the gentle Etowah rolls enticing sands through the charming gorges of the Blue Ridge. When the gold excitement of the Pacific coast aroused the country he started Westward, taking his course up the Arkansas, passing along the eastern base of Pike's Peak, and so northward to the emigrant trail. He observed at that time what seemed to him indications of gold-gravel, but did not pause to verify it. When, therefore, a few years later, he retraced his steps, he halted long enough in Colorado to assure himself of the richness of its bars, and then proceeded homeward to organize a party to return with him to this point. Two brothers, some friends, and a few Cherokee Indians joined him.*

---

* The Cherokees had previously been through here searching a promised land for their tribe, and had themselves reported gold. They concluded to remain in the Indian Territory, but left their name attached to several springs, mountains,

Following up the Arkansas river, they were joined by adventurers, until finally the party numbered thirty or forty, and reached the base of the mountains early in the summer. Finding nothing in the neighborhood of Pike's Peak, they advanced up Squirrel creek, and then across to Cherry creek, where they built a village, near its head. Sluicing there proved of small consequence, however, and finally they worked down to the site of the present city, where Cherry creek empties into the South Platte. Here, building a camp, they prepared to spend the winter. Exaggerated reports of their success having gone back to the border States, recruits came steadily, until, by the time cold weather really set in, three or four hundred persons (only three of them women) were gath-

ered in the camp. The settlement was christened Auraria, after the mining town of that name near Dahlonega, Georgia; and straggling immigration during the winter brought in many merchants and artisans as well as gold-seekers.

Meanwhile the story of the new discoveries of gold in Pike's Peak

etc., as a memento of their visit of inspection. Little is known of this interesting journey "looking for a home," in which about half the tribe participated, the remainder staying in Western North Carolina, (for all the mountain region was known by that name, though the Peak itself was seventy - five miles from the diggings) hastened eastward, gathering marvels as it ran, and was attested by sundry goose-quills full of dust. Just following the financial distresses of 1857, thousands of men were ready for anything, and the spring of 1859 witnessed the beginning of such an emigration across the plains as had only been equalled by the wildest hours of the rush to California a decade before. Council Bluffs, Atchison, Kansas City, and all the other outposts of civilization became filled with excited crowds hastily preparing for the two months' journey across the plains, and an almost

"PIKE'S PEAK OR BUST!"

continuous procession of wagons of every description filed out from their streets to undergo the hardships and perils of that eager race to be first at the gold-fields. He who could not pay for the swift stage became driver or escort of a freight-wagon, or followed along with his ambulance; while thousands rode on horseback, or walked, trundling their luggage in a handcart or wheelbarrow, or slung upon their backs. *Those* were the storied days when the motto "Pike's Peak or Bust!" was inscribed on many a wagon-sheet by jubilant owners, and those also the days when the same wagons, hopelessly bogged in some treacherous fording of the Arkansas, or broken down among the rocks of a stony bit of butte-road, were grimly labelled "Busted, by Thunder!"

The vanguard of this exodus reached the Platte in April, and it is estimated that nearly a hundred thousand persons followed during the summer. We are told that they were in the main from the better classes of men at home, but that nineteen-twentieths were entirely ignorant of gold-mining. Thousands were disappointed, of course, and a thin returning stream met, but failed to discourage, the new-comers, who pressed across the weary, bone-marked plains, sure that their lot would be an exception to all the misfortunes described.

As soon as the snows were sufficiently melted the Russells and others pushed into the mountains, reasoning that, if these outer streams contained a sediment of drifted gold, some source of the riches must remain in the rocks whence the waters came. One party, under the leadership of J. H. Gregory, started up Clear creek to a point just above where Black Hawk now is, and began prospecting in the gulch. " He climbed the hill," says a written account of the incident, " where he believed the wash or gold-dirt would naturally come from, scraped away the grass and leaves, and filled his gold-pan with dirt and took it down to the gulch. Upon panning (washing) it down there was about four dollars' worth of gold in it ! He dropped his pan, and immediately summoned all the gods of the universe to witness his astounding triumph. That night he could not sleep."

Whether any immortals obeyed the summons the record fails to inform us, but it is certain that it was a very few days only before the rugged trails, slippery with ice and gagged with snow, became

EVENING ON THE PLAINS.

thronged with the well-nigh disheartened emigrants, fired with a new hope. Almost simultaneously discoveries of rich bars and veins were made at Idaho Springs, Boulder, Golden, and elsewhere ; and the mountains, from Estes Park to the Sangre de Christo, began to be overrun with prospectors ; while gold and silver ledges and placers were discovered so rapidly, that no one could keep track of them, and thousands of claims were taken up on both sides and among the very summits of

A RACE TO NEW DIGGINGS.

the Snowy Range,* under laws and regulations framed by the miners themselves. Valleys hitherto undisturbed except by the light tread of the moccason and the scarcely timid game it followed, cliffs that had echoed to no other sound than the noise of the elements or the voices of bird and beast, now resounded with human energy, and were despoiled by the ruthless shovel and axe. The sage-brush yielded place to wagon-tracks, and the splendid spruces were felled to lie docile in the walls of log cities that sprung into shape with the startled swiftness and decision of magic.

---

* Fine mines of silver—which are still worked—were opened a few years later on the brow of Mount Lincoln, at an elevation considerably over 14,000 feet, in the midst of perpetual snow.

There is much of romantic, picturesque, and human interest in the story of these early years of gold and silver hunting in the Rocky Mountains; but I have said enough to show that, while thousands turned back, tens of thousands had good cause to remain, and that this widely scattered, nomadic army needed and naturally would come to have a central point, where supplies could be gathered and dispensed; where a post-office and express-office might be established, and where the convergent interests of this new and isolated world might find a focus. How Denver fulfilled these conditions, and became, from the very first, the metropolis of the mountains, it is now time to explain.

When the Georgians built their cabins for winter-quarters among the lofty cottonwoods between the Platte and Cherry creek, they thought "Indian Row" a good enough name; but when a settlement grew up around them, and more men kept coming, they surveyed a town-site and named it "Auraria," as already stated. At the same time a few persons crossed to the east side of Cherry creek and built a group of cabins, which they called "St. Charles;" and a few others "located" on a ridge northward under the name of the "Highlands." These last two were abortive attempts at city-making, however; and during the winter of 1858-'59 a party, with General Larimer at its head, came to St. Charles, "jumped" the now deserted settlement, laid out a nine hundred and sixty acre town-site of their own, and christened it Denver City, in honor of the Governor of Kansas, of which territory all this region soon became a county, known as Arapahoe.

This last deliberate movement was a direct recognition of the advantages which this point offered as a town-site. It lay midway between the routes of travel to the Pacific coast along the North Platte and by the way of Santa Fe. It was at the junction of two water-courses, along which grew abundant timber and unlimited pasturage. It was a situation central to the half-dozen passes and cañons which then, as now, constituted the gate-ways through the mountain barrier into the interior valleys and parks. Lastly, it had priority, and was fast getting the advertising which has ever since been so liberally accorded to it, and to which it owes, in no small degree, its present success.

Each of the forty-one share-holders was required to erect a cabin at once, and General Larimer was the first man to put up his roof. Denver thus sprung at one bound into rivalry with Auraria; but the strife for supremacy was brief, and resulted in a consolidation by which the older sister of the twain lost her name, and became simply West Denver; or, when spoken of with contumely, simply, "'Cross the creek."

2

Those were wild days in the young city's history. Thousands of excited people thronged her streets, living in tents, in wagons, in dug-outs, and in the rudest of log-huts and shanties—the best way they could. Everything eaten had to be brought across the plains, except game and some cattle that Mexicans would drive up from Santa Fe. Yet there was no great scarcity; and though prices were almost uniformly ten times as much as at present, gold-dust and coin were abundant, and wages in proportion. If a man thought it cheap to be able to buy a sack of flour at ten dollars, he felt outraged if he was not getting fifteen or twenty dollars a day for his labor.

The fall of 1859 saw Denver very city-like and busy. Machinery poured in, and with it every appliance of civilization possible at such a distance from the frontier of even the Western States. All kinds of business enterprises were projected, and among others a newspaper. The Honorable William N. Byers—a gentleman who has been identified with the best interests of Colorado—was the moving spirit in this latter venture, and its history is a good illustration of ways and means in " Pike's Peak " twenty years ago. Mr. Byers and his associates heard that there was lying idle at Belleview, near Omaha, such a printing-office as they wanted—a relic of a starved-out journal. Mr. Byers went there and secured the property, leaving Omaha with it on the 8th of March, 1859. The streams were all flooded, snow and rain storms frequent, and the third day out the trains waded through a frozen sheet of water three feet deep and two miles wide, breaking the ice as they progressed. The wagons carrying the press and types had a variety of mishaps, and at the end of the month had only reached Fort Kearney, 185 miles from Omaha. Beyond there, however, the roads were firm, and faster time was made, so that on the 20th of April the precious press and types entered Denver. The name of this fair-sized and nicely-printed weekly was *The Rocky Mountain News*. To-day it is an eight-page daily, and owned by another company, but the name remains, and is widely known. Its salutatory is worth quoting, as a piece of brave crowing, for that very week was the time of the remarkable stampede which carried back in a panic four-fifths of the emigrants who had set out for the promised land, scared by a cry of fraud and certain starvation :

" We make our *début*," said this introductory paragraph, " in the Far West, where the snowy mountains look down upon us in the hottest summer day as well as in the winter's cold; here, where a few months ago the wild beasts and wilder Indians held undisturbed possession— where now surges the advancing wave of Anglo-Saxon enterprise and civilization—where soon, we proudly hope, will be erected a great and powerful State, another empire in the sisterhood of empires."

This was plucky, and partook of the character of "bluff," for really the stoutest-hearted had intelligent doubts about the truth of the boast; but the journal can take to itself much credit for staying the stampede, and bringing capital and brains to the development of the new camp.

It was not long before rivals sprung up, and in May of the following year a daily edition was begun, to which a second daily, *The Herald*, opposed itself within a few weeks. At first the nearest post-office was at Fort Laramie, 220 miles northward, and the mail reached there from the East only once or twice a month. About the 1st of May, 1859, a messenger was induced to go to this post-office, and through an utter wilderness he brought a mule-load of letters and newspapers, which were delivered on payment of twenty-five cents each for the former, and fifty cents for the latter. Nor did affairs speedily improve. More than two years passed before Denver had its own post-office, all mails being carried from the East on the overland coaches, which came regularly after June, 1859, and letters were charged for as express matter, at twenty-five cents apiece.

There is a whole book to be written some day—and a book of thrilling interest—on the overland coach lines, the pony express, and the fast-freight arrangements, which preceded the trans-continental railways. Their histories might properly come in here, but would take up so much space that I prefer passing them by altogether to making an unsatisfactory mention. Denver owed much, in its infancy, to the enterprise and pluck of its stage and express managers.

At this time the War of the Rebellion was raging in the East, and a general Indian war harassed the plains. In 1863 mails were so irregular that weeks would elapse without one, and what was received came by the way of Panama and San Francisco. The freighting business was demoralized, so that many a hundred pounds of paper cost a hundred dollars for its transportation alone; and wrapping, tissue, and even letter paper were used to keep up the daily issues of the *News*, which often shrunk to a mere bulletin of military orders, etc., for lack of something to print upon. In 1861 the telegraph reached Fort Kearney, where it rested two years. Then the Denver journals begun taking news despatches, which were printed here only four days after their origin in New York. This increased the competition between the papers, and the most bitter personalities were indulged in through the editorial columns. It is great fun to read these old files; it is like witnessing a battle between men of straw. Both offices established pony-express lines to the principal mining camps in the mountains, and their daily editions were delivered in Black Hawk, Central City, and other neighborhoods, forty or fifty miles away, more quickly than the steam-cars now manage to do it. Under these circumstances twenty-five dollars a year was not a high subscription rate, the retail price being twenty-five cents a copy; but this was in gold, which, at that time, was worth twice as much as currency. There was no lack of local news, of course, in so wide-awake a community, and these journals were more successful than is usual in manufacturing "items" on their own account.

In 1859 the town became overrun with gamblers and cut-throats, who thought themselves too far from authority and too strong in numbers to be interfered with; but one night several of them were hanged, and the next night others. Rumors of a Vigilance Committee got abroad, and the leading desperadoes found it to their advantage to depart. As a consequence the reign of terror, which forms a part of the early history of all the Pacific Railroad towns, never amounted to much in Denver. Still there were plenty of bad men, and the carrying of fire-arms was a universal custom. Gambling, too, was as open and prevalent as it now is in Leadville, Durango, or Cheyenne; and "tangle-foot whiskey," at two bits a drink, was to be had on every corner, and two or three times between. As a natural result quarrelling and bloodshed were of so frequent occurrence as to excite no notice; and when anybody was killed,

> "They piled the stiffs outside the door,"

and went on with the game, under the impression that it served the dead man right for not being quick enough to "get the drop" on the other fellow.

A single incident of the beginning of a higher sentiment on the subject may be worth the space to print it.

One night, in 1861, when *The Rocky Mountain News* was a few months old, a man named Harrison shot a companion across the card-table in one of those "silver exchanges" which in the young metropolis were a good deal closer together than chapels. Though well aware of the existence of the general ideas which made such a state of affairs possible, the *News* was so utterly lost to all regard for Mr. Harrison's sensibilities that it denounced the case as Murder (with a big M), and called for proper punishment. The accused man took it good-natured-ly; but some of his friends, having drunk themselves into a state of belligerency, concluded that this slur upon the honor of a citizen must be avenged. Mr. Byers, the editor of the *News*, sitting quietly at his desk that afternoon, was considerably surprised, therefore, to find himself suddenly grasped by three men in a way that rendered him powerless. They cursed him in the foulest manner, and threatened him with six-barrelled revolvers. Keeping his wits about him, nevertheless, and coolly opening a parley, Mr. Byers secured a little time, until the ruffians were alarmed by the click of a gun-lock, and looked up to see three or four rifles, the possessors of which were only waiting to get an opportunity to fire without killing the editor. The *News* office had reckoned upon the character of the men it had been writing against, and for weeks every printer and pressman had had a musket at his elbow ready for emergencies.

Mr. Byers, however, promised to go with the men to see Harrison, the alleged murderer; and between the two desperadoes, flourishing their revolvers and momentarily threatening to kill him, he walked up to the saloon. The instant they entered Mr. Byers saw that the outrage had not been instigated by Harrison, who evinced his displeasure most emphatically, and demanded the instant delivery of the editor into his own custody. Then, taking him into a back room, he warned him of the danger from these uncontrollable ruffians, and opened the rear door. Mr. Byers took the hint, and made haste to return to his office, but not to his desk—a very wise precaution.

Finding their prey escaped, Wood and Steele, the would-be avengers, started out to collect a mob, but kept carefully out of range of the office-windows of the newspaper. Finally, however, Steele mounted a swift horse and dashed by, firing his revolver through the window at Mr. Byers's desk with an aim which would have been fatal had the editor been sitting there. Receiving portions of two charges of shot from the printers as he passed, he dashed on through West Denver, brandishing his pistol in the face of all opposition, and returned across the Blake Street bridge for a second attack. Just here, however, riding ahead of him, was a friend of Mr. Byers. Hearing Steele approach, this gentleman quietly turned in his saddle and, asking no questions, sent a rifle-ball through the "terror's" brain.

Meanwhile, an impromptu "law-and-order" *posse comitatus* had arrested Wood; a court was extemporized and a hasty trial conducted, in the presence of a crowd whose temper emulated that of the mob which dragged Captain Porteous from the Heart of Midlothian. Yet there were plenty of desperate sympathizers with Wood, and whispers of an attempt to rescue him were heard; but a hundred rifles and six-shooters clicked ominously, and the idea was abandoned. Even then the sentence of Judge Lynch was not death, but banishment. Wood was given his arms, a horse, and twenty minutes to get out of town. A mounted escort showed him the way with grim politeness, and he vanished forever over the hills to the northward.

There are many old citizens who look back to those days from our tamer times with a certain longing interest, as to the golden age of Denver's history. This was the kind of city which Horace Greeley saw, and wrote to *The Tribune* about, and which Albert D. Richardson describes in his book. Yet there was a deal of quiet family comfort, too, even in those days, only it was hid beneath the turbulence of the surface-life.

Although Auraria had long before lost its identity, yet the west side remained the business part of Denver until 1864; and the circumstance which caused a change of base was the memorable flood of that spring, one of the events from which Denver people date. For several days a mixture of rain and snow had fallen over the whole region in an almost continuous storm, and Cherry creek, ordinarily an insignificant, civil stream, was full to the top of its banks. At last there came an unprecedented fall of hail, followed by an hour or two of warmth, and then by a thunder-storm. Hundreds of small reservoirs up on the Divide were thus unlocked at a stroke, and in pitchy darkness, rain, thunder and lightning their loosened contents swept down the valley of Cherry creek, and struck the town in a series of prodigious waves. Uprooted trees, drifted houses and barns, and floating *débris* of every sort were borne along upon the swift water; and the inhabitants of half the city, particularly on the west side, were driven from their swaying houses by this unexpected, black, and icy flood. It was a night of destruction of property and horror to mankind throughout the whole region, for Cherry creek was only one of many that rose into majestic proportions, and asserted themselves as the channels of awful power. Yet less than a score of persons lost their lives, and it was all over in a few hours. The most serious loss sustained was that of the county's safe, wherein were deposited a large number of deeds, leases, mining records, and other important documents, the destruction of which has been the source of a vast deal of litigation. Shrewd ones suspect that the safe was found long ago; but that those who prefer that it should never turn up have paid so much more highly to have it buried again than the public authorities offered for its production, that it never will be seen until exhumed by some future antiquary.

Cherry creek has "boomed" without warning three or four times since then, and will do so in future; but the guards along its banks and channel are such as, it is hoped, will ward off disaster. When the water is heard and seen coming down in a mighty flood, crested with great waves and spreading from one trembling bank to another, the fire-bells ring and the creek-side becomes thronged with spectators and men with ropes, grapnels, and hooks. As night advances they build great bonfires at the end of each street which touches the creek; and the angry, chocolate-colored, swift-racing waters run this long gauntlet of fires, that throw their rays far across the turbid waste and lend new vividness to what is always an exciting picture.

Meanwhile, Denver had grown to possess fifteen hundred or two thousand people. More and more persons had gone into the mountains, and every available point near the town had been pre-empted for ranching. The Arapahoes of the plains and the Utes of the mountains, seeing this inroad of white men, were far from pleased, and by the spring of 1864 their depredations had culminated in united war over the whole length and breadth of the plains. The transportation of merchandise from the East became impossible, except in great companies, under armed escort, and even then hundreds of men lost their lives. My memory teems with thrilling incidents as I write. The mail-service along the Platte became broken up, and Colorado was practically cut off from the Atlantic coast. Even the city itself was fearful of attack and massacre. Knowing this, it is strange that so complete a panic should have occurred as happened one memorable night early in June, when the report that an army of Arapahoes were about to sack the town spread through the streets. It was a wonderfully propitious moment for the savages. Most of the able-bodied men of the town were away in the mountains, with teams on the plains, or doing service in the three regiments that Colorado sent into the Union army. At Camp Weld, a mile away up the Platte, were only a corporal's guard of sick and disabled soldiers, and a large number of families who had been rendered homeless by the recent flood. The barracks lay right in the track of the Indians, and a messenger started at a breakneck pace to give warning. The wife of the officer in charge was sitting quietly sewing, in company with another lady, when the door suddenly burst open, and a soldier, his knees knocking together and his face pale with fright, gasped out, "D-d-on't be fri-frightened, ladies; there are only th-thr-three thousand Indians a mile and a half from Denver!" and vanished. The barracks resolved itself at once into Bedlam, where hysterics developed a clamor which might well have frightened away even a war party of Arapahoes. The acting commandant was away; but Mrs. Sanford, thinking that he would come out to the post, decided to stay where she was, and persuaded several other ladies to the same sensible course. Before long the captain came, sure enough, and marshalled the few women and children for the dreary walk into town. The darkness was intense, the plain was rough and full of cactus and bayonet-grass, and everybody was overburdened and fearful. In town bells were ringing, men were organizing into armed corps, and the women and children, many in their night-clothes, were being crowded into the only brick building on the west side—the large three-story structure now occupied by the Lindell Hotel. The building had been considered unsafe, even to stand alone; but no one thought of this, and in packing it full of people hazarded the greatest peril of the evening. So our friends from Camp Weld made their way out as hurriedly as they got in, and took refuge in a log-hut until something more alarming should appear than had yet shown itself. It was a night as full of dread and terror as that of the flood, and more so, for it affected everybody; but plenty of comical things happened. A dozen or so cravens among the men crept into the old brick building, cowering among the women, who were not soothed by their abject faces; and one fellow was found hiding beneath his wife's wide-circling skirts. One little party, fleeing in from the suburbs, heard the noise of what seemed a thousand hoofs, and saw a host of dark forms sweep over a ridge of the prairie. They knew their time had come, and dropped upon their knees in the prickly-pear, clasping imploring hands to—half a dozen mules!

These are not the customary examples of Far Western heroism, but, unfortunately, are "ower-true tales."

Well, after a night of scouting and patrolling, waiting and watching, praying and cursing, fear and fury, morning dawned; but no Indians, or traces of Indians, showed themselves. Everybody went back to their work, and in the course of the day it leaked out that the whole scare originated with a nervous old couple, who were surprised at milking-time by the advent of a band of horses. Never stopping to see that they were unsaddled, and driven by only a Mexican boy or two, they leaped into their wagon and rushed off to tell Denver that three thousand Arapahoes were ready to cut its throat.

The outcome of all this excitement was the proclamation of martial law, and the sudden organization of a regiment for Indian fighting. The " Sand Creek " campaign followed, and secured instant peace to the harassed settlers and miners, over whose heads the tomahawk had been suspended for months.

The flood, or the Indian scares, lost to West Denver its pre-eminence, and business moved to the east side, building up Blake, Holliday, Larimer, and Fifteenth streets. Its expansion has been eastward and northward ever since. When, in 1874, our expedition was fitting out, the city itself was too well built up, and the environs either too unsuitable or too expensive to afford space for the rendezvous camp; accordingly, it was fixed in a grove of cottonwoods, six miles from town, on Clear creek. There the tents were set up, all the baggage and stores distributed among the various divisions, the new hands given their first taste of roughing it, and the animals brought together and prepared for the campaign.

III.

IT goes without saying that, in making original explorations through so lofty and broken a region as is comprised in the term Rocky Mountains, wheeled vehicles are out of the question. Before they can be used to any extent roads must be laboriously built; and it was one object of the Surveys to discover the most practicable routes for these prospective highways. Explorers, meanwhile, had to trudge afoot or take to the saddle.

The Survey, during its many successive years of service, acquired a large herd of animals, which were kept from season to season, whenever worth it. The labor required was severe, and a superior grade of stock was needed. The great majority of these animals were mules, for their endurance is greater than that of horses, and their size and build are better suited for bearing burdens. This is so well understood by all mountaineers that, whereas you can buy a fair pack-pony for fifty dollars, or less, you must pay three times that amount for a good mule.

The rendezvous camp having been organized, the laboring-men hired (usually the same muleteers, year after year), and the stores collected, the first thing done is to distribute the live stock. Herewith begin both the fun and the peril of the expedition.

The herd of a hundred or more animals, that have been ranging the open plains in the wildest license all winter, have just been "rounded up," and are at last penned in a corral by themselves. The head packer now looks them over as they go careering round the confined space, and selects the quota of each division of the Survey. Some will require to be re-shod; and those bravest of men, the frontier blacksmiths, who would fearlessly straddle a thunder-bolt if it needed an iron tip, unhesitatingly do the job, whether the mule consents or not. Then the animals go back to the corral to fight and play, and to mature, by long consultations, the evil designs which they propose to execute during the coming campaign.

By this time the saddles and *aparejos* (Californian pack-saddles) have been repaired and distributed, the stores divided, and, as far as possible, stowed in bags, in order to be most conveniently lashed upon the mules' backs ; and each man has studied how to bestow his bedding and small personal outfit most compactly.   In place of trunks or valises every- thing is stuffed into canvas cylinders, each about the size of a section of stove-pipe, which close by means of puckering-strings at the top.   Near- ly everything that each one carries must be enclosed in this one war- bag ; but, for the few fragile and shapely articles needful, a pair of pan- ier-boxes is given to each party.   My writing-kit I stuffed into a small,

STUFFING THE WAR-BAG.

soft travelling-bag, the last time I was out, and it carried very well.   Of course such arrangements preclude " boiled shirts " or starched goods of any sort.   Your war-bag, like everything else, will be placed in that part of a mule's load where it will ride best, and the utmost strength of two men will be expended in drawing the lash-ropes tightly across it. Anything more linen than a handkerchief or whiter than an under-shirt is, therefore, treated with scorn and derision in camp, and old trousers and coats, heavy flannel shirts, coarse shoes, and broad-brimmed felt hats are the *mode*.

Finally comes the gala-day, when the mules are to be saddled for the first time after their long vacation, and everybody is on hand to see the fun.

The Western pack-mule is small, sinewy, and, like old Joey Bagstock, "tough, sir, tough! but de-e-vlish sly!" Most of them are bred from Indian ponies, and are born on the open plains. Having previously been lassoed and branded, when three years old they are driven (or inveigled) into a corral, and exhibited for sale as *bronchos*. An untamed horse is a model of gentleness beside them. Sometimes they are accustomed at once to the saddle by one of those wonderful riders who can stick on the back of anything that runs, and more rarely they are broken to harness; but ordinarily their backs are trained to bear the pack, which is generally the only practicable method of transporting freight through these rugged mountains.

The first time the pack-saddles are put on the excitement may be imagined. The green mule, strong in his youth, having been adroitly "roped," or lassoed, is led out into an open space, stepping timidly but quietly, not seeing any cause for alarm. Before he understands what it all means he finds that a noose of the rawhide lariat about his neck has been slipped over his nose, and discovers that his tormentors have an advantage. He pulls, shakes his head, stands upright on opposite ends, but all to no avail. The harder he pulls the tighter the noose pinches his nostrils; so at last he comes down and keeps still. Then a man approaches slowly and circumspectly, holding behind him a leathern blinder, which he seeks to slip over the mule's eyes. But two long ears stand in the way, and the first touch of the leather is the signal for two frantic jumps—one by the beast and one by the man, for packers are wise enough in their day and generation to fight shy of the business-end of a mule. The next attempt is less a matter of caution and more of strength; and here the animal has so much the advantage, that often it must be lassoed again and thrown to the ground.

It is a fine sight to witness the indignation of such a fellow! He falls heavily, yet holds his head high, and essays to rise; but his fore-feet are manacled by ropes, and his head is fast. Yet he will shake almost free, get upon his hind feet, stand straight up, and dash down with all his weight in futile efforts for liberty. Secured with more ropes, allowed but three legs to stand upon, and cursed frightfully, he *must* submit, though he never does it with good grace. It is not always, however, that this extremity is resorted to. Some animals make little resistance while the strange thing is being put upon their backs and the fastenings adjusted—all but one. When an effort is made to put that institution called a crupper under a young mule's tail language fails to describe the magnificence of the kicking! The light heels describe an arc from the ground to ten feet above it, and then strike out at a tangent. They cut through the air like whip-lashes, and would penetrate an impediment like bullets. But even mule-flesh tires. Strategy wins. The crupper is gained, and the first hard pull made upon the *cincha* (as the girth is termed), which holds firmly every hair-breadth, and finally will crease the contour of the mule's belly into a semblance to Cupid's

SUBMISSION TO THE APAREJO.

bow. But this one pull suffices to set him springing again—bucking, now, with arched back and head between his knees, landing on stiff legs to jar his burden off, or falling full weight on his side and rolling over, to scrape it free. He will sit on his haunches and hurl himself backward; duck his head and turn a somersault; finally will stand still, trembling with anger and exhaustion, and let you lead him away, conquered. So much is enough for one day; having fitted the aparejo, the putting on of the burden will come easier.

Let me turn now to the matter of supplies—shelter, bedding, food, and arms—which were accumulated at the rendezvous camp.

Those old heroes who made a beginning of exploration in the Rocky Mountains, nearly a century ago, as trappers and hunters for the fur companies, would have thought themselves in Paradise could they have seen our stores in 1874; but a casual reader may not be moved by any such envious feeling. The trappers used to make their head-quarters mainly at Fort Benton, at the head of navigation on the Upper Missouri. Everything civilized had to be taken twenty-five hundred miles up the river from St. Louis in batteaux; and for the last five hundred miles these heavy boats must be hauled mainly by men, who walked along the shore with ropes over their shoulders. The value of the cargoes by the time the three months' voyage was completed may be imagined. Flour was unheard of at Fort Benton, sugar was a wild extravagance, and tea and coffee were only fit for the nabobs who conducted the business of the post. The journey was too frightfully long and difficult to admit of many articles of food being transported, since all available space in the overladen mackinaws needed to be reserved for the indispensable whiskey.

Going out into the woods for a tour of lonely trapping, lasting four, five, or six months, and extending hundreds of miles beyond even this extreme outpost of civilization, these half-savages took nothing in the way of food except a little salt and pepper, and perhaps a trifle of tea, as an occasional indulgence. An iron skillet and a tin cup comprised their only furniture; if they needed anything more they made it out of poplar-bark or soapstone. For months together these men would live wholly on the flesh their guns brought them, varying this diet now and then with berries, sweet roots, or a pungent decoction of sage-leaves and the bark of the red willow or other plants that would serve the purpose of tea. The red willow bark, mixed with kinnikinnic, made very good smoking, too, after the trapper's tobacco was exhausted. It often happened in the northern mountains (where little alkali occurs) that a trapper would even have no salt for his meat; but in this he fared no worse than the Indians, who, indeed, have to acquire a taste for it. "White men big fools," they say; "want fresh meat, fresh meat, all time —then put heap salt on it!" The history of these trappers adds to the record of human endurance and abstinence; but we had no desire to imitate them, though in the earlier years of the government expeditions the fare was primitive and scanty enough wherever game proved scarce. Latterly we lived better, and finally even attained to four-tined forks!

Dr. Hayden's survey was divided into several working divisions of five to seven persons, each of which had a cook, and spent the season in a field of work by itself. Whether or not one thinks these cooks had a hard time of it depends upon the point of view. It seems to me they had, because they had to rise at an unearthly hour in the morning; but, on the other hand, they were not obliged to climb snowy and back-breaking peaks, and half freeze on their gale-swept summits in "taking observations," nor to chase a lot of frantic mules and horses that chose to be ugly about being caught up. However, upon a fairly satisfactory cook depends a large portion of *your* good time.

The camp cook presents himself in various characters. There are not many colored men in the West in this capacity, and few Frenchmen; but many Americans have picked up the necessary knowledge by hard experience, not one of whom, perhaps, regards it as a "profession," or anything better than a makeshift.

It is considered by the ordinary mountaineer as a rather inferior occupation, and, as a rule, it falls to the lot of inferior men, who have tried and failed in more energetic, muscular, and profitable pursuits. Of course there are exceptions, but, as a rule, they are men who are not even up to the level of picturesque interest, and are worthy of small regard from the observer, unless he is hungry. We are hungry—therefore we pursue the subject.

Roads being non-existent, and it often being necessary to go boldly across the country, without regard for even Indian trails, the *cuisine*, like everything else, had to accommodate itself to the backs of the sturdy mules, on whose steady endurance depended nearly all hope of success. The conditions to be met by kitchen and larder were: ability to be stowed together in packages of small size, convenient shape, and sufficient strength to withstand without injury the severest strain of the lash-ropes, and the forty or more accidents liable to happen in the course of a thousand miles of rough mountain travel. The only sort of package that will meet these requirements is the bag. When it is full it is of that elongated and rounded shape which will lie well in the burden; as fast as it is emptied space is utilized and the weight remains manageable. In bags, then, were packed all the raw material, except the few condiments in bottles and flasks, for which, with other fragile things, a pair of panniers was provided. Even the few articles of ironware permitted to the camp cook were tied up in a gunny-sack.

I V.

LET me omit the rough methods and vexatious delays of the first morning's setting out. Let me simply suppose the party fairly away, beginning its summer campaign; and let us leave for the later expe- riences of actual mountaineering the details and routine of daily life, when the animals have quieted down, and we have hardened to a com- mendable regularity of work. Starting from near Denver, it is a day's march to the foot-hills, and, for the beginning, a long march, as you find at the end, somewhat to your surprise if you are an eager novice.

The smooth, level plains, rising almost imperceptibly to the black wall of the forest-clad foot-hills, are covered with short, bunchy buffalo- grass, already (though in May) grown sere; and the wagon-track you follow dips and rises over greenish gray ridges in monotonous succes- sion. There is little to charm the eye, save the gleaming peaks uplifted ahead—the glorious beacons for our progress. In spring the weather is likely to be misty, so that the mountains do not stand out with as sharp and definite outline as they will later in the season; but the more prom- inent heights are very plain a hundred miles away. Long's Peak shows all his gigantic proportions, everywhere mantled in snow; and in clear moments I can catch sight of the silvery crests of snow-covered moun- tains behind, away in the interior of the Snowy Range.

Rising abruptly from the plains, standing in orderly array, north and south, the peaks crowd together and tower up among the storm-clouds that drift past them, until, as you watch, it is the mountain peaks which seem to be moving, cutting the clouds asunder and dashing the flurries of snow from their fronts, as ships before a gale part the white spray of the waves. This grandeur of the tremendous contest of the elements among the serried ridges is better witnessed in this season of thunder- storms, when winter disputes every step of summer's advance, than at any other time. The mountains are still piled high with snow, only the black crests of the cliffs streaking their white cones. And while you are watching the pure gleam of the snow, or the rosy play of sunlight upon it, an indigo cloud, dense and square-fronted with rain, will march up from the valley at one side, cutting off all the rest of the landscape, while a similar phalanx will sweep up on the left hand, hiding the other mountains behind its black veil, and together they will assault the mountain whose white and lofty head stands out between them firm and clear against the angry sky.   But as the storms strike the monarch's flank and climb his sides and close about his base, sounding the long-roll in their thunder and hurling the bolts of their lightning, the dense blue-black of the rain is changed to the misty white of snow, the darkness gradually vanishes, the ammunition of the lightning is exhausted, and the mountain emerges from the battle whiter than ever with fleecy trophies of victory; while triumphant banners of crimson and gold are hung upon the clouds so blackly defiant a moment ago.

Beyond some grand exhibition like this, the pranks of a few ill-packed mules, or the early vagaries of the beast you ride, there will be little to amuse you.   This first day, indeed, is likely to be tiresome and unsatisfactory.   You have not become accustomed to your mule, nor he to you.   You are sunburnt, your eyes smart with the hot alkali dust—for the cool mountains are not yet reached—and your muscles ache with the unwonted labor of riding.   If it happens to have been wholly in the wilderness, you have got along without much trouble, perhaps; but if your road has led you through the miserable outskirts of civilization, you have been gazed at in an annoying way, and chaffed on your "green" appearance.   The mules have exerted themselves to enter every gate and door-way, to go anywhere and everywhere but where they ought; and the amount of caution, invective, and hard-riding necessary to keep them together and under their respective packs has been vexatious and fatiguing, conducive neither to observation of scenery nor to the cultivation of Christian virtues.

Indeed, on this initial trip, you get some new ideas on the subject of mountain mules.   You learn, for instance, that they love company, cling together, and enjoy walking one behind the other in long file; but no mule has independence of judgment enough to lead a train, even with a bit in his mouth.   On the other hand, all mules are "stuck after" a horse, as the muleteers phrase it, and advantage is taken of this to cause them to travel steadily, and to keep them together at night, by having a horse to lead the march.   The horse has a stock-bell round its neck, and is ridden by the cook, who is thus debarred from anything except steadily plodding along; while the others can ramble off from the train as much as they please.   At night the bell-horse is

3

hobbled, and all the mules are turned loose to graze about the neighborhood, the tinkle of the bell giving us information of their position in
the morning ; for there is little fear that they will wander away from the
horse, unless stampeded, and that rarely occurs. Mules will go absolutely daft over a horse, and there are always fierce contests between the
animals on the first day a train starts out as to which shall have the
coveted place next to the leader. It often happens that for weeks afterward the victor has to maintain his position by constant exercise of
heels and teeth, and with much mulish profanity. I have seen two
mules fight so incessantly for the place next the bell-horse, when feeding, that they forgot to eat all day.

This quarrelling among the animals, and the continual loosening of
their burdens, due to the fulness of their bellies, the stiffness of the

FIRST STAGE.—ADJUSTING THE PACK.

new lash-ropes, and the weight of the loads, make frequent stops necessary, and more than one chase occurs after a panic-stricken runaway,
which must be caught and repacked, while the remainder wait most
restlessly.

Here let me say a word about the art of "packing." Years ago everybody used the old Mexican saw-buck saddle, and it still bestrides the lacerated spines of unfortunate *burros;* but generally it has yielded place to the Californian stuffed aparejo, the shape of which is seen very well in the cut on page 19. This is fastened firmly to the long-suffering beast by all the strength of two men, who tighten the girth by bracing their feet against the upright mule's ribs. Then a long lash-rope, having a broad, strong girth at one end terminating in a wooden hook, is thrown across the aparejo, and the packing begins. The burdens are laid on so as to balance properly, and are held in place until all, or the main part, is in position. Then the ends of the lash-rope are handed back and forth by the man on each side, twisted and looped loosely in a way very

SECOND STAGE.—"MODERATE PULLING."

THIRD STAGE.—"GIVE IT TO HER!"

dexterous but utterly indescribable, and finally, by moderate pulling, the whole net-work is tightened. The load is now criticised and balanced anew, small articles are tucked in, and it is pronounced ready. One man goes to the left side of the animal and seizes a portion of the rope which passes round the hook, while the other, on the opposite side, turns his back and passes the end of the lash-rope over his shoulder, so as to give him the greatest possible pulling power. This done, he calls back to his invisible mate,

"All set?"

"All set."

"*Give* it to her!"

Then results a sudden and mighty strain in concert, a dreadful groan escapes from the poor mule, there is a stifled sound of creaking and crushing, and in an instant more the fastening is made and the work is done. This lashing is all one rope, but it is crossed and entwined till it seems half a dozen. On the top of the load it forms a rectangular or diamond-shaped space, which gives the process its name among the packers. To know how to do it is a passport to mountain society, and establishes your credit. I remember once being alone at a stage station in Wyoming. I wore a partially civilized coat and hat, and hence was under suspicion among the party of men assembled. Foolishly venturing an opinion upon some subject, I was judged by the clothes I wore, and promptly snubbed.

"What right have *you* to know anything about it?" a big Klamath man hurled at me. "You're a tender-foot!"

"Perhaps I am," I answered, meekly; "but I can put the diamond-hitch on a mule."

"Can you do *that?* Then, sir, you are entitled to any opinion you please in this 'ere court!"

Even this lashing will not always hold firm, however, against equi-asinine contortions; but it is incomparably superior, both for the welfare of the mule and the safety of the burden, to the antiquated and cruel saw-buck.

A day of such rough experiences is only wearisome, and at night, very likely, you curse your folly in having come out, and find that the first irregular camp in the foot-hills is not worth description.

Divide Colorado into nearly equal east and west halves, and you will have two districts of entirely different physical characteristics, that on the east being the edge of the broad plains stretching away to the Missouri river; while the western half rises abruptly into piles and ranges of great mountains, which, intersected by frightful cañons, and embracing some extensive table-lands, cover the whole to the borders of the State and beyond, exhibiting the most startling development in the great uplifts where the Rio Colorado takes its rise. This great mountainous system was the *terra incognita* which the Surveys opened to the light, and the foot-hills are its outposts.

Leaving Denver, which is situated on soft sandstones and marls (at the base of which formation occur the extensive coal-beds of Colorado), you pass over "hog-backs" of upturned rocks, running in a north-and-south direction, at the base of the foot-hills. In these you find the edges of all the upturned series of underlying sedimentary rocks, till you reach the deep, crystalline rocks of the mountains themselves. Among the oldest of these strata that have been set upon edge by the upheavals that elevated the range are the triassic "red-beds," whose thin vertical walls stand, with grandeur so theatrical, at the gates of the Garden of the Gods—fit portals to that geological play-ground. The coal from the base of the mountains comes from the beds of this horizon. At Golden—now a thriving manufacturing and railway town— you observe a noticeable peculiarity in the geology, for it is the only place east of the mountains where basaltic lava occurs. Here, too, one gets a good idea of the amount of erosion that has taken place. The top of Castle Rock, a bluff six hundred feet high, close to the town, was once the bed of a valley! Going up Berthoud Pass, you soon get away from all the sedimentary rocks, and advance through an immense thickness of metamorphosed pre-Silurian schists, gneisses, granites, etc., among which occur the lodes of gold and silver. This was the route of my first entrance to the mountains. Now a good wagon-road goes across, and there is even talk of a railway; but at first a mere muddy and rough path traced the little-frequented course to Middle Park.

The hills grow more and more precipitous as you near the mountains, the higher ones being crowned with fantastic pinnacles of shattered rocks, or showing a bold escarpment of granite along the crest of a ridge. The slopes of the distant hills are thickly clothed with resinous woods as far up as timber grows—that is, 10,500 to 11,500 feet— and the watercourses are marked by the lighter foliage of a species of aspen, with occasional currant and gooseberry bushes; but close to the road the trees have been cut down and converted into firewood for the mines, piles of which you pass along the way. This stripping of the hills, and the familiar marks of the axe, detract from the wildness while enhancing the desolation of the scene. I do not remember to have noticed anything, so far, which was picturesque or pretty, except certain night effects in camp, which, rather, are weird. It is all on so large and grand a scale as to produce less immediate satisfaction and pleasure than one probably would derive from a week's trip among the Catskills or Adirondacks; but there is a breadth, and height, and depth to a day's experience among these silent, sky-piercing peaks that you cannot take in at once, but must make an effort after, and grow to the appreciation of, through a lifetime. For example, approaching Black Hawk we descended two thousand feet in one hill. From the top of this hill, itself a depression among foot-hills, I could take in at a glance the icy summits of Evans, James, Gray and Torrey, Chief and Squaw,

Arapahoe, and a dozen other peaks, named and nameless, whose separating valleys were two miles above the sea. In the majestic calm of
that presence all else dwindled; yet I heard a man swear in hot anger
because, forsooth, a strap had loosened! It seemed more than profanity.

Much of our way after this lay down the side of a long range, everywhere punched with the "prospect-holes" and tunnels of gold-diggers,
into the deep valley of Idaho Springs, a hot watering-place, where, notwithstanding my exaltation over the mountains, I was glad to pay a
dime for a glass of poor lager. We camped for the night quite near the
village; and whereas we had before been set down as a prospecting
party, and afterward chaffed by the small boys of Central City as fisher-
men, here in Idaho we were classed with a circus company which was
just leaving town. Now we were at the base of the main range, and our
climb really began; but it was easy at first, for we followed the wagon-
road to Georgetown and Empire City.

All through here these mining camps were the most interesting thing
visible to us new-comers. The miners build their hasty villages in the
spots least likely to prove valuable for mining purposes; yet I have
seen many places where they would dig the streets and yards up, leaving their houses perched on pillars, or would tear them down altogether,
to get at the gold in the heavy soil underneath. All the hill-sides are
furrowed with ditches bringing water to the mines from some upland
spring; or pitted with holes about the size of graves, where some search-
er has tried to find the lode that should make his fortune. Far and
near only stumps show where trees once stood, and the fair snowborn
creeks are polluted with the mud of "tailings," or diverted from their
beds to feed the flumes.

A Rocky Mountain mining camp, indeed, is about the newest and
roughest place, at its beginning, to be found in the world. When a successful "strike" has been made, no matter how far from anywhere it
happens to be, thither rush scores and hundreds of miners and other
restless money-makers, and every one houses himself as best he can
until lumber can be sawed and other regular building materials prepared. Some dig little caves in the hill-side, roofing them over in front
with a sort of porch and door-way; others put up a framework of poles,
and stretch their tents over them, laying down a floor of slabs, and
banking up the sides with dirt; some haul logs and construct square
cabins, ten or twelve logs high, roofed with poles and thatched with
mud, which soon supports a crop of weeds. This is the dwelling of an
aristocrat; yet it has only a rough stone fireplace, continued outside

into a big mud-and-stone chimney, surmounted by a corn-cob structure of fagots, a headless barrel, or an old powder-canister. The floor is dirt, the door a couple of slabs, or perhaps only a pendant gunny-sack; and the bed a bunk of poles, covered with hay and army blankets. On a shelf above the small window stands a row of empty whiskey-bottles, and some bitters and liniment. The table, chairs, and stools are knocked together by means of a few nails and an axe. The kitchen requisites consist of copper pails, tin cups, and iron knives and forks; the library of a pack of cards, a copy of the "Mining Code," and perhaps a well-thumbed copy of Bret Harte's "Luck" or Mark Twain's "Roughing It." I once found Byron's poems, Dickens's "Nicholas Nickleby," Shakspeare's plays, and an old *Harper's Magazine*, as the entire library of a Colorado camp.

Such a collection of flat-roofed, wide-verandaed log-houses perched up among the rocks beside a foaming stream, skewed out of shape, and devoid of any color or appearance of civilization, is exceedingly picturesque, reminding one of a distant view of Swiss hamlets. But here there is little green in the landscape—only the dull olive of the sage-brush and buffalo-grass, and dark-hued rocks. Perhaps the white fence of a sad little graveyard in a corner of the picture will be the only light in it. All is desolation.

The inhabitants of these towns were a curious lot—bearded miners, dirty laborers, strong-armed bull-whackers, thin-lipped gamblers, men of every character, and women of no character. Sunday is unheard of, or devoted to the dance-hall. Clothes wear out, and are superseded by buckskin jackets and breeches made of army blankets; while the women renew their "linen" by saving the flour-sacks, labels and all. I remember, once noticing among a lot of red shirts and heterogeneous textures hanging on a quaking-asp pole to dry, in a Wyoming mining camp, a garment answering the purpose of a chemise that some woman had made out of two flour-sacks. On one side was printed, in large blue letters, "Hard to Beat;" on the other an azure legend, "Rough and Ready." These were the brands of the mills. Salt-bags, being stouter, are used to patch trousers, care being taken to have the grocer's advertisement outside. One week such a town would be overflowing with people, and money in plenty, whiskey triumphant, contractors busy, everybody aflame with news of wonderful gold discoveries near by, and excited with anticipations of marvellous riches and a great city to spring up there in a night. The next week the dazzling "finds" had proved "blind leads," real estate had fallen one hundred per cent., and

everybody was selling his extra boots to get out of town, leaving the
"city" with empty houses, a high-sounding title and reminiscences—
nothing else. There are dozens of towns throughout these mountains,
once the abode of hundreds of eager people and the scene of thriving
business, that are now as fully given to the moles and the bats as Baby-
lon was ever threatened to be. They were once graphically described
to me, by one who knew them well, as "towns where there are two
or three whiskey-shops and a lot of dead-beats." It was a good defi-
nition.

Such a relic was the town of Empire, lying on our road to Berthoud Pass. Now it has become a railway station, and is somewhat
revived, but then it was the merest ghost of a town. There were houses
and stores enough — barns, and fences, and gardens; Clear creek ex-
panded into a pond above the strong dam that supplied ruined mills
yet standing on its banks, but the people had departed. Yet its decline
had been less rapid than its rise, if one might judge from the look of
hasty construction about all the buildings, mainly unpainted structures
of loose boards or simple log-cabins. With the high hope of a sudden
great city which animates the breasts of all Western men "where two
or three are gathered together," the town seems to have been elabo-
rately laid out, and the broad streets run at equal intervals, and intersect at right angles all across the valley, hemmed in by precipitous hills
beyond which snow-capped peaks make a horizon. Ten years before,
fifteen hundred people, attracted by the mines which were discovered
in the vicinity, built the town with almost magic haste, and its streets
were busy with congregated men and women. The valley was a pleasant one, the mines proved productive, the trades and industries to supply the demands of this population were just established, when suddenly new mines were opened at Georgetown, Buckskin Joe, Idaho
Springs, and elsewhere, and almost in a day the miners had gone.
Robbed of their customers, the shops were quickly closed; the blacksmiths, coopers, and carpenters locked up their tools, to begin again their
nomadic life; and the school-house (newly built) did not even see
the benches that were to be whittled by jack-knives of pupils who never
came. The apothecary-shop was the last to succumb, but even that
went long ago, for this is a healthy country; and now the tavern, which
was also the post-office, was the only public place. Half a dozen families
comprised the entire population, and these all lived in the best houses,
as though they had taken their pick of the abandoned tenements. Cav-
ernous mansions were so common that they had lost, with the absence

of isolation and novelty, the fearfulness which hangs about empty houses, and the few children played in them with unaffected glee.

These are pictures of a by-gone time, however; and, though you may find plenty of ruins, you may search far for a similar life to that of the old camps. Civilization has been brought too near by railway and telegraph and a crowd of travellers, to make possible the wild scenes which were the result of extreme isolation and outlawry. Yet in some of the new and distant silver camps, even now, a brief period of disorganized revelry and roughness will exist, and there will be wickedness and terrorism enough to satisfy the most sensational appetite.

V.

AFTER leaving Empire we began the real ascent of the mountain-pass, properly speaking.

The trail led upward by a gradual ascent along the sides of heavily-timbered mountains, with almost unattainable heights overhanging on one hand, and an immense depth dropping from one's track on the other. There was little chance for extended vision till the higher portions were reached ; but the luxuriant growth of mosses, lichens, and ferns under the damp pines, and lovely flowers and grasses along the path, formed a contrast to the sombre massiveness of the opposite mountain that was never wearisome. At one point the ridge of the other mountain, far above timber-line, was hollowed into a great amphitheatre, opening out-ward. From this a slender stream trickled down to the invisible creek in the bottom of the cañon, as I could trace by its foam. Like all these snow-torrents, it was very narrow, and flashed out from the dark background of pines as if somehow a zigzag of lightning had become fixed there ; when, farther up, I could look down into this amphitheatre, I saw that the source of the stream was a delta of brooklets from a semicircle of snow-banks.

On the way I met one of the surveyors of the new wagon-road into Middle Park—an old man, clad in homespun, with long, gray hair and beard setting off his brown face and sweeping his bent shoulders. He carried a levelling-rod, and drove before him a sedate little ass, as homespun and grizzled as himself, on which was packed his small roll of butternut blankets. He was all neutral tint, like the mountain, but as picturesque as one of its weathered bowlders.

That night we encamped at timber-line—always the pleasantest of bivouacs—under Parry Peak, named after Dr. C. C. Parry, the botanist, whose party built a monument on its summit some years ago. It is easily climbed ; but I chose to ascend an opposite spur in the gray of the long evening, and here I had my first tramp above timber-line.

We were so near the limit of tree-growth that it was short work to get out of the scattered spruce-woods. Then came some stiff climbing up ledges of broken rocks standing cliff-like to bar the way to the summit. These surmounted, the remainder was easy; for from the northeast—the side I was on—this mountain, and nearly all others visible, present a smooth, grassy slope to the very top; but the western side of the range is a series of rocky precipices, seamed and shattered into chaos.

Just above the cliffs grew a number of dwarf spruces, some of them with trunks six inches or more through, yet lying flat along the ground, so that the gnarled and wind-pressed boughs were scarcely knee-high. They stood so close together, and were so rigid, that I could not press between them; but, on the other hand, they were stiff enough to bear my weight, so that I could walk over their tops when it was too far to go around. Two or three species of small brown sparrows lived there, and were very talkative. The sharp, metallic chirp of the blue snowbird was heard also as it flitted about, showing white feathers on either side of its tail in scudding from one sheltering bush to another. Doubtless careful search would have discovered its home, snugly built of circularly laid grasses, and tucked deeply into some hollow by the root of a spruce. There would be young at this season, for it was now the beginning of July.

Proceeding upward a few hundred feet at a slow pace—for any exertion quickly exhausts the breath at this great altitude—I came to the top, and stood upon the verge of a crag which was being rapidly crumbled by water and frost. Gaping cracks seamed its face, and an enormous amount of fallen rock covered a broad slope at its foot.

The first moment I arrived here I heard a most lively squeaking going on, apparently just under the edge of the cliff or in some of the cracks. It was a strange noise, somewhere between a bark and a scream, and I could think of nothing but young hawks as the authors of it. So I set to work to find the nest, but my search was vain, while the sharp squeaking seemed to multiply and to come from a dozen different places. By this time I had crawled pretty well down the rough face of the cliff, and had reached the talus of broken rock, when I caught a glimpse of a little head, with two black eyes, like a prairie-dog's, peering out of a crevice, and was just in time to see him open his small jaws and say *skink!* about as a rusty hinge would pronounce it. I whipped my revolver out of my belt and fired, but the little fellow had dodged the bullet and was gone. The echoes rattled about among the rocks, wandered up and down the cañon, and hammered lustily at half a dozen stone walls before ceasing; but when they died away not a sound was to be heard. Every little rascal had hidden himself. So I sat down and waited. In about five minutes a tiny, timid squeak broke the stillness; then a second, a trifle louder; then one away under my feet, in some subterranean passage. Hardly daring to breathe, I waited and watched. Finally the chorus was as loud as before, and I caught sight of one of the singers only about ten yards away, head and shoulders out of his hole, and doubtless commenting to his neighbor in no complimentary way upon the strange intruder. Slowly lifting my pistol, I fired. I was sure he had not seen me; yet a chip of rock flying from where he had stood was my only satisfaction — he had dodged again.

I had seen enough, however, to know that the noisy colony was a community of conies, or Little Chief hares (*Lagomys princeps*), as they are called in the books. They live wholly at or above timber-line, burrowing among the fallen and decomposing rocks which crown the summits of all of the mountains. Not every peak by any means possesses them; on the contrary, they are rather uncommon, and always are so difficult to shoot that their skins are rare in museums, and their ways little known to naturalists. During the middle of the day they are asleep and quiet; but in the evening, and all night, when the moon shines, they leave their rocky retreats and forage in the neighboring meadows, where they meet the yellow-footed marmot and other neighbors. About the only enemies they have, I fancy, are the rattlesnake and weasels, except when a wild-cat may pounce upon one, or an owl swoop down and snatch up some rambler. In midwinter, of course, their burrows are deep-buried in snow; but then they neither know nor care what the weather is, for they are hibernating, snugly ensconced in the warm bed of soft grasses and downy weeds that they have thoughtfully provided against this very contingency. If he can catch a cony, an Indian will eat it; he likes to use its fur, too, to braid his locks; but the lively little rodents are pretty safe from human foes— even when armed with Colt's revolver!

Although it was getting a trifle dusky I chose to explore a new way back to camp, which seemed to obviate re-climbing the peak. Following a stream down a quarter of a mile or so, I found I was all right, but must go through a bog and get my feet wet—an accident of too little consequence to cause much hesitation.

I did not have such an easy time on a subsequent occasion, when we delayed our return to camp until darkness overtook us—always a dangerous risk. This happened near the head-waters of the Rio Grande, where, just for sport, four of us added to our day's work a postprandial climb of about two thousand feet, with nothing in the way of view or novelty at the end of it as reward—one of the stiffest climbs I ever made, too. We began it by creeping up a narrow defile through the vertical escarpment of granite and basalt which hemmed in the valley and carried the mountain-top on its shoulders. Coming down the darkness overtook us, and we had to trust to luck to find the stairway-like passage through the cliff, for we could see nothing, and of course there was no path. Proceeding cautiously as best we could, the margin of the crag—the jumping-off place—was at last reached, but no passage down appeared. Below there, half a mile away, we could see the faint sparkle of our camp-fire, and wish for our blankets, but the situation promised little hope of reaching them before daylight the next morning. This was a hard prospect, for even an August night is freezing cold when you are without fire or shelter in the high Rockies.

Working our way along the cliff, however, we finally came to a small chasm in its face, within which a spruce-tree was growing, whose top came just a little above the surface of the bluff. The tallest of trees would reach only a fraction of the way down; but where this was rooted there might be a shelf and another break in the wall. So it was decided that I, being the lightest and most nimble of the party, should go down this tree and explore. In almost pitch-darkness, therefore, my sense of feeling my only guide, I began the descent. To get to the lower branches was easy; then, grasping firmly the bulky trunk, I "swarmed" down the rough shaft for perhaps twenty feet before I touched the ground and shouted back, "So far so good." There was a considerable ledge here, which creeping along I speedily found a way to a second lower shelf, whence I could dimly see that by scrambling down the smooth trunk of a dead pine, which had fallen against the cliff, we could reach sloping rocks, and thus extricate ourselves. Making a trumpet of my hands, I howled these facts up to my companions, and waited until, one by one, they had all descended. Then, with a few broken shins and barked elbows, we made our way safely back to our somewhat alarmed cook and his camp-fire, deciding not to try mountaineering at night again, except in an emergency.

Here in the wet grass—to return to my bog in Berthoud's pass—the beautiful white-crowned sparrows, brothers to our common Eastern white-throated sparrows, or peabody-birds, were singing away in great

glee. Besides some *chips* and *chucks*, they had a very sweet strain, frequently repeated, which said

These sparrows were just leisurely migrating from their Southern
winter-homes to their breeding-places, almost altogether north of Colorado. Eastward of the Plains, indeed, their nests are built rarely south
of Labrador, but in the Rocky Mountains the birds stay in summer

HOME OF THE WHITE-CROWNED SPARROW.

among the cool uplands almost
down to the 40th parallel. I myself had the pleasure of discover-
ing one of the earliest nests of
this bird ever taken in the United
States. It was fixed in the tall
grass growing on the bank of a
lovely trout-brook in Southwest-
ern Wyoming, and could not be
seen from above, for the yellow
grasses arched over it like a roof,
and the bird crept in through a
concealed tunnel.

It had been pretty rough coming up the pass, but the descent
from this summit was ten times worse. The road was merely a bridle-
path, and had never been improved in the least respect from the way
Nature left it. On the contrary, every animal that passed left it worse
than before, so that the whole road was a succession of deep holes, full
of mud and water, of big bowlders, with angular edges and slippery sides,
and of bogs, across which we had to build corduroy bridges, and then
thrash the mules, to keep them from leaping on one side into the mire.
The whole was steeply descending, and wound through a dense forest,
so that the getting down was an experience to be remembered. As
soon as the mules began to drop their loads in the torrents that rushed
across the trail, and do their level best to kick them to pieces; as soon
as they began to throw themselves headlong on the sharpest rocks they
could find; as soon as they got well mired in sloughs such as Bunyan
never dreamed of; as soon as they rolled, load and all, a hundred feet

or so down into a gulch, the day's sport began, and there was no in-
termission till the broad prairies of Middle Park gladdened our eyes at
evening.

Some farther characteristics of the genus *mule* were well brought
out by that day's struggle—for instance, strength. Our pack animals
were loaded with from two to three hundred pounds each; yet, while
everything went well, they climbed about as though they were free.
We found them very sure-footed and plucky under their loads so long
as they kept on their legs. This was particularly true in fording rivers,
and I once had one take me out of a very awkward predicament in
that way; but let one fall, and his courage seems to leave him.

In a bad place to go through, like a bog, mules are desperately stupid.
The very first of our mishaps that day was when the leading mule got
a trifle mired on the edge of a mud-hole, became frightened, and fell.
No power could prevent every single one of the eight pack animals following from piling themselves into that same hole in a determined effort
to get past or over the prostrate body of their leader. There they were
—nine of them—floundering on their backs in one mire, spoiling their
harness, breaking their shins against the rocks, and kicking their packs
to pieces! Safely out of that, and re-packed, the next move was for the
big mule carrying the kitchen kit to fall off the shelf-like path and roll
over and over down the hill-side about sixty feet.

These tough beasts can stand more than that, though. One of our
parties had a mule fall, by a series of bounds, an almost vertical distance
of about two hundred feet. It being supposed, of course, that he was
done for, one of the men went down with a rifle to put the animal
out of its misery, if perchance it still lived. But he found the tough
beast pretty comfortable, the pack having acted as a cushion to most of
its tumbles; and when released the acrobat followed along into camp
little the worse for its accident.

His mule is the mountain-man's mainstay. He treats it much more
kindly than he does himself, and respects it far more than he does his
neighbor. Finding all sorts of excuses for an habitual cutthroat, he
simply *hangs* the mule-stealer.

VI.

EMERGING from Berthoud's Pass and its Gehenna of trails (nevertheless, I traversed far worse afterward, down in the San Juan country and up among the Wind Rivers), we came out, just before sunset, into the grassy savannas of Middle Park, and overtook a party of the Survey that had preceded us, resting in a little grove of pretty quaking-asp trees.

Knowing where the camp is to be placed, the most of us—there are half a dozen, all told, in the party—gallop ahead and unsaddle our riding animals, each putting his saddle, gun, coats, etc., in a heap at the foot of a tree. By that time the train has come up, and every one turns to help remove the packs and place the cargo in orderly array. This operation the sagacious mules undergo with the most exemplary quietude; and a little later, when the animals have cooled, the aparejos are taken off, the bell-horse is hobbled, and the whole herd are turned loose for the night. Their first act is to roll, removing the perspiration and scratching the backs grown hot and irritated under the heavy loads, which, at first, often average 250 or 300 pounds. Then how they eat! The sun sets, twilight fades, the camp-fire is replenished, and still they munch, munch at the crisp grass; the stars come out and the riders go in, but the last glimpse of the mules in the darkness shows them with their noses to the ground. A pack train intelligently cared for will actually grow fat upon a trip of this kind, though they never get a mouthful of grain during the whole four or five months.

The very first mule unloaded is the staid veteran distinguished by the honor of bearing the *cuisine*. A shovel and an axe having been released from their lashings, the cook seizes them, and hurriedly digs a trench, in which he builds his fire. While it is kindling he and anybody else whose hands are free cut or pluck up fuel. We are so stiff sometimes, from our eight or ten hours in the saddle, that we can hardly move our legs; but it is no time to lie down. Hobbling round after wood and water limbers us up a little, and hastens the preparation of dinner—that blessed goal of all our present hopes! If a stream that holds out any promise is near, the rod is brought into requisition at once; and, if all goes well, there are enough fish for the mess by the time the cook is ready for them.

IN THE EDGE OF MIDDLE PARK.

Flies, as a general thing, are rather a delusion to the angler than a snare for the trout. The accepted bait is the grasshopper, except when there are great numbers of this insect, in which case the fish are all so well fed that they will not bite. The best fishing had by any party that I was with was in Wyoming, along the head-waters of the Green river, and in eastern Idaho, on the tributaries of the Snake. That region, the entomologists say, is the nursery of all the "'hopper" hordes which devastate the crops of Dakota, Colorado, and Kansas; but when we were there it was so difficult to find bait, that we used

4

to keep our eyes open all day, and pounce upon every grasshopper we could find, saving them for the evening's fishing. The usual catch was salmon-trout, great two and three pounders, gleaming, speckled, and inside golden pink — that sunset color called "salmon." They were not gamy, though—really it was more exciting to capture the lively bait than it was to hook the trout—and we were glad of it, since the object was not sport, but the despised "pot." In the southern Rocky Mountains we took true brook-trout, of smaller size, but of excellent flavor. The largest I ever saw came from the upper Rio Grande, where a charming little ranchwoman fried them for us—in commemoration of which the cañon where they lurked was named "Irene." Rapid decapitation and splitting finished the dressing. The flesh was always hard and firm and white, as it ought to be in a fish born and bred in snow-water. If by chance any were left over from dinner, they made most toothsome sandwiches for the next noon-day lunch, especially if (as was once our happy lot) there was currant jelly to put between the bread and the backbone.

But all this happens while the cook gets his fire well a-going. That accomplished, and two square bars of three-quarters inch iron laid across the trench, affording a firm resting-place for the kettles, the stove is complete. John sets a pail of water on to heat, jams his bake-oven well into the coals at one side, buries the cover of it in the other side of the fire, and gets out his long knife. Going to the cargo, he takes a side of bacon out of its gunny-sack, and cuts as many slices as he needs, saving the rind to grease his oven. Then he is ready to make his bread.

Flour is more portable than pilot-biscuit; therefore warm, light bread, freshly made morning and night, has gratefully succeeded hard-tack in all mining and mountain camps. Sometimes a large tin pan is carried in which to mould the bread; but often a square half-yard of canvas kept for the purpose, and laid in a depression in the ground, forms a sufficiently good bowl, and takes up next to none of the precious room. When a bread-pan is taken it must be lashed bottom up on top of the kitchen-mule's pack. If it breaks loose and slips down on his rump, or dangles against his hocks, there is likely to be some fun; and when a squall sweeps down from the high peaks, and the hailstones beat a devil's tattoo on that hollow pan, the mule under it goes utterly crazy. The canvas bread-pan, therefore, is preferred. Sometimes even this is dispensed with, the bread being mixed up with water right in the top of the flour-bag, and moulded on the cover of a box or some other smooth surface. Baking-powder, not yeast, is used, of course. This species of leaven (of which there are many varieties) is put up in round tin boxes. You find these boxes scattered from end to end of the Territories, and forming gleaming barricades around all the villages. The miners convert them to all sorts of utilities, from flying targets to safes for gold-dust; and one man in Colorado Springs collected enough of them, and of fruit-cans, to shingle and cover the sides of his house. There seems now to be found no region so wild, no dell so sequestered, that these glittering mementos do not testify to a previous invasion. On the highest, storm-splintered pinnacle of Mount Lincoln I discovered a baking-powder can tucked into a cranny, as a receptacle for the autographs of adventurous visitors.

TOSSING THE FLAPJACK.

Sometimes the cook used the Dutch bake-oven—a shallow iron pot with a close-fitting iron cover, upon which you can pile a great thickness of coals, or can build a miniature fire. Having greased the inside of the oven with bacon-rind, bread bakes quickly and safely. A better article, nevertheless, results from another method. Mould your bread

well, lay the round loaf in the skillet, and hold it over the fire, turning
the loaf occasionally until it is somewhat stiff; then take it out, prop it
upright before the coals with the aid of a twig, and turn frequently. It
is soon done through and through, and equally on both sides. Sometimes we had biscuits made in the same way; but these were more
troublesome; and the one great anxiety in the preparation of dinner,
after a day's riding or climbing, is speed. Men must eat heartily in
this oxygen-consuming West, and are eager to discharge that duty. I
invariably found myself travelling in a particularly hungry latitude.

The table-furniture, and a large portion of the small groceries, such
as salt, pepper, mustard, etc., are carried in two red boxes, each two and
a half feet long, one and a half feet broad, and a foot high. Each box
is covered by a thin board, which sets in flush with the box, and also
by two others hinged together, and to the edge of the box. Having
his bread a-baking, the cook sets the two red boxes a little way apart,
unfolds the double covers backward until they rest against each other,
letting the ends be supported on a couple of stakes driven into the
ground, and over the whole spreads an enamelled cloth. He thus has
a table two and a half feet high, one and a half feet wide, and six feet
long. Tin and iron ware chiefly constitute the table-furniture; so that
the mule carrying it may roll a hundred feet or so down a mountain,
as occasionally happens, yet not break the dishes.

His table set, John returns to his fire, and very soon salutes our
happy ears with his stentorian voice in lieu of gong: "Grub Pi-i-i-le!"

Coffee is the main item on our bill of fare. It is water, and milk,
and whiskey, and medicine combined. Ground and browned in camp,
made in generous quantity over the open fire, settled by a dash of cold
water and drunk without milk, it is a cup of condensed vigor, the true
elixir vitæ, a perpetual source of comfort and strength. Tea is pronounced "no good," and chocolate is only used to distinguish Sunday
by. Oh, what a bitter trial it was, after one particularly hard day's
work in Wyoming, and a stormy day at that, to have the steaming and
fragrant coffee-pail kicked over by a clumsy foot! There was an irre-
pressible howl of execration, and one man's hand impulsively clutched
his revolver.

But coffee, though the main-stay, is not all of our feast. For meat
we have bacon and generally steaks or roasted ribs of elk, mule-deer,
or mountain sheep, with fresh, crisp bread, or sometimes wheaten flapjacks, made in the orthodox way, and properly thrown into the air
during the cooking. When, as occasionally happens, two parties meet,

the rival cooks toss the flapjacks to each other, when they require turning, so that every cake begins at one fire and is finished at the other.
In the mining camps (it is said) they toss them up the chimney, and
catch them right-side up outside the door! Butter there is none, nor

A CAMP-DINNER.

milk, nor potatoes, nor vegetables, except rice and hominy; but there
is plenty of fruit-sauce — apricots, peaches, prunes, etc., which, being
dried, are very portable, and, being Californian, are wonderfully good.
Occasionally, also, there is a corn-dodger by way of variety, when a
pound cake of maple-sugar will be melted into sirup, for a feast. For
dessert we have nothing at all (yet are content), save when, now and
then, the cook makes a plum duff to put our digestions to the test.

Here, in this Middle Park camp, just as we were sitting down around the table, using bowlders and war-bags and sacks of bacon as chairs, we saw approaching at a leisurely lope over the prairie, a large, lean sorrel horse that showed good points, but seemed to have been roughing it quite as much as his rider. The horse bore a gayly-rigged ranger's saddle, behind which was slung the carcass of a black-tailed deer, whose flapping head and heels seemed not to disturb him in the least; and in the saddle sat a remarkable man—a person of medium height, but of so powerful a build that his breadth of chest and massive loins seemed better fitted for a giant. His hair and beard were curly, and yellow as corn-silk; his face fiery red, through incessant exposure to sun, and snow, and alkali-dust; but his eyes were blue as the little *Lycæna* butterflies flitting in thousands over the blossoming prairie. Across his shoulder he balanced a heavy, double-barrelled rifle; his waist was girdled by a red-white-and-blue cartridge-belt; from his boot-leg protruded the horn handle of a hunting-knife, and a six-shooter was strapped to the pommel of his saddle. He was dressed throughout in buckskin, from every seam of which depended a six-inch fringe of the same material; but his hat was a colorless *sombrero*, badly crushed.

This was "Mountain Harry" Yount and his horse "Texas." He was a professional hunter, with whom later I became well acquainted through months of companionship in hard work—a notable man, of a type almost as foreign to the Eastern States as is a native of Japan.

Yount's parents were Swiss, but he was born at Susquehanna, Pennsylvania, and so came by double right to his deep affection for the mountains. When he was a child his father moved to Kansas, introducing the boy at an early age to pioneer life. But, wearying of the plains, when eighteen years old Harry joined an emigrant train, and pushed out to Pike's Peak, driving oxen. Gold-mining, however, was not his vocation; and, stimulated by his innate passion for the freedom of unfenced nature, Yount quickly abandoned the rocker for the rifle, beginning the wild and lonely career he has since led. At that time such a life was far more lonely than at present, notwithstanding that he was able to get his game much nearer to the main settlements than is now possible. Yet the towns twenty-five years ago were far between, and wanderers among the snowy ranges or interior parks very few. Harry hunted principally in the Medicine Bow range, the lofty crests of which are about the only peaks of the Rocky Mountains the traveller on the Union Pacific Railway catches a glimpse of after Cheyenne has been left an hour behind. Here roamed the mountain buffalo, the broad-antlered wapiti, the agile black-tail, the shy, covert-loving Virginia deer;

OUR HUNTER.

every valley was haunted by antelopes, and all the crags were homes of the mountain sheep. Where there was so much tender flesh of course many beasts of prey were present—Harry once unexpectedly stepped into a convention of seven grizzlies—and hard experience with these creatures added deliberate courage to the skill learned from seeking wary deer and trapping the small, shrewd game whose furry coats were coveted. To find out all the passes and game-trails through these unknown mountains—all the resources of living alone anywhere, and at any season; to elude or conciliate the Indians, all of whom were to be dreaded; and, most of all, to become thoroughly acquainted with the distribution and habits of the animals and birds, was the task before this young hunter, and one looked forward to with eager pleasure.

He was armed with stout hands, keen powers of observation, and strong enthusiasm. Never killing for sport, all his energies were directed toward making every grain of his costly ammunition yield a profitable return. He shot buffaloes for their robes, and what meat he could send a wagon after from the nearest mining camp, many a time slaughtering a whole herd by keeping himself concealed while he shot them one after another, or by riding them down in a long chase on Texas's back. Antelopes he hunted for the sake of the flesh. They were abundant on the plains everywhere, and his method was to drive a span of mules and a wagon to some point and hunt in a circle around it, killing a load, and then driving back. There is far more skill than appears in this kind of work. He once shot seventy antelopes in one day, in a match with a crack shot from the East, who was mightily skilful in scoring bull's-eyes, but found hitting a nimble prong-horn an entirely different matter. Difficult as this feat was, and much credit as it reflected upon him, Harry was always ashamed of it. It went against his heart to kill so many innocent creatures only for the glory of markmanship.

Harry was (and *is*, for he still lives in the West, as game warden of Yellowstone Park—and here's to you, old fellow!) a quiet, simple-hearted man among a generation of ruffians fortunately growing less. Constantly supplying the workmen along the new trans-continental railways with meat, he never joined those orgies that used to characterize their hours of leisure, or took part in the series of bloody quarrels that never ended so long as any combatants were alive. By nature a gentleman, under his sinewy frame and tireless strength there glows a heart which hates cruelty. His eye is open to every beautiful feature of the grand world in which he lives—his heart is alive to all the gentle influences of the original wilderness. Having been much alone, he is

timid in new society, reticent, thoughtful, and given to framing fanciful
theories to account for such phenomena as he does not comprehend.

What stories he could tell round a camp-fire at night, when dinner
was over, the big blaze had been built, and the pipes lit! I had many
a discussion with him concerning points in natural history, wherein he
opposed life-long experience to the statements of the books in not a
few instances. He has read much, particularly about the West, and
written somewhat for newspapers, even indulging in rhyme now and
then. A handsome man, but holding in great contempt the long-haired
fops of the plains who ape the style (because they cannot rise to the
heroism or skill) of Kit Carson or Buffalo Bill, Harry is as vain as a girl
about his personal appearance. His belt, holster, knife-sheath, bridle,
and saddle are all set off with a barbaric glitter. I have known him
to pay seventy-five dollars to a Shoshoné squaw for the adornment of
a single buckskin jacket, which was a marvel of fringes, fur-trimming,
and intricate embroidery of beads. Yet his is not a peacock-like, strut-
ting vanity, but a simple, genuine delight in bright colors and pretty
things. He laughs quietly at it himself, but says he likes it. And why
shouldn't he dress as suits him?

"Mountain Harry" could on no account be induced to leave his be-
loved hills. He is happy as a man on broad estates—indeed, he feels
that he owns such, as, in truth, he does, to all purposes. He has an
idea that he belongs there, and that those rough and desolate slopes,
those mighty cañons and towery walls of lichen-stained rock, those forests hiding the sources of mighty rivers, those white peaks striking up
into the azure, would miss him and grieve for him, as he would for
them, if once he got beyond the invigorating chill of their snow-banks
and the resinous fragrance of their pines. It is such a character as his
that Thoreau addressed:

> "O man of wild habits,
> Partridges and rabbits,
> Who hast no cares,
> Only to set snares;
> Who liv'st all alone
> Close to the bone,
> And where life is sweetest
> Constantly eatest!"

VII.

DINNER over (and, much as our bodies ached with ten hours in the saddle, or a day's climb to make some topographical station, the brief rest and the help of the food has freshened us remarkably), the remaining hour or two of daylight is employed in odd jobs—exploring the neighborhood, to get an idea of next day's route or in search of the natural science of the place; in fishing, mending saddles or clothes (*hoc opus, hic labor est!*), in making beds, writing letters, and, if it looks like rain, in putting up the little dog-tents, of which there is one for each two of us, except the cook, who has a tent to himself and his comestibles.

Under how many varying circumstances, then, this evening meal is eaten! Sometimes, when the camp is stationary for two or three days, in a pleasant bower; next, out on the dry plains, before an illimitable landscape of sere grass stretching away to where the delectable mountains lie on the snow-silvered rim of the world; again, it is in a hot valley of Arizona, and the scalding alkali dust blows in your face and filters through your food; or at high timber-line in Colorado, where sleet and snow contest the passage down your throat with rapidly cooling coffee and chilly bacon; or beside the Yellowstone in August, with its millions of ravenous flies and hordes of thirsty mosquitoes; eaten anywhere and everywhere, with the royal vigor of appetite that comes of this out-door life, and the marvellous grandeur of the Rocky Mountains as garniture for your dining-hall.

Then the times afterward, when

> "The day is done, and the darkness
> Falls from the wings of Night!"

That is the pleasant hour of camp-life, and you forget that a little while ago you were vowing that if ever you got safely home you would never again be caught out on such an all-work, no-play expedition as *this*. After-dinner reflections take on a rosier hue, and your pipe never tastes sweeter than now, as you idly creep about among the brookside willows till its smoke warms the wings of the birds seeking an early roost.

The most noticeable bird, by-the-way, in this part of the mountains, haunting our track all through the pass, and not quite deserting our fireside here in the park, was the Canada jay. My first sight of it was at the summit. As soon as the smoke of the camp-fire began to drift away toward the rocky peaks over our heads, and the odor of the juicy and hissing bacon, mingling with the warm fragrance of the russet-backed biscuit, essayed to rise among the spruces, then the Canada jays began to assemble to share in the coming meal.

"What are those birds, Steve?" I asked our old head packer.

"Well," he replied, "in Oregon we used to call 'em 'camp-robbers;' in Californy I've heerd 'em called 'meat-hawks;' and up North we called 'em 'buffalo-birds.'"

He had never heard the name "whiskey-jack" (said to be a corruption of a Cree Indian word), or "moose-bird," both of which are the common designations of the bird in the Canadian and Maine lumber camps; nor had it occurred to him that they closely resembled the other jays, which he knew very well. The scientific name is *Perisoreus canadensis* of Bonaparte.

This bird is nearly eleven inches in length, and strongly built; its head and neck and the forepart of the breast are white; beginning dull lead-color at the back of the head, a general ashy tinge covers the whole upper parts, interrupted by a whitish collar; there are two narrow white bars across the wings, and the edges of some of the wing-quills and the extremity of the tail are obscurely whitened; underneath, its color is smoky gray, and the bill and feet are black.

Belonging to the Arctic regions, it spreads in summer over the whole of British America to the shores of the Frozen Sea, and is common enough; while in winter it retreats southward only so far as the shutting up of the polar world by darkness obliges it to, and only stragglers get as far south as Pennsylvania, except along high ranges. In the Rocky Mountains, however, the Canada jay lives all the year round, even south to Arizona; since those Alpine heights supply, through altitude, that congenial climate which, nearer the level of the sea, he can only find in high latitudes. The Canada jay is not alone in thus extending southward its Arctic range into a warmer climate, along the peninsula which the snowy tops of the mountains afford. There are many other birds that do the same thing—for instance, the white-crowned sparrow, of which I have already spoken; the horned lark, the ptarmigan, and various others. The same advantage is shared by many sorts of insects, particularly beetles; and on some of the peaks occur isolated colonies of moths and butterflies, which otherwise you will not find south of the Arctic circle. So, too, it is reported that the rare mountain goat—a lover of ice-fields, like the Alpine ibex and chamois—works his way even to the borders of Arizona along the cold and lofty crests of the sierras, though nowhere found, even at the level of timber-line, south of the headwaters of the Mackenzie river.

The Canada jay is smaller than the familiar blue jay, and has no crest like his; but the lighter-tinted feathers of the head are moderately long, causing a fat, rounded appearance, as though a white hood were drawn over the ash-gray mantle of the rest of the body. Around the neck is a band of dark lead-color, like a blackish cape to the hood. This, with his black feet and bill, make him like a brigand; and, in fact, he is one—the terror of the smaller birds of the woods, whose homes he robs ruthlessly of both eggs and young. I have a record of a case where a single pair of these jays destroyed the fledglings in four nests of snow-birds in one day. The narrator emptied both barrels of his gun in the direction of the marauders, and naïvely remarks that he is "inclined to think they have killed no young birds since." The small birds hate them, therefore, as they do owls and crows, and mob them at every safe opportunity. A lost straggler of this species was seen many years ago, in midsummer, in the upper part of New York City—of all curious places!—where he was surrounded by a group of sparrows and warblers poking no end of fun at the bewildered stranger, just as the city newsboys would at a country lad.

This jay is never seen out of the forests of the high mountains—say from nine thousand feet upward—where he picks up a precarious existence; and in winter the poor bird is often reduced to mere skin and bones. "At such times it will frequently weigh no more than a plump snow-bird or sparrow, and undoubtedly starves to death sometimes. During the latter part of autumn its hoarse croaking is almost the only sound to be heard in the cold, sombre forests that lie near timber-line." The moment the hunter camps in the dark spruce forests the jays flock about and peer at him with great curiosity. They are so tame that they perch just over his head, and walk about among his luggage, chattering to each other about the matter, and cocking their head on one side and the other just as a gigantic chickadee might do. If the hunter leaves camp for a moment the birds flock in and snatch at any scrap of meat or other eatable morsel, even pulling the frying bacon out of the skillet sometimes; and if he cuts up a deer, then he is sure of their interested and inquisitive company.

The Canada jay afforded Wilson an opportunity to fire a shot at Buffon, whose self-conceited fancies he was never weary of ridiculing. He says: "Were I to adopt the theoretical reasoning of a celebrated French naturalist, I might pronounce this bird to be a debased descendant from the common blue jay of the United States, degenerated by the influence of the bleak and chilling regions of Canada, or, perhaps, a *spurious* production between the blue jay and the cat-bird; or, what would be more congenial to the Count's ideas, trace its degradation to the circumstance of migrating, some thousand years ago, from the genial shores of Europe—where nothing like degeneracy or degradation ever takes place among any of God's creatures. I shall, however, on the present occasion, content myself with stating a few particulars better supported by facts, and more consonant to the plain homespun of common-sense." Then follows his account, most of the facts of which he obtained from Hearne's "Journey."

In the Arctic regions (where it is a great nuisance to the hunter, stealing the bait from his traps) the jay builds a stout nest in a dense evergreen-tree, woven of sticks and twigs, inside of which is a well-packed inner nest of soft mosses, lined abundantly with feathers. Though it lays its eggs and hatches them out before the snow has left the woods in the spring, it is able to feed its young out of hoarded stores of food. Our Rocky Mountain variety breeds in the elevated spruce forests, but I was never there early enough to take its nest, which is always a rare thing to find.

Though noisy and thievish, the camp-birds are amusing fellows, and we liked well to have them around the often cold and desolate camps made just under the snow-line. It was hard to believe that they were so perfectly wild, for their actions suggested those of a trained parrot —every motion implied a spectator.

VIII.

THE march across the Middle Park was decidedly uninteresting. On this side the mountains you come upon the cretaceous formations which were deposited as *débris* from the worn-down summits, when they were only islands here and there in a boundless ocean. These creta-ceous strata were folded and flexed before that great upheaval lifted the Rocky Mountains bodily throughout their whole extent. Here, too, are many dikes and palisades of eruptive rock, all of which about this dis-trict can probably be referred to a line of small volcanoes lying south of here. These lava-bluffs, resting on sedimentary strata, have been carved by water and frost into all sorts of queer shapes, reminding one of the Garden of the Gods. The heights bounding the Park were pictu-resque, but the ground travelled was only a bare, rough plain, after all, and I was glad to get to Hot Sulphur Springs, where a little settlement was beginning to exist, under the care of Mr. William N. Byers, the plucky Denver editor already introduced to my readers. These springs, and the land about them, were early pre-empted by Mr. Byers, who built a cabin, and placed a log roof over the principal basin. It is one of the most remarkable localities in Colorado. Close to the bank of the Grand river there boils out a great central spring of hot sulphur-water, the deposits of which have built up a mass of white rock many feet high and yards square, in the centre of which is the vent, and an oval basin about forty feet long and twenty wide. At the lower end the wa-ter is only knee-deep, perhaps; but at the upper end, where the stream pours out, it is seven or eight feet deep. You step in at the lower end, and find the temperature very pleasant; but as you advance there is a rapid increase of heat, until you must have been long parboiled before you can stand close up at the vent, whence water of about 110 degrees of heat gushes in a strong stream.

The springs have been resorted to for their medicinal properties from time immemorial by the Indians, who still come here during the summer in large companies. Such a bath is, of course, the best possible help for rheumatism, a disease from which all Indians are great sufferers; and the Utes were greatly disgusted to see the white owner assert his rights by roofing the basin in and putting a lock on the door. The fact that he gave them every reasonable privilege for bathing freely, while he charged the prospectors and tourists who happened along six "bits" for an entrance, did not satisfy them; and they were so grieved and angry about the matter at first that it almost came to war.

I believe this was not all selfishness and rheumatism on the part of the Indians, but partly a superstitious feeling that a sacrilege was being committed—something that moves an Indian very quickly, and which once put me in a dangerous place, as I shall have occasion to mention farther on.

The Utes have a tradition about these springs, told me by Antelope, one of the sub-chiefs whose band was encamped there. He said that long ago, before any Europeans ever came to the West, there lived a chief of the Utes who was not only an heroic warrior but also a wise and saintly man. His voice was always for peace, and under his moderate guidance the whole tribe prospered. When he had grown aged, though, the restless young men urged the making of war upon the neighboring Indians of the plains, the Arapahoes, and won a good many votes in the council in its favor. The old chief resisted and begged and argued; but at last the hotheads conquered, not only disregarding the aged man's admonitions, but scornfully deposing him from his presidency. Broken-hearted, the old chief sank away into feeble health, and upon the news of the first defeat of his braves he died. Yet it was with sorrow, not anger; and; true to his beneficent life, his spirit entered into the heart of a lofty hill, whence instantly burst out the healing waters of these varied and copious springs.

The indignation of Antelope's Utes—which was almost at boiling-point when we happened along—therefore had this semi-religious foundation; and a half-drunken old squaw, hideously scarred by a husband who had cut off her nose years ago to mark her forever as an adulteress, expressed about the temper of the tribe when she rushed at two of us with a knife, made from the end of a broken scythe, as if to cut us in pieces.

Close beside the spring used for bathing is a second one, also of hot sulphur-water; and near to these several other springs, both hot and cold, varying in their mineral character; and in addition cold springs of sulphur-water, with others of pure water whose temperature is almost at freezing-point. Ah, what delicious draughts came from that round little fountain up on the hill—princess of all the springs in the world in my recollection!

The natural history of this place was very interesting — even the little that a two-days' stay afforded the superficial observer. There used to be plenty of elk and deer here, but now they are very rare. The howl of the mountain-lion is sometimes heard, and one day a small cinnamon bear came rattling down the hill-side and stampeded a pair of valiant explorers in magnificent style, paying for it with his life, however, as soon as they had got their breath.

But I was after smaller game. In the outlet of the hot sulphur-bath, for example, I went searching for mollusks; and there, and also immediately in the cooler alum, salt, and magnesia springs, I found abundance of little *physa* snails, although they seem to occur nowhere else in the vicinity. The rocks that encroach upon the Grand river here, and form the first indication of the magnificent cañon through which its waters rush furiously a few miles below, are full of niches and small grottoes, the last of which are the homes of innumerable bats. This was attested by their presence in the evening, when they went squeaking and diving about over the river, hawking after insects; and also by large deposits of their dung, which closely resembles tar.

The niches in the rocks were occupied by large colonies of barn-swallows—the only place I ever found them breeding away from civilized structures, as, of course, they were all obliged to do before the coming of white men to America. Sometimes the niches in the lime-rock (the whole mass of which had been built up of deposits from the mineral waters) were so close together that there would be half a dozen in a square yard; yet every one had its burnt-breasted tenants, and the twittering silenced the gurgle and sputter of the rapid stream at the ledge's base. The floor of each niche was hollowed out, so that it only required to be softly carpeted to constitute it a perfect nest. For this grass-stems and a few large feathers were used, precisely as in our Eastern barns. But here the birds had greatly economized labor by occupying the niches, for they needed not to build the firm underpinning and stout high walls which become necessary in the barn, or on an exposed rock-shelf, to prevent the eggs and young from rolling out; all these happy birds had to do was to furnish a house already made. These were the *Hirundo erythrogastrum*—the true *barn* swallow, with orange breast, which builds on the beams or in angles of the rafters *inside* of the barn; but on the opposite bluff—which, being native rock, and not this lime-deposit, had a smooth face—lived the familiar *cliff*

5

or *eave* swallows (*Petrochelidon lunifrons*), whose cup-like or bottle-shaped abodes cling in a long row outside our barns under the shelter of their eaves.

Climbing a high point back of our tents, which were in the midst of a sage-brush flat, close to the river, I had a queer little bit of good-luck one evening. It was just at nightfall, and as I reached the top a large owl came swooping down and perched on a crag some distance off. Drawing my revolver, I held it up and walked slowly nearer, expecting neither to get within range nor hit the bird if I fired; but he let me get so near that at last, about thirty yards off, I blazed away, and down came the owl. Rushing up, I could see him lying in the brush a little way below; but it was some time before I got courage enough to reach down and take hold of him, for a bite or talon-grasp from a wounded owl is no joke. He proved to be stone-dead, and it was a long time before I found out the bloodless wound, the bullet having gone in at the base of the skull and out of the open mouth, without tearing any of the feathers. He was a fine barred or "cat" owl, about two feet long.

From this pinnacle, in daylight, there is visible a picture of blue mountains whose sharp, serrated outline indicates a portion of the main range in front of Long's Peak. Among those immutable yet ever-changing bulwarks lies a lake in a circle of guardian peaks whose heads tower thousands of feet above it, and whose bases meet no one knows how far below the surface of its dark waters. It is Grand Lake, a spot *taboo* among Indians and mysterious to white men. The scenery is primeval and wild beyond description: Roundtop is one mountain at least that has suffered no desecration since the ice ploughed its furrowed sides. The lake itself lies in the trough of a glacier basin, and its western barrier is an old terminal moraine, striking evidences of glacial action occurring on all sides in the scored cliffs and lateral moraines that hem it in. Its extent is about two miles by three, and its greatest depth unfathomable with a line six hundred feet in length. The water is cold, and clear near the shore, but of inky blackness in the middle. In the reflection usually pictured upon its calm bosom all the cloud-crowned heads about it meet in solemn conclave; but not seldom, and with little warning, furious winds sweep down and lash its lazy waters till the waves vie with each other in terrible energy. On such treachery hangs one of the many tales told by the camp-fire of this singular lake.

Some years ago—so the story goes—a party of Utes, with women and children, were camped upon its banks, trout-fishing. Suspecting nothing, and unprepared for war, they were one day surprised by a strong band of Arapahoes, their ancient and implacable enemies. Looking first of all to the safety of their wives and little ones, the best and quickest way seemed to be to set them adrift upon rafts in the centre of the lake till the victory should be won. This done, they returned

GRAND LAKE.

to repel the attack. The battle waged. Engrossed in its excitement, none noted the rising winds, till the patience of the elements failed, the unleashed storms rushed down upon their prey, and the rafts were submerged. Never to this day has the lake given back a single one of its victims. In their consternation the Utes fell an easy prey to the Arapahoes, and only one of all that company escaped to tell the fearful

tale. What wonder that the Indian counts such signal and swift destruction as a special manifestation of the Great Spirit's anger, and
avoids the place as a dreadful and fatal spot?

The outlet of the lake is one of the forks of the Grand river, following which brings me back to where I started from. It is fortunate that
I can follow river-courses, or I should get totally lost!

IX.

A DAY'S march down the Grand river from the Hot Sulphur Springs takes one to the junction of both the Blue and the Muddy rivers, flowing in from opposite directions, through a wide, marshy plain. There is a knoll that juts out into the valley, from which the finest view is obtained. You naturally face the north there, and at your right hand the Grand winds five or six miles down from where a bend in the river limits the view, through meadows of that deep-green grass seen only in wet ground, and on both sides series of hills sweep up higher and higher till they merge into the dark mountains behind them. These hills are covered with sage-brush, whose dense, ashy foliage makes them appear carpeted with drab plush. From this cinereous tint there is a gradation into the indigo of greater heights; and, as though to set these out, the indistinct outline of peaks in the main range is visible in the wondrously clear air—a rear rank of mountains. At one point they rise into a mass, among which Roundtop, at the side of Grand Lake, is but a dwarf beside the towering height of Long's. Farther to the right a near hill, Elk mountain, hides a quarter or so of the horizon, which contains some of the highest peaks in the range; but to the left you can follow the line of bald hills around to the north, where, through the break in which the Muddy comes down, you can discern Rabbit Ears and its neighbors of the Medicine Bow range, dim with distance and embroidered with snow. Between them and you some remarkably abrupt hills will attract your attention, and just in front long, brown palisades of indurated clays form the prominent object in the picture. Running your eye along the hills to the left, you catch sight of the jaws of the Grand Cañon of the Grand, a tremendous rent through granites and eruptive rocks, three miles long and 1500 feet deep,* where in

---

* This gorge now appears on the maps as Gore's Cañon, and the Denver and Rio Grande Railway has run a narrow-gauge line through it, adding one more to the long list of views of splendid scenery this company offers the traveller.

many places you may drop a stone plumb from the edge of the cliff to the river below.

Now turn around. At your feet is another river wriggling through the grass and willows, just as the Grand does, till it joins that stream in the centre of the valley. It is named the Blue, but its waters are yellow with the mud from the streams at its head. Its hither banks are mere sage-brush plains, lovely in the distance and uncomfortable close by; but on its farther bank stand the Park mountains, the finest range in the region, with their heroic head, Mount Powell—the most mountainous they seem to-day of all the mountains I have yet seen. The whole range is rugged and inaccessible in the extreme, and of a deep-blue color, whether seen one or one hundred miles away. Behind Powell stand almost his equals, isolated by "great gulfs," all bare and ragged and black save the long, thin locks of snow blown back from their ancient foreheads. Climbing 2000 feet to the top of an opposite hill, we photographed these mountains and their foreground. During the time we were there snow-storms drifted through, banks of clouds filled their gorges, rain came from them and scudded across the valley, their pinnacles swam one moment in the glow of sunlit haze, and stood out the next sharp and cold against a steel-gray winter sky.

One day we had a lively experience of this same "winter sky." It treated us to an all-day, steady down-pour of rain and sleet, through which we rode in dripping and disconsolate silence. The train had gone ahead, as usual; and when my friend and myself reached the place of encampment it was pitch dark, the storm increased in force, and our tents were not even raised. In this plight we cooked and ate our food under such shelter as a willow bush afforded; and, erecting the tent, with a big ditch around it, crept out of our rubber ponchos into our blankets, and slept in spite of wind and rain.

"Rheumatism next morning?"

"Not a bit of it; never felt better in my life."

It is fifty miles from the mouth of the Blue river to Breckenridge— a little mining town — where we crossed over the Park range to the head-waters of the South Platte, through the Hoosier pass. This pass admits you into South Park. The descent—nothing remarkable, however—is rather steep, and near the base you come face to face with very high, vertical walls of smooth, black granite, perfectly marbled by veins of quartz intersecting each other in every direction, and measuring from a tenth of an inch to six feet in thickness. Right here, in the ruggedest of rugged gorges, where it would seem impossible for goats to spend the night comfortably, is the village of Montgomery, whose glory, like that of three-fourths of these mountain towns, is departed. The miners seem to take delight in forming their "camps" in such a way as to exclude every possibility of anything nice or inviting. In a choice of two objects they invariably take that which is most rude and uncomfortable. But this contributes to picturesqueness, and I can think of nothing which exhibits this element of beauty more than one of these towns perched among the *débris* of a primeval earthquake.

Down this gorge came the South Platte, a brawling, bounding youth of a stream, just released from the icy fetters of the mountain where it takes its rise. It was not late when dinner was over, and, lighting my favorite pipe, I unfolded my bed, stretched it out in a convenient place without any special making up, and then walked down to the bank of the river. Just as I reached the margin a little drab-colored bird flitted across the stream and dived into the water. The bird looked like a sparrow. But who ever saw a sparrow dive like that? I went nearer, and saw it come out; so there could be no doubt about its having gone under. An instant later a second came flying down the creek, dropped upon the water, where I could see it plainly, sank to the bottom, and with outspread wings began to move about the pebbles as unconcernedly as if he was picking up grubs on shore. I knew him then. He was the water-ouzel, or dipper—a bird now very well known to naturalists (and popularly), but then more of a novelty. Anxious to get a better view, I incautiously walked out on a log that spanned the current, when in a flash my cap and pipe went one way and I the other. Ugh! how cold that water was! and deep, too! By the time I struggled up I was completely saturated with ice-water; and by the time I had succeeded in extricating from the depths of my war-bag any dry clothes I was almost too stiff to put them on, for a cutting wind swept down from the heights. But this accomplished at last, I began to run back and forth as briskly as my chilled muscles would permit, when down came an icy blast and a heavy fall of wet snow. Snatching our tents, we laid them across our half-made beds and crept under, supposing we should be out again in a quarter of an hour or so; but that squall settled into a storm, and we had to undress ourselves in those confined quarters, wriggle the blankets into shape as best we could, and stay there under six inches of snow till morning. This was the very next night after the rainy day on Rattlesnake creek; and during the succeeding one I slept out alone on Mosquito pass, without any bed at all, as you will presently hear.

X.

My first year's campaign taught me some points in camp-life which would have lessened the hardship, if known earlier, information upon which may prove useful to some future wanderer.

Any one, for instance, who is of the opinion that it is not hard work to ride on mule-back in the Rocky Mountains an average of twenty miles a day for three months, is respectfully referred to practical experience for an answer. It is noteworthy, though, that the wisest entertain widely different views on the point of hardship at 6 A.M. and 6 P.M. At sunrise breakfast is over, the mules and everybody else have been good-natured, and you feel the glory of mere existence as you vault into your saddle and break into a gallop. Not that this or that particular day is so different from other pleasant mornings, but all that we call *the weather* is constituted in the most perfect proportions. The air is "nimble and sweet," and you ride gayly across meadows, through sunny woods of pine and aspen, and between granite knolls that are piled up in the most noble and romantic proportions. But later you toil up a mountain thousands of feet high, tramp your weary way through the snow and loose rocks heaped upon its summit, "observe," and get laboriously down again; or search through forty ledges and swing a ceaseless hammer in collecting fossils; or march all day under a blazing sun, or in the teeth of a dusty gale, munching only a sandwich as you plod along—till gradually your "glory of existence" oozes away, and the most dismal reflections arise to keep company with your strained muscles. How welcome after that is the evening bivouac, when there is rest for the aching limbs, and no longer need to tighten the belt! The busy hour between the end of the march and sitting down to dinner quickly passes, and the meal is not hurried; after that, leisure and the solid comfort of camping.

It is astonishing how greatly recuperated one feels after half an hour's rest and his dinner, following the most tremendous exertions all day. Sometimes it seems, when camp is reached, that one has hardly strength to make another move; but after dinner one finds himself able and willing to do a great deal. This, as I have already said, is the hour for exploring the neighborhood, preparatory to next day's work; for investigating the natural history of the locality, or putting up the specimens accumulated during the day; for mending harness and arms and clothes, and writing memoranda, or perchance letters, against a possible opportunity to send them out to the civilized world by some Indian or friendly trapper. But the most important work is the making of your bed. It is the one thing in this wandering life that you cannot afford to neglect, and which, *if* neglected, is the cause of more hardship, distress, and possible illness than any other one thing which it is possible to guard against. Nevertheless, unless the camp is to be fixed in that spot for several days, it is not usual to put up the tents, except when the weather is stormy.

These tents are of the army pattern known as "dog-tents"—just large enough for two persons to stretch themselves out, side by side, but not more than three feet high, even under the ridge. The canvas is of good quality, however, and will stand a severe rainfall without wetting through, so long as the inside of the cloth is not touched. If the precaution is taken to dig a ditch around the tent, so that the water will run away and not spread underneath the edges, making pools on the floor, you will find yourself secure from all storms. But, as a rule, one doesn't bother to put up a tent.

No matter how firmly resolved you may be upon roughing it, you soon find that it pays to keep your bed dry and warm, and to spend all needed time in making it up. Hardship enough will be inevitable; needless exposure is foolish. The proper supplies in the way of bedding consist of the following articles: a piece of moderately heavy canvas-ducking, water-proofed, fourteen feet long by four feet wide; a buffalo-robe, trimmed into a rectangular piece sufficient to lie at full length upon; two pairs of thick California blankets, and a small pillow. This appears to be the list settled upon by the best experience. All are light and warm, and can be rolled up inside the canvas and strapped into a cylindrical bundle, so compact as easily to be carried in one hand, and so tight that it may be rained upon all day and not be wetted through. The California blankets are expensive, but it is better economy to buy them. A pillow is a great comfort; lacking it, one finds a fair substitute in his boots, saddle, war-bag, or even in a piece of wood. A thick night-cap is more convenient than your broad-brimmed hat to sleep in; and nothing warms chilled feet so much in bed as dry woollen socks, which may be kicked off later in the night.

At every opportunity air the bedding thoroughly in the sunshine. Then, before the evening dew comes, stretch out your long piece of canvas, lay the buffalo-robe smoothly on the upper end, double your blankets, and place them one over the other upon the robe.   After

THE DOG-TENTS.

smoothing out every wrinkle, the two blankets together are evenly folded once over lengthwise, the remainder of the canvas (seven feet) is drawn up over the foot, so that the toes cannot push through, and the bed is made.   You have a canvas, buffalo-robe, and four thicknesses of blanket under you, and (except the robe) the same over you, the blankets passing full thickness behind your back, which you will learn to place to windward.   Then you fully undress, put your rifle, revolver, and clothes under the flap of the canvas cover, to keep the frost off, slide gently into your rough, clinging blankets, pull the edges together in front, jerk the canvas over your ears, and—pleasant dreams to you!

Such is scientific bed-making: but there are niceties. It is important, for example, that the surface you lie on shall be, not soft—that is a little matter—but level; sloping neither toward one side nor from head to foot. Unless you are sure about this you will slide out of bed in some direction. Common-sense would tell you to clear all stones and nodules away (though sometimes this is impossible); but only experience, or a wise friend, will teach the camper that his rest will be tenfold better if he digs a depression underneath his bed where his hips come. The reason why persons become so stiff who pass an accidental night on the floor, or on a railway bench, is mainly because they have had no support for the spine, such as the yielding bed affords; all night long many muscles have had to keep on duty, bearing up the less prominent parts of the body. The spring of a mattress cannot be found in the ground, but it can be imitated by sinking the hips until the small of the back also rests upon the earth. Always dig a hole under your bed.

A GOOD-NIGHT WHIFF.

If you are in fear of the cold (frequently an altitude is attained for which the bedding sufficient below is an inadequate protection, particularly if a heavy wind is blowing or the snow is flying), a good plan is to fold your blankets, turn up the bottom as usual, and then stitch the whole together into a bag. Another way is not to erect your tent, which is little or no protection against cold, but to spread it over you

and peg it down, or pile enough rocks around the edges to keep it from
blowing away.   The former plan I tried in 1877, with great success; but
it was the hardest work in the world to get into my bag, which was just
large enough and no larger.   I had to insinuate my body as gently as
a surgeon probes a wound, in order to keep the blankets from drawing
out of shape before I was inside.   When once I had wriggled in, how
snug it was!   I could not turn over without rolling the larger part
of my bedding with me.   Yet those very same nights, away up on the
bald brow of a lonesome peak, when every man piled on as many extra
canvas *mantas* and buffalo-robes as he could find, the mosquitoes were
so thick that we had to build miniature tents of netting over our half-
frozen heads to get any sleep at all.   It was the most startling con-
junction of winter and summer, zero and insects, that I ever heard of.

But at such altitudes one must expect often to find it very cold at
night, even in midsummer.   Often, down in the San Juan country, near
the head-waters of the Rio Grande, we woke up to find the canvas over
us frozen as stiff as sheet-iron.   When one rises under those forbidding
circumstances he gets into his frosty trousers with considerable celerity.

I think the very coldest night I ever had in the mountains was on
the occasion of a little adventure in Mosquito pass, long before Leadville,
to which that pass has since been made a highway, was ever dreamed
of.   It was then a very high, rough pathway over the range—merely
a place where it was possible to get up and down, and used mainly
by donkeys—but I had to go across that way, and started.   It was
a long, unfamiliar road; I was alone; a storm came up; I went widely
astray from the dim trail, and had a variety of minor adventures, which
I have chronicled elsewhere.   The result was, that when I got over the
gale-swept crest and down to timber-line on the right side it was dark;
and, after thrashing through half a mile of wet thickets and dense
woods, my horse and I at last came to an utter stand-still in front of
where a tornado had piled fallen timber across the already half-obliter-
ated trail.   It was useless to go farther, so I unsaddled at a little open
spot among some spruces.   Securing my exhausted horse by his long
lariat, I dragged the heavy ranger's saddle to an evergreen, and dived
into the pouches after matches, for if you are warm being hungry does
not greatly matter.   Alas, there were none!   For the first and—*cela va
sans dire*—for the *last* time in the West I had not a lucifer!   Then I
took an inventory of my goods, which were not designed for such an
evil fate as this.   First, there were my saddle and saddle-bags, which
contained only a stupid flask, empty of everything save odor, a tanta-

lizing pipe which could not be lit, and a pair of woollen socks, which I pulled on as an attempt at a night-dress. This saddle was my pillow, and a thin, worn-out saddle-blanket, with my rubber poncho, constituted my bedding—rather scanty for eleven thousand feet or so above the sea! I spread my poncho under the drooping branches of the spruce, just where partridges love to hide, gathered the ragged blanket about my legs, belted an army overcoat tight about me, and lay down. I was very weary; my nag's steady crunching was the only disturbing sound, and I soon fell asleep. My nap was not a long one, however, on account of the cold; but, re-arranging the coverings, I again slept an hour or so. This time I awoke thoroughly chilled, yet dozed a little longer, until I shook in every member, and had just sense enough left to raise myself up and move about. My poor horse was standing, head down, the picture of lonesome misery. With a low neigh as I approached, he came to meet me, and followed me with his nose at my shoulder as I walked back and forth. What a night it was! All around the glade stood a wall of forest, black except where, on one side, a group of burnt trunks held aloft their skeleton-white arms. The grass was pale and crisp with frost, which crackled under my feet as I walked. Overhead the stars seemed fairly to project from their jetty background, like glittering spear-points aimed at my cantonment. I noted the slow wheeling of that platoon of nebulæ, the Milky Way. I studied the constellations, but got little comfort. Corona only suggested

"That a sorrow's crown of sorrow is remembering happier things,"

and the Pleiades seemed to beg me to sympathize with their lost sister. At one side a bit of the creek valley was visible, over which faintly gleamed the whitish snow-crest of some mountain. It was profoundly still. Icy water gurgled softly under the elders; tall, muffled trees swayed gently; an occasional ringing snap of frost was heard, like fairies clinking glasses; but these sounds were so consonant with the whole scene that they did not break the stillness. There was nothing particular to be afraid of, my walking warmed me, and, giving myself up to imaginative thought, I came readily to enjoy the novelty of the experience, and the calm delight which the sweet influences of the night ever exert. Thus quieting myself, drowsiness weighted my eyelids, till, scarcely feeling what I did, I again laid my head on the saddle, and did not awake until the blue ridges were sharply and grandly outlined against a glowing background of auroral light.

The reason for my being alone here was, that I had cut across the

range by this route, while the rest of the party went around through
South Park and over to the Arkansas by the way of Trout creek, in order that I might get our mail at Granite—a mining camp and post-
office.   I reached there too late to attend the proceedings in which it
was decided not to hang two Chinamen, whose only crime was that
they wanted to come there and work; but I saw the court, and came
very near seeing the pigtails hung anyhow!   They left town in a great
hurry, at all events, and that night there was a ball at the Trans-continental Shades saloon.

This opportunity for unbending was embraced by pretty much all
the population of the camp.   I think the only families unrepresented
were those of the justice of the peace and the proprietor of the hotel;
and as they contained all the women there were in town, *to speak of*, it
is needless to say that the male element predominated in the ball-room,
to the entire exclusion of anything else.   The genial proprietor of the
Shades united within himself the duties of both bar-tender and floor-
manager; but in the former capacity he was ably assisted by a fiery-
headed youth popularly known as "Reddy."   As for the "floor" he
managed, it was only hard-trodden earth, and the decorations of the
walls were old coats, old hats, discarded elk-antlers, rifles, and some
pictures from the *Police Gazette*, in which there was always a sufficient
breeze blowing to lift the pretty girl's petticoats a trifle above her boot-
tops.   To these hangings was speedily added a row of boots of gigantic proportions, which were hung on wooden pegs or piled under the
benches along the wall as soon as the dancing began.

Beside thirty or forty gold-washers, rough and big enough to satisfy all conventional requirements for the type, there were present
three or four gamblers, who set up a faro-table in one corner; the fiddler—a young freighter from Fairplay; two or three cut-throat-looking
Mexicans, who had driven up some beef-cattle from Saguache; a lank,
peaked-bearded lawyer or two, in rusty regimentals of broadcloth; a
Herald reporter from New York, who had just returned from South
Africa; and myself.

By the time the crowd had taken an average of two drinks all
round the bar-man ordered the fiddler to "whoop 'er up," and yelled a
general invitation to "clinch."   The crowd fell back to the benches,
the wicks of two or three smoky oil-lamps fixed in the logs were turned up, two stalwart Missourians grasped each other's hands and waists,
where six-shooters dangled in lieu of tassels on a silken sash, and began
to pat the clay with stockinged feet to the time of a lively waltz, where-

in the musicians were assisted by a jolly soul who drummed on the bar with a beer-glass. In a moment another pair had joined them, then a third, and so on until the floor was full of nimble miners, spinning and whirling, executing interludes of pigeon-wing and double-shuffle, each leap accented by a whoop or shriek, to which the delighted spectators responded with approving yells and clatter.

When the dancers were out of breath—which comes hard in this thin air—the bar-keeper invited them to a " What'll ye have, gentlemen?" The fiddler took brandy in "his'n," while the majority of the spectators drank on each other's account, and let the other pay for it, intending to return the compliment themselves after the next dance.

This time a quadrille claimed the floor—two of them, indeed, and we outsiders climbed upon the benches out of the way. After this an adept in the jig business—whose Irish mug proclaimed his good right to know the steps—gave an exhibition that elicited loud applause, but ruined his socks; and then the Greasers were invited to show how they did it at the fandango down in " Mayheeko," and thought it prudent to comply, though with bad grace.

And so the fun continued, tanglefoot whiskey flowing at two bits a drink, until everybody was satisfied to go home; but long before this I had stolen away. I heard next morning that there had been a murder during the night; but I do not believe that the dance had anything to do with it.

That night I slept in a bed, and on a spring-mattress; yet it was a very uncomfortable rest, for somehow I couldn't keep the bedclothes snugly about me as I did my blankets out-of-doors. If I had known then that the kind host had put himself and his family to sleep on the kitchen-floor, in order to give me his only bed, I should not have slept half as well as I did.

XI.

THIS part of Colorado was then the seat of the principal mining for gold, the process of which may as well be described here, in order that future allusions may be understood without special remark.

The person who travels through many parts of the Rocky Mountains, and of the Sierra Nevada, will observe along the banks of the streams vast piles of bare gravel. Through the midst of these heaps of pebbles—among which, now and then, there towers up the round back of a bowlder, or rises a little grassy island, bearing some charred stump—one may often see remains of wooden machinery and the ruins of abandoned huts; or he may even meet with men at work, and learn how the hasty little stream is made to pause and pay toll in service as it rushes downward from the snow-fields where it was born.

All these appearances are signs of gold-mining, by the method known as "placer-washing" or "gulch-digging." It is the simplest and, in some respects, the most interesting of all the processes by which the precious metal is got out of the earth. It has been practised for a very long period. History does not go back far enough to tell us when gold first began to be used, but it is supposed that all the gold the ancients had was procured in this way. Wherever that mysterious country Ophir may have been, no doubt it was a placer district.

When gold has been discovered in any region (and this usually happens through some lucky accident) adventurous men rush to the spot in crowds, and at once look for more signs of it. This search is called "prospecting," and it is done by parties of two or three, who go along the creeks flowing down from the hills, and test the gravel in the banks until they find what they seek. The prospector's outfit consists of as much provision as he can carry on his back or pack on a donkey—a couple of blankets, guns and ammunition, a few cooking-utensils, a shovel and pick, and a gold-pan. The last is the most important of all these, excepting food. It is made of sheet-iron, and is shaped much like an extra large milk-pan. The prospectors (who call each other partner, or "pard" for short, agreeing to divide all they find) trudge along all day beside their Mexican donkeys, keeping their eyes keenly upon the lookout, and slowly climbing toward the head of the ravine or gulch down which the creek plunges. Finally they come to a point where the gulch widens out a little, or perhaps where a rivulet flows down from a side-hill, and a high bank of gravel has collected. Then they let their donkeys feed upon the short, crisp grass or nibble the white sage, while they climb a little way up the bank and dig a pit a few feet deep.

PANNING-OUT GOLD-GRAVEL.

You may see these "prospect-holes" all over the mountains, for many times nothing has been found at the bottom of them to justify farther operations there; and a man who is unlucky enough to dig many of these fruitless pits gets the reputation of being a "gopher," and finds himself laughed at.

Their prospect-hole dug down to where the gravel is firm, they scoop up a panful of dirt and carry it down to the margin of the stream. First having picked out the large pieces of stone, one of the prospecters then takes the pan in both hands, dips up a little water, and, gently shaking the pan, allows the water to flow over the edge and run away, carrying with it the lightest portions of the soil. This is done repeatedly; but, as less and less of the heaviest dirt is left behind, greater care must be used. It requires much dexterity and practice to keep the bottom of the pan always lower than the edge and at the same time dip up and pour out the water without throwing away more earth than you wish to. Tender management for eight or ten minutes, however, gets rid of everything except a spoonful of black sand, and among this (if you have been successful) gleam yellow particles of gold, which have settled at the bottom, and have been left behind in the incessant agitation and washing away of the earth, because they were heavier than anything else in the pan.

This operation is called "washing" or "panning-out;" but it is not quite done yet, for the "colors," or particles of gold, must be separated from the black grains, which are mainly of iron or lead. By passing a magnet back and forth through them these will be dragged out, sticking to it, after which the gold left behind is weighed and its value estimated. If a prospector finds he can average three cents in every panful of dirt, he knows he can make money by the help of machinery; but if he is to do his work wholly by hand he must collect at least ten cents from each pan, and in the early days this would have been thought very moderate pay. There used to be mines in Colorado known as "pound-diggings," because it was said that a pound's weight of gold a day could be saved by every man who worked there.

After testing here and there, our prospectors decide upon the best part of the gravel-bank (which they would call a "bar"), and take possession of a small tract, or "claim," the amount of which is regulated by law, which "claim" they mark by driving down stakes upon which are written the names of the claimants and the boundaries pre-empted.

Our miners, let us suppose, prefer not to get their gold by the slow method of panning. They therefore procure some pieces of board and hammer together a "rocker," or "cradle." This machine takes its name from its resemblance to an old-fashioned baby's cradle—the "old-fashioned" referring to the furniture, not to the infant. It is mounted upon two rockers, and its head-board is high enough to serve as a handle for moving it. Inside is arranged a series of three or four sieves, upon inclined supports, one above the other, the coarsest sieves being uppermost. There is no foot-board, for in its place projects a long spout out of which the waste water runs, which is fitted with cleats or "riffles" like those I shall explain farther on when I speak of the sluice. Into this cradle one man shovels the dirt and gravel, while his partner rocks it and pours in the water, which he dips out of the stream with a long-handled dipper. The big stones all shoot off from the surface of the cradle, but the dirt and small pebbles fall through upon the second sieve, through which, in turn, the finer half goes, and so on until the bottom and the spout catch the gold and retain it alone, while the water drifts the worthless stuff away.

The cradle is an old contrivance, and many forms of it are in use, some having only a single perforated partition to screen off the largest stones. It can be carried about wherever the miner finds it convenient to work, and it does not require a vast deal of water; lastly, it calls for much less skill than most

MINER AND CRADLE.

other methods of washing. Nevertheless the day of the cradle is nearly gone by, except where a single poor man goes off by himself to some retired spot and works, not so much for wealth, as merely for the hope of getting a living. In its place the "sluice-box" has come to be the great instrument for gathering gold out of a placer-bar.

In order to operate a sluice to advantage there must be plenty of material to be handled and plenty of water. It is upon a sure supply of water that placer-mining depends, and it often happens that a bar that is worth very little might be worth a great deal, if only a stream could be turned through it. Sometimes the gravels are in the very bed of the creek, or on a level with it, and the poor stream, tortured out of its course, is sent into a dozen new channels, while the old beds are rocked through the creaking cradles, or go rattling down the stretching lengths of the hollow sluices. But, as a rule, it is necessary to bring the water in a ditch from some lofty point in the mountains down to the highest part of the placers. Sometimes all the miners stop work and unite in making the ditch, which they then own in common; at other times one or two men will pay for the construction of the ditch, which they then own, and from which they lease water to the miners. You may see these little canals curving under the brows and along the retreating slopes of the hills, seeking in and out of all the windings a slant by which the water will steadily run downward. Now and then a rocky headland must be skirted or a deep gully crossed, and here the water is carried in a wooden " flume," supported upon a trestle-work of poles and props. These aqueducts become a striking addition to the naturally strange scenery, in their rough out-

THE FLUME.

lines, as they straggle, all mossy, rude, and dripping, over and around great bronze-brown cliffs and along the green, velvety hill-sides.

Now let us examine how the ditch is made useful. When it is completed, as many gates are made as there are mines to be supplied. Through these water can be drawn off. Then the water is let on, and flows gurgling and sparkling through the canal, bright and limpid as a natural mountain torrent.

Meanwhile each miner has built his sluices. These consist of long, narrow boxes made of planking—one plank high on each side and two planks broad at the bottom. Sometimes only two or three of these boxes or troughs are placed end to end, sometimes a long line of them ; but all along on the bottom, particularly down toward the lower end, are nailed, crosswise, strips of wood like cleats, which are known as "riffles"—I suppose because they make a series of little waves or riffles in the water as it flows over them. Usually, also, in addition to the cleats, the bottom is paved with cobble-stones, so as to offer as many chinks and crannies as possible. Now all is ready for extensive placer-mining; and opening the gate which admits to the little channel that leads to the sluices, down comes the clear blue water, and goes dashing and foaming through the confined trough and worries past the riffles, until it finds itself free, at the " tail," to run on down the valley whither it will. It is pure and sparkling when it enters, but in a moment becomes brown as chocolate with mud, for the miners are shovelling the earth and gravel into the sluice-boxes, and the rivulet's play-day is over—its work of gold-washing has begun.

After my description of the cradle, I need hardly trouble you to read an explanation of sluicing. It is perfectly plain to you that, when the gravel is shovelled into the sluices, the swift current sweeps away all the light stuff, and rolls the round stones out at the end, while the heavy grains of gold sink rapidly to the bottom, and are caught behind the cleats, or between some of the paving-stones. Usually the men help this process along by continually stirring up the bottom of the sluice-box with a shovel, so that too much besides the gold shall not stay behind; and frequently some quicksilver is sprinkled in the bottom, to attract and hold the gold more surely. This seems a very rude and clumsy contrivance in working after so precious a prize; indeed, it never seems quite right to dig and toss and treat so carelessly the rich soil of these mines; but experience has shown that gold is so sure to sink through all this agitation and mass of waste rock, and is so indestructible, that these rough methods are good enough for this kind of mining. It used to be quite a common thing in California and Montana for a speculator to buy a cabin where gambling had been carried on, or the banking business had been done, and burn it down, for the sake of panning out of the ruins the fragments of gold-dust which had been spilled. I was told of a cabin in West Denver which thus yielded twelve hundred dollars and over.

The proof of this efficacy comes at night, or at the end of the week, when the clean-up is made. Then the water is shut off, the sluice is drained dry, and all the big stones are thrown out. The black iron-sand and other sediment in the bottom is scraped out of all the corners and crevices, and carefully washed. A rich panful of gold remains—perhaps hundreds of dollars' worth—which is separated from the iron by the use of a magnet, as before, and poured into the little buckskin bag which forms the miner's wallet. Last of all, it is weighed and divided between the various partners who are working the claim together.

By the amount of the "clean-up" they judge of the worth of the claim, if anybody proposes to buy it of them. The general supposition is, that a claim will average the same yield of gold all the way through; but this does not always hold true. The gold occurs in "pay-streaks," and two claims, side by side, may be of very unequal value. The effort of every miner is to get to "bed-rock" as soon as he can—that is, to the rocky floor upon which the gravel has been drifted and piled—for the reason that in the process of that drifting the gold has a chance to fall through the bowlders and sift down to the bed-rock. He will tell you that it is paved with a sheet of solid gold, but often he finds hardly more than he met with on the way.

Sometimes it is only a certain layer in the bank which is "pay dirt"

and profitable to work.   Then he pushes a tunnel into the side of a hill,
and brings his gravel out on a wheelbarrow to wash at the opening.

Men work all day in these tunnels, sometimes lying almost at full
length upon their sides; and accidents occasionally occur, by the roof
falling or otherwise.   In digging down to bed-rock it frequently happens

THE SLUICE AND PUMP.

that the hole or shaft becomes so full of water that no more work can
be done.   It would cost too much to pay a man to pump it out, and
very likely one man, or even a dozen men, would be unable to do it.
But here is the water in the neighboring creek, or, if that is wanting,
the stream from the big ditch, waiting to be harnessed to do the work,
So the blacksmith is consulted, and an axle-tree, trunnions, and some

other bits of iron-work, are forged. Then a framework is raised, a small water-wheel knocked together and hung in it, a flume laid, which pours a stream of water upon the wheel, and a rough gearing of poles so arranged that every time the wheel goes around the plunger of the pump is raised, and the water is pulled out. Sometimes the connecting-rod between the water-wheel and the pump is a line of aspen-poles, a hundred or two hundred feet long. This is supported, every dozen feet or so, upon standards, which are fastened on pivots to firm blocks on the ground, so as to move backward and forward with each lifting and sinking of the pump.

When a company of men find a new gold gulch, and begin to work it, they call the village which grows up there a camp, and give it some name, which is just as likely to be absurd as it is to be appropriate. Dutch Flat, Red Dog, Bough Town, Buckskin, and dozens of other comical names, are examples. The miners hastily throw up little log cabins, six or eight logs high, covered with a roof of poles and dirt, and having nothing better than the hard-tramped earth for a floor. In one end is the fireplace (the chimney is outside, like that of a negro's hut in the South), and at the other end are rough bunks, where the owner stuffs in some long grass or spruce boughs or straw, and spreads his bed or blankets. These rude little cabins are packed close together up and down the sides of the gulch, so as to be as near as possible to, and yet out of the way of, the mining, and they give a very pretty look to the wild scenery of these mountains. As the camp grows larger merchants go there with goods to sell; stage-coaches begin to run to and from older settlements; shops, hotels, restaurants, and churches are built, and the camp becomes a town. I have known of such a gulch-mining settlement in a single year converting an utter wilderness in the mountains, long miles away from anywhere, into a city of ten thousand people or more. One of the most remarkable examples of this was the settlement in California Gulch, which antedated Leadville by almost a score of years and occupied nearly the same site. I will sketch it.

After the rush to Pike's Peak, in 1859, which was disappointing enough to the majority of prospectors, a number of men pushed westward. One party made their way through Ute pass into the grand meadows of South Park, and, crossing, pressed on to the Arkansas valley, up which they proceeded, searching unsuccessfully for gold, until they reached a wide plateau on the right bank, where a beautiful little stream came down. Following this nearly to its source, along what they named California Gulch, they were delighted to find placers of gold. This was in the midsummer of 1860; and before the close of the hot weather ten thousand people had emigrated to the Arkansas, and $2,500,000 had been washed out, one of the original explorers taking twenty-nine pounds of gold away with him in the fall, besides selling for $500 a "worked-out" claim from which $15,000 was taken within the next three months. Since that time this same "exhausted" gravel is being washed a third or fourth time with profit.

The settlement consisted of one long street only, and houses even of logs were so few that the camp was known as "Bough Town," everybody abandoning the wicky-ups in winter, when the placers could not be worked, and retreating to Denver. During the summer, however, Bough Town witnessed some lively scenes. One day a stranger came riding up the street on a gallop, splashing the mud everywhere, only to be unceremoniously halted by a rough-looking customer who covered him with a revolver, and said, "Hold on, there, stranger! When ye go through this yere town, go slow, so folks kin take a look at ye!"

No money circulated there; gold-dust served all the purposes of trade, and every merchant, saloon-keeper, and gambler had his scales. The phrase was not "Cash up," but "Down with your dust;" and when a man's buckskin wallet was empty he knew where to fill it again. It was not long, however, before the placers were all staked off, and the claims began to be exhausted. Then the town so dwindled that in half a dozen years only a score were left of the turbulent multitude who, in 1860 and 1861, made the gulch noisy with magical gains and unheeded loss. Among the last of their acts was to pull down the old log gambling-hall, and to pan two thousand dollars out of the dirt where the gamblers had dropped the coveted grains. This done, everybody moved elsewhere, and the frightened game returned to thread the aspen groves and drink at the again translucent streams of California Gulch, where eight million dollars had been sifted from the pebbles.

Not all the camps have so fleeting a life. Almost all the large cities and towns of California and the Rocky Mountains began as placer-camps. But it usually happened that, about the time it was found that all the gold in the gravel-bar had been washed out, and people had begun to leave the place, some shrewd rich man, or company of rich men, bought out several claims, until they had a considerable area of the gravel-bank in their possession. Then they erected machinery, and pursued what is known as hydraulic mining; for they could make money by this means out of gravel too poor in gold to pay for panning or cradling, according to the gold-diggers' high ideas of profit.

In hydraulic mining a stream of water is brought into the mine through iron pipes, from so high a source as to give immense force to it when it leaps out of the nozzle. The fall must be from one hundred and fifty to two hundred feet, usually, to furnish the necessary "head," and upon the power which the water has depends the success of the enterprise. The pipe consists of stout iron, and is a foot or so in diameter. It is made up of sections, each about twelve feet long, and therefore can be lengthened or shortened, bent or moved about, as required. Into its upper end, away up on the steep hill-side, flows the water of the high-line ditch, or perhaps the current of a mountain snow-fed torrent. At the lower end of the pipe is arranged a very strong iron mouth-piece, like the

HYDRAULIC MINING.

nozzle of a steam fire-engine, only three times as big, which swings upon compound joints in its attachment to the pipe, so that it can be moved in any direction — upward, downward, or sideways. So much for the water-power or *hydraulic* machinery. Now, observe how they employ it.

Down at the edge of the creek there is room enough to lay their pipes and set up the "Little Giant," as they call their nozzle. In the creek-bed a little distance below has already been built a great sluice-box, sometimes a hundred yards or more long, and much more capacious than the sluices used in hand-work. Leading down to this, a steep channel is arranged from the gravel-bank, and all is ready. The flood-gates are opened, the big nozzle is pointed straight at the bank, the water resounds through the humming pipes and rushes forth from the nozzle in a solid, straight, ice-white beam, which bores its way into the bank and tumbles the bowlders out very much as a steady stream of cannon-balls would do it. It is great sport to watch this fierce attack

of so much water, remembering that it is only its weight, and the force
it accumulates in its eagerness to escape from the close pipes, which
is hurrying it on at this fearful speed.   The bank crumbles, and bits of
hard clay, small stones, and fragments of petrified wood are tossed high
in the broad fountain which flies backward from the point where the
water strikes, and falls with a constant roar and rattle.   The white,
mist-hidden beam of water bores its way deeper and deeper, the mass
of foam and broken earth changes and grows as the face of the cliff
and the direction of the nozzle are changed, and so the Little Giant
rapidly eats his way into the gravel, and at the same time sweeps
the loose material into the sluices by the very flood which his energy
creates.

I used to delight to watch this work down below Leadville, where
the same wilderness of pebbles and bowlders was being gone over that
were tossed about by thousands of eager hands a score of years ago.
It was fascinating to note the fearful power and effect of this concen-
trated beam of water, with no propulsive force behind it but its own
weight; and none of the romance was destroyed in finding that here
and there the water cut down into some cabin—a relic of Bough Town
that had become utterly buried in *débris*.

While all this picturesque enginery is in operation above them,
down along the rough channel stand men aiding the separation of
the gold.   They are picking the large, worthless stones out of the
stream, and piling them in an out-of-the-way place ; they are walking
about knee-deep in the raging, mud-laden flood, continually poking
out the heavier rocks, and stirring up the bottom with shovels, in order that no gold may settle there.   Through the stout sluice leaps a
swift and noisy current, bearing in its thick waters thousands of minute
flakes of gold, with now and then a nugget.   These quickly sink to the
bottom, and are caught by the riffles ; so that the clean-up of an hydraulic sluice ought to be, and usually is, very rich, for a hundred times more
earth is sent through it each day under the tearing strength of the
Little Giant than ever shovels alone could handle.   Moreover, it often
happens that there are five or six pipes and nozzles firing at the same
bank.   Then the destruction is very rapid, great masses of gravel being
quickly undermined, and falling with a noise like thunder.

The gold is collected from the sluice by shutting off the water,
taking out the riffles, and scraping the bottom.   Some quicksilver has
usually been sprinkled in the sluice previously, and more is now added,
the better to collect the gold, for which it has a strong attraction.   The

union of the two metals forms what is known as an amalgam, and there are two ways of separating them again. If the miners do not care to save the quicksilver (which is the same thing as the mercury of our thermometers), they put the amalgam in a bag, and strain out the quicksilver by squeezing, just as you press the juice out of grapes when jelly is to be made. Then the gold and the trifle of quicksilver remaining is placed upon a shovel and held over the fire until all the white metal passes off in vapor.

If, however, it is desired to save the mercury, the amalgam, as soon as it is cleaned out of the sluice, is put into a chemist's retort and heated. The mercury turns to vapor, which rises through a tube passing at a short distance through a box of ice or cold water, and is there condensed or turned back to liquid again, when it runs into a jar and is ready to be used a second time. In this way the same mercury may be used over and over again, with but little loss.

Sometimes several thousand dollars are the profit of a single week of hydraulic mining, but several hundreds would be a more ordinary estimate.

Conducted on whatever system, gold-mining is not always so profitable a business as it seems at first glance. After all, an ounce of gold is worth only so much, and a pound only twelve times as much. To get a pound of gold requires much hard work, and a considerable outlay of money for food, for wear and tear of clothes, for rent of water, for purchase of machinery, etc., etc. Sometimes the gains are enormous, but it is only a few who have become rich in gold-digging out of thousands who have struggled and failed. Nor, exciting and romantic as it seems to live in this wild, out-door, picnic style, and to dig the shining, precious, poetic mineral out of the ignoble gravel where it has so long lain neglected, is it altogether enjoyable work. You must be almost continually wet, and the water in the mountains is cold; you must handle all day long rough stones, heave huge bowlders, and shovel heavy dirt; you must swing the pick till your back aches, and waggle that rusty gold-pan till your arms grow lame and your fingers are sore, while the sun beats down straight and hot, or the chill wind cuts through your wet garments; you must work early and late, hard and fast, often defending your property by a little war, if you would equal your neighbors and hold your claim.

Then see how the gold-miner lives. His cabin is low and dark and dirty. The climate is too severe and the ground too rocky for him to raise a garden if he cared to, and he has no time for such pleasantries.

His hard work permits him to wear none but the very roughest of leathern and woollen clothes, and his fare is of the plainest kind, such as he himself can cook. I have known a placer-camp to be without a potato, or a drink of milk, or a bit of butter for nine months at a time; but nowadays miners live somewhat better than they used to, because grocers have learned how to pack food in such a shape that it will keep well, and can be carried far into the mountains.

The amusements of a mining-camp are almost all connected with liquor and gambling. It is in such dissipations that gold-miners spend nearly all the great wealth they get, so that often they will make and lose a dozen large fortunes in as many years. There are some, of

THE PROSPECTOR AND HIS BURRO.

course, who save, hiding away their little buckskin bags of gold-dust; but they are careful not to let any one know of it, for if they did they would very likely be robbed, and perhaps shot, by some desperado. Gold-digging is hard, dangerous, and life-wearing work, yet always fascinating.

Did it ever occur to you to ask how the gold got mixed up in the gravel? Perhaps I can give my younger readers a hint as to how to study the matter out fully.

The gravel-banks were piled in the places where they are now found either by the streams, which formerly were vastly larger than they now are, or else by great moving masses of ice, called glaciers. If you should read Professor Tyndall's little book, "Forms of Water," you would get a very good idea of this ice-power, and much entertainment besides. Whatever the way, the broken fragments of the mountain, which the action of the atmosphere and trickling water had undermined, frost had cracked off, or lightning had splintered to pieces during thousands of years, became rolled down the bed of the ancient river and rounded into pebbles and cobble-stones, just as is still being done in the bed of every rapid stream.

Now, scattered all through the granite rock of which these towering Rocky Mountains are built up, are veins or streaks of quartz—a white, crystalline rock in which the gold is found, though it by no means follows that every quartz-vein carries the royal metal. When, by the action of frost, rain, lightning, and ice, the rocks are shattered and rolled down the bed of the stream, the quartz goes along with the granite, and of course, if there is any gold there, it also is torn out and grinds along with the rest, until it finds a chance to settle and help build up the bar that, ages afterward, our prospectors seek and dig into. Therefore placer-gold is sometimes known as "floated" gold; and high in the range, at the head of a gulch which contains good gravel, are to be found quartz-veins whence the riches below have come, and where the undiscovered gold may be dug out and separated from the mother-rock by the various processes known under the head of quartz-mining, which are far more expensive and complicated than anything done in working the placers. It is the general belief that in the United States the placers have been pretty well exhausted, and that most of the gold of the future is to be expected from the quartz lodes, and sought for hundreds of feet underground, deep in the heart of the mountains.

XII.

WELL, to go back to my trip to Granite, I may dismiss the matter by saying that I got no letters for myself or anybody else, much to our disgust. It was nearly four weeks since we had had a word of news either from home or from head-quarters.

Starting away early, I rode about fifty miles before night. It was almost all accomplished by keeping my poor tired horse at a dog-trot— a pace which is less than a trot and more than a walk. All his muscles seemed lax, and he went on, like a machine, at about five miles an hour, without any apparent effort. Now and then he would rouse into a gallop, and at noon he had an hour's rest.

The next fortnight was not productive of many adventures or noteworthy incidents, though it contained plenty of hard work. Our track led across into the head of the San Luis Park, and so on down to Saguache—a Mexican town near the Rio Grande. There was a pleasant bit of natural history picked up along here, though.

The plover of these interior valleys does not seem to care for marshes, like the most of his race, but haunts the dry uplands. It is closely related to the golden plover, and is named in books *Ægialitis montanus*. (See cut, p. 60.) A flock of these plovers dropped down on the plain one day, and I determined to get them for dinner, if possible. Jumping off my horse — who would stand stock-still wherever I left him—I approached to where they had dropped, and finally caught sight of one by distinguishing the dark dot of its eye against the light-tinted surface of the ground. Even then I really could not follow with my eye the outline of the bird's body, so closely did the colors of the plumage agree with the white sand and dry grass. I shot it; then found another, shot that; and so on until all were killed, none of them flying away, because their "instinct," or habit of thought, had taught them that when danger threatened they must invariably keep quiet; movement would be exposure, and exposure would be fatal. I and my gun formed a danger they had had no experience of, and here their inherited "instinct" was at fault. When I had shot them I was unable, with the most careful searching, to find all the dead birds. Hunting for a black pin on a mottled carpet, or a sixpence in a skating-rink, were an easy task compared with finding those color-protected plovers on the San Luis barrens.

Several days gave no special incident that I remember. The Sangre de Christo range, along the western side of which our road led us to Saguache, is, perhaps, the most beautiful in Colorado, as we viewed it, because the range presents a perfectly straight line of the most lofty and shapely peaks—blue triangles, with white tips. Down at the southern extremity the splendid rank terminates in the Sierra Blanca—king

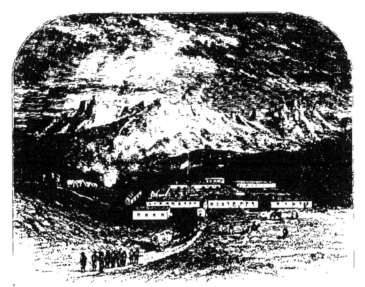

FORT GARLAND AND SIERRA BLANCA.

of Colorado's peaks in respect to height. Afterward I went all round its base, but never scaled its almost inaccessible summit, mindful of the terrible dangers and suffering which our party encountered who measured it. Among other things, they were obliged, in order to reach the topmost pinnacle, to creep for a long distance upon a ridge of rock falling on either side to frightful depths, which was so narrow and sharp that in many places it was possible to sit astride it.

From Saguache—an old Mexican village, inhabited chiefly by cattle-men and shepherds whose herds range in the Rio Grande valley—the trail took us over an exceedingly water-worn and desolate region, and then, through the beautiful pass of Cochetopa creek, into the valley of

ALONG THE COCHETOPA.

the Los Pinos. Here there was the Southern Agency of the Utes, and we came suddenly, at a turn in the road, to a view of an immense collection of Indian lodges, with all their attendant herds of horses and crowds of women and children, spread below us on the green river-plain. The sight of six hundred lodges and three thousand savages, all together, was to me a most novel and inspiring one.

Though we passed on to a point near the Agency house to fix our camp, yet, as we stayed here a week, I had abundant opportunities to visit the red men and become familiar with their summer home-life.

This Agency—which, I believe, has lately been removed—is on the direct trail from Saguache to Antelope Park and the San Juan region, to which we were bound. It is said to have come here by accident, and the story goes that the officer who had charge of locating the Agency was instructed to put it on the Rio Los Pinos, one hundred miles or so south-west of here; but he said, "Put it anywhere, and call it Los Pinos." So here it is.

The valley of the Cochetopa is eight or ten miles long at this point, and three or four wide. Being full of good grass, and surrounded by

high, timbered hills, it has always been a favorite summer halting-place
for the Indians, and here Ouray (I spell it as has been the custom, but
it is pronounced Oo-ráy), the chief of the seven tribes that formed the
Ute confederation, had his head-quarters. Ouray was a remarkable
man, and I am glad I knew him; but there proved finally to be too
many rascals in his nation for the strength of his influence.

It is difficult, of course, to estimate a man in his position by the
standards we apply to civilized leaders; but it seemed to me that his
hold upon his tribe was always precarious, and that he accomplished his
ends, when he *did* succeed, by artful devices, patience, and the force of
the side he took, rather than by any power as a ruler. He was not
wholly popular with this federation, though followed faithfully by his
own tribe—the Weeminoochees. The Northern bands, which had their
head-quarters at the White River Agency, always looked upon Douglas
as their chief, though acknowledging the nominal supremacy of Ouray,
since he had been recognized at Washington as "head chief."

Ouray continually lost popularity with a large number of his men by
his persistent endeavor to keep peace with the whites, to prevent war
of any sort, in short, and his steady advocacy of the principle that the
prosperity of the tribe lay in their adapting themselves to the manners
of the white men. He was the apostle of progress and liberality among
a people too thoroughly cast in its traditions, too inflexibly moulded,
to willingly consent. This appeared very strongly in several incidents
which occurred while I was at the Agency.

The division of the Survey that I accompanied at this time was
the photographic party, under the charge of Mr. W. H. Jackson, whose
beautiful and highly artistic pictures have done more, perhaps, than
anything else to make the Survey widely and attractively known. Our
purpose was to photograph portraits of Indians and scenes in their life.

Ouray was informed of this, by a visit paid him at his cabin at the
Agency, where he lived with his pretty wife in an attempt at civilization, and he acquiesced heartily, promising to sit himself, and have his
wife and his brother-in-law (I believe he was) also sit, with all their best
regimentals on. That afternoon, therefore, there was a large gathering
on the veranda of the house of the Agent, the Rev. Mr. Bond, a Unita-
rian clergyman from Boston.

Ouray ordinarily wore a civilized dress of black broadcloth, and even
boots, though he had never cut off his long hair, which he still bound up
in two queues, Indian fashion. But now he came out in buckskin costume of native cut, full and flowing. with long fringes trailing from his

7

arms and shoulders, skirts, and leggings, until they dragged upon the ground. These garments were beaded in the most profuse and expensive manner; and as he gravely strode through the circle of spectators and seated himself in a dignified and proud way, his many medals flashing, he looked every inch a monarch.

His wife, Sowabéeah,* was that day about the most prepossessing Indian woman I ever saw, and Ouray was immensely proud of her. She evidently had prepared with great care for this event, yet at the last was very timid about taking her place before the camera; but the encouragement of her husband and assistance of Mrs. Bond soon overcame her scruples, and she sat down as full of dimpling smiles as the veriest bride. The doeskin of which her dress was made was almost as white as cotton, and nearly as soft as silk. From every edge and seam hung thick white fringes, twelve or fifteen inches long, while a pretty trimming of bead-work and porcupine-quill embroidery set off a costume which cost Ouray not less than $125.

The third negative made was that of the brother-in-law, and chief medicine-man of the tribe, whose dress was more resplendent than even his royal brother's, being almost wholly covered with intricate patterns of bead-work. He was a tall, straight, broad-shouldered fellow, and had not an unpleasant face, but it was thoroughly painted in vermilion and yellow—a bit of savage full-dress which Ouray and his wife, with liberal taste, had discarded. The most noticeable thing about this great sorcerer, however, was the evidence of his prowess in war. The fringe on his coat, from shoulder to elbow, consisted wholly of locks of human hair—the black, straight hair of Arapahoe and Cheyenne scalps that had fallen to his valorous share in battle. The heart he wore upon his sleeve was a dauntless one.

We made good pictures of all three of these, singly and in groups, and had much fun out of it; but the consequences were dire.

At the conclusion I sat on the chief's porch, and asked him some questions as to the origin of the Ute nation. Ouray told me that they first occupied a little district at the southern end of the Uncompahgre mountains, about the sources of the Rio San Juan and Rio Uncompahgre, where, according to tradition, they were without horses, had no arms other than bows and arrows, and used stone implements exclusive-

---

* I learn, too late to ascertain the real fact of the case, that possibly I am wrong in this name; or, at any rate, that she had another name by which she was more widely known beyond the Agency.

ly. I asked him many questions about the method of making the stone tools, but got no satisfactory answers. After the advent of the Spaniards, who introduced metals, the use of weapons and implements of stone gradually declined, until soon they wholly disappeared. Having only bows and arrows, no horses or dogs, and yet trusting to the chase for their maintenance, they secured all their wild game by driving it into ambush along the runways. They had at this primitive time no goats, sheep, or cattle; nor was there any current means of exchange, legal tender, or money, unless the buckskin in which the medicine-men were paid might be called such. This pay was for teaching the young men traditions and knowledge of national import, in addition to the regular family instruction practised by the parents.

The only enemies of the tribe at this time were the Indians of the plains, and some mountain tribes to the northward. From these they were constantly obliged to defend themselves; but they made few aggressive raids beyond their own narrow limits. South of them were the Jicarrilla Apaches, with whom they were always on friendly terms, and even intermarried. But, curiously enough, it was always an Apache girl marrying a Ute, and never a young Ute girl giving her hand to an Apache brave. There was no law about it—only usage had confirmed a custom. (It is a common feature of Indian society, from the Atlantic to the Pacific, that members of the same band or tribal family shall not marry; but I do not remember to have seen such a secondary fact as the above-mentioned recorded elsewhere.) Through the Apaches the Utes communicated with the Spaniards, who had already settled south and west of there, in what is now eastern Arizona, and from them obtained a few horses and dogs, which by being carefully bred soon multiplied until they had accumulated a sufficient stock. This was the first step toward their subsequent prosperity.

They now changed their attitude of defence to one of offence, and pushed the war hotly against their old ·enemies, refusing to fight the Spaniards, as nearly all of the village tribes south of them were doing. It was in these raids that they first obtained, and learned to use, firearms, capturing them from the plains Indians who had been visited by traders. Gaining in strength, numbers, and courage with new victories through long years and weary battles, they finally drove their foes eastward to the open plains, and were possessors of all the territory now included in Utah and Colorado, between the Wahsatch mountains and the main range.

Of course, it is difficult to tell how long ago all this happened; but that the main account is a true history of the tribe I have little doubt. The rest we can form a definite idea of, for Ouray tells me that he can remember when the Utes first met the white man (that is, Americans—the Spaniards had been seen long before), in the vicinity of Del Norte, on the Rio Grande. His father, Salvador, was then chief of the tribe, and his mother an Apache. These white men were, of course, traders; but they were soon followed by others, and the Utes soon became familiar and friendly with them; and, Ouray added, "It is their boast to-day that a Ute in good standing never killed a white man." I knew that that was not quite true, but I did not argue the point just then. Now, since the White River massacre, and several other bloody scenes, the assertion is farther than ever from the facts.

The head men of the tribe are constantly watching the behavior of the boys and young men. When they see one who is intelligent and progressive, whose ideas are in conformity with the policy of the nation, and who shows a capacity for carrying on their affairs with credit and advantage, he is looked upon as a captain without farther ceremony. From the captains the head chief is elected. Such a man was young Ouray, and he at last became chief, with the consent of all the tribe, altogether through his own merits and not because his father was chief, for no hereditary honors are recognized. He first succeeded Benito as war-chief in 1863, perhaps at the nomination and certainly with the sanction of the United States Government, which had become convinced of his ability during the negotiation of the treaty at that time. This election and the terms of the treaty together so dissatisfied old Nuvava, head chief, that, with all his band, he left the Southern Utes and reported thereafter at the White River Agency. Subsequently there was a split in his band, and some three hundred and fifty, under the leadership of Peeah, went to Denver to receive their supplies. It was this same rascal, Peeah, who later got us into trouble.

The day after Ouray was photographed was "issuing day" at the Agency, and we were down bright and early to view it. Beginning at sunrise, parties of Indians, with their wives and little ones, were to be seen riding leisurely over the rolling plain up from the village about six miles away. There was a wagon-road down there, but most of them came a straighter way by the trails, half a dozen of which, like so many cow-paths, ran side by side. So they poured in, until by nine o'clock nearly the whole village was there—perhaps two thousand men, women, and children. They loitered about the court-yard within the quad-angle of the Agency, swarmed inside the buildings and at the trader's store, and loafed in the stables. Finally, old Shavano, the war-captain of the tribe—but, 'pon my word, he was the mildest looking, most grand-fatherly savage I ever saw in my life!—appeared on the ridge-pole of the government's storehouse, and struck an attitude of great dignity, with his blanket impressively looped up about him, like a regular bronze statue in a cocked-hat and feather. Whether we speak in loud tones because we have acquired the habit of doing so through living in the midst of the incessant racket of our manifold industries; and whether, conversely, it is because the savage dwells in such mighty silence, that he speaks in tones so moderate, I leave for your specula-tion: but I know that one of the most noticeable traits in all the dozens of Indian tribes I have met has been, that their conversation was almost in whispers. I have often wondered how it was possible for the person addressed to hear, yet he never failed to do so; and now, when Shavano gave out the directions for forming the array to receive the annuity goods, he did it in a tone which I had to strain my ears to catch even the sound of, yet which was understood in every word by all the Utes far and near. So much sharper are savage ears than civilized. Having referred to the captains, sub-chiefs, and head chiefs, it may be a good place in which to explain their respective posi-tions and duties, while the women and children, with much merriment, are seating themselves in three large semicircles, one behind the other, converging toward the storehouse door, where the Agent and his assist-ants were about to dispense the goods.

When anything of national interest is to be deliberated, as the open-ing of a war, notice is given and a general mass-meeting called of all the men in the tribe. There all the *pros* and *cons* of the matter are discussed and weighed against one another. The matter is then re-ferred to a council of the aged and influential men of the tribe, many of whom have some authority and are termed sub-chiefs, who render a decision and arrange a mode of action, the execution of which be-longs to the captains. In these deliberations no woman has any voice; or if by chance the sage advice of any woman is heeded the source is never recognized. When they go to war everything is in common. All the plans, tactics, and strategy to be employed are thoroughly un-derstood by each man, who, acting on this intimate knowledge of the plans, looks out carefully that his own share of the work is well done. Thus all details of organization are rendered unnecessary, and the act-ual authority of the captains is so small as to amount to nothing. It had been learned from the experience of wars with Indians of the plains that when much authority is delegated to one man he is likely to abuse it for his own personal advantage; and, moreover, that jealousy toward him is sure to arise. It was especially pressed upon me to observe that the charge brought against them by those ignorant of their customs, that there was no system in the conduct of their affairs, and that they had no capability of organization, was untrue. On the contrary, their customs are uniform and universally respected, and they exhibit in their leaders just as much capacity for government as do any of the civilized nations of the earth. The only difference, the chief insisted, is, that civilization presents greater complications. Poor old Ouray—he is dead now, after an administration full of trouble! Very likely he wished his capacity for government a trifle greater, or his " complications " less.

When all had been seated and were quiet, several of the older Indians came forward to help distribute the flour, beans, coffee, tobacco, and whatever else was given out. But before it began Shavano (who had remained lofty and statuesque on the ridge-pole) said something which sent a little murmur around the circle and caused everybody to turn their eyes upward, where I now descried Mr. Jackson and his assistant perched on the roof of a second building, with their camera aimed at the expectant crowd. Shavano held up a warning hand, as though he were pronouncing a benediction; and in an instant it was over, and the distributing began, amid great excitement and unintelligible but not unmelodious gabble.

But there was one man there who was displeased excessively at this trick of the photographer, and proposed to put a stop to such foolishness. Meanwhile, however, he had some fun on hand.

As soon as the goods had been pretty well given out the male Indians threw aside their blanket-robes, mounted their ponies, took rifles and revolvers in hand, and gathered in groups about the great gates of the corral. Then the gates opened, and, goaded by an onslaught of frantic youngsters in the rear, out rushed a score or more of wild-eyed, long-horned, sleek-hided Texan steers. They were received with excited yells by the redskins on horseback, and each group, selecting a steer, at once improvised a mimic buffalo-hunt, their ponies entering into the full zest of the chase.

The steers, indeed, were wilder than buffaloes, and dashed away at high speed, surrounded by a little crowd of shrieking Indians, whose fringes and bright blankets flashing in the sunlight, with the rapid movements of the horses, made a very lively picture. It lasted only a few moments, however, before the rifles and revolvers began to be heard, and the agonized cattle dropped in their tracks, yielding up their hides almost sooner than their souls.

This over (of course it was unphotographable), we attempted to take some pictures of groups of redskins at the Agency, when opposition began to be evident; and the murmurs grew so strong that when Mr. Jackson came out with a second plate he found his camera surrounded by a mounted guard of Indians, armed with lances, who not only kept everybody away but threatened the destruction of the instrument. So no more negatives were made that morning. They had a superstitious reason for this behavior; or at least they alleged one, though I have always thought it merely a move for popularity among the malcontents of the tribe by the wily Peeah. They said that to photograph a single man was bad, but not necessarily fatal; to photograph a squaw was wrong and immodest; but to take a picture of a group of Indians (unless of a whole town, for example, at long range) was the worst kind of bad medicine. "Make heap Injun heap sick," they asserted. When asked why, it was gathered that they believed that in order to produce an exact likeness on the photographic plate some witchery must be exercised by the sorcerer who hid his head so mysteriously under the black cloth, which drew out of the "subject" enough of his actual soul and substance to construct the semblance on the plate. This loss of soul a brave warrior might not miss; but certainly a weak squaw had no such strength to spare; and great evils had been known to follow the photographing of a dozen or so persons at once.

XIII.

UNDETERRED by our bad-luck of this morning, we went down to the camp on the day following, determined to make another effort, and by flattery succeeded in getting several good general views, and even pictures of Peeah himself and some of the other head men in their ceremonial toggery of crown and long train of the feathers of the golden eagle, which is the war-eagle of all Indians.

For several years the Utes have been supposed to live upon the reservation, which embraces some 14,000,000 acres, in south-western Colorado, and is the largest Indian reservation in the country.* But the

FIRST GLIMPSE OF THE INDIAN CAMP.

fact is that they are in its valleys only in the winter, roaming during the summer all over the Territory, particularly in the park country.

---

* This was written before the very recent sale and reduction of a large part of the reservation in Colorado, and the consequent movement of the whole tribe north-westward into the White River region.

From about the 1st of August until it is time for them to retire to their winter-quarters in the Uncompahgre valley they keep near their respective Agencies, and live on the rations which are dealt out to them by the government. This is the best time to see them at home, for then there are often sixty or eighty lodges in one camp. Their lodges are all nowadays made of cotton cloth furnished by the government, are conical in form, and supported on several slender poles meeting at the top, where the cloth is so disposed as to make a sort of flue or guard, set by the wind, in order to cause a proper draught. A little, low opening on one side makes a door, which is usually closed by a flap of hide or an old blanket. The white cloth soon becomes begrimed with smoke at the top, which in time extends downward and deepens, until you have a perfect gradation of color, from the white base through ever deepening smoke-browns to the sooty blackness of the apex, adding greatly to their beauty. Besides this discoloring, for which their owners are not directly responsible, the lodges are often painted in bright colors, particularly about the door-ways, and in a band about the base; and usually there will be one or two blue, yellow, or striped lodges in a camp, giving a picturesque variety to the scene. About each teepee (lodge) or group of teepees — for they cluster together here and there in no sort of order—you will ordinarily find several little huts of evergreen branches, called wicky-ups; fires, with queer kettles hanging over them; frames hung with skins in process of tanning and softening; buffalo-robes staked on the ground to dry or to be painted by the squaws at leisure times; piles of all sorts of truck—Indian, Mexican, American, and nondescript—among which papooses play, ponies stroll and entangle long lariats of braided raw-hide, dogs bark, and indifferent warriors in gay suits smoke with stoical laziness.

Their utensils consist almost entirely of what they have bought from the whites, iron and tin ware; but some peculiarly Indian manufactures are still in use, as, for instance, gourd-shaped water-jars, holding from two quarts to a gallon, made of close wicker-work, well pitched, one of which, it is said, it takes a squaw four days to make. They have little paint-pots, too, of black pottery, and stone pestles, but these things are almost entirely superseded by civilized manufactures. The boys practise with bows and arrows, and use them largely in getting small game; but the older ones are all well-armed with Sharp's and Ballard rifles and the latest improved Winchester carbines. They have plenty of cartridges, too, and always wear revolvers, so that a boyish game, something like quoits, is about the only use they find for their arrows.

The noises which strike your ear are equally varied, running all the way from the squealing of a poor little papoose strapped in its coffin-like cradle, or the really melodious laughter of a squaw, to the hoarse whinnies of a hundred horses and the ringing report of a revolver. The one sound, though, which will attract your attention, and which you never fail to hear, is the monotonous droning of drums in the medicine-man's tent, generally accompanied by the more monotonous chanting of a series of notes in the minor key which is neither song nor howl nor chant, and which could go on endlessly if it wasn't occasionally stop-ped by a yelp from the leader. The young bucks enjoy this singing, and swing their bodies in time with a seriousness of countenance that is very funny to a white man. I have seen two different drums among them; one nothing more than buckskin tied tightly over the mouth of a jar, and the other made of raw-hide stretched very tense over a broad hoop, so that its shape was that of a sieve.

One of the little cradles mentioned seemed a trifle different from the ordinary style, and I began to sketch it, as it stood up against one 'of the lodge-poles, while the mother sat on the ground near by croon-ing a low ditty, and sewing on a pair of moccasons. But the instant she saw what I was about she snatched her infant up and set it out of sight. I changed my position and tried again, and soon found myself walking round and round the lodge after a highly alarmed squaw. It struck me just then that I was acting an impertinence, but I had no time to desist gracefully, for I found my arms pinioned to my side by half a dozen sturdy young men, who crowded me so closely that I could not make a stroke. I laughed and shut my book, but would not let them take it; and when one essayed to draw my revolver slyly from its case I resented it most emphatically.

Just then it began to rain, and I accepted the hospitality of Peeah's teepee, where we all of us sat around, on skins, until the shower was over. The shelter was miserable, streams trickling down everywhere. The squaws kept pretty quiet, as usual; but Peeah talked a good deal, and an old grandfather was very voluble. Peeah occupied the time in making his toilet. From the depths of an otter-skin pouch, which was his carry-all, he drew forth a small, round looking-glass with a tin back and cover, and a little shallow box, hollowed out of a single piece of wood, which contained vermilion. He was a short man, with a very small head and face; and as he squatted upon his haunches and grinned facetiously at me over the top of the glass with his little piggish eyes, he seemed more like a masquerading boy than an influential man.

INTERIOR OF A WICKY-UP LODGE.

Greasing the palms of his hands with a little tallow, he vigorously smoothed down his jet-black hair until it was pasted to his diminutive skull and shone as though varnished. Behind, his hair was plaited into two braids, into which were entwined strips of otter-skin, thus lengthening the plaits until, partly hair and partly fur, they hung down to his hips. These braids he did not disturb, but contented himself with tinting the geometrically straight parting in the middle of his crown with yellow-ochre. This done, he folded a bit of buckskin over the end of his finger, dipped it in a vermilion paint, and began rubbing it upon his cheeks, where two large red spots speedily ornamented his extraordinarily dark complexion. To these he added some flourishes upon the forehead, and two or three vertical dashes upon the chin. Then, with a last critical smirk in the glass (the shower having now ceased), he replaced his toilet articles, gathered his Navajo blanket around his half-naked shoulders, and stalked out of the lodge with the gait of a tragedy-king. I followed, and made a bargain with him for his blanket, which I bought for twelve dollars, cash down.

The tribe possessed (in 1874) some six thousand horses—and about six hundred thousand dogs — fine stock, too, which they had largely captured from the Cheyennes and Arapahoes, who in turn stole them from Texas ranches and Mexican herds. They take immense pride in this horse-wealth, and each manages to have a racer in his stud, on the speed of which he will bet, not only his "bottom dollar," but his bed and board, if he thinks there is the least chance of winning. I was present at one of their races, and it was an exciting scene, I assure you. The track is always a straight one, and the distance only a few hundred yards. The owners bestride their own nags, and at a signal all start together and come flying down the track, arms outstretched or frantically plying the three-lashed quirt of leather, heels digging every pony's ribs, and mouths yelling like so many devils. Sometimes a horse won't stop at the end, tearing over the prairie a regular runaway; but the spectators only laugh, and the rider doesn't seem to care.

For the last few years the nation has been decreased in numbers, probably, especially by the ravages of small-pox, which was purposely communicated to them, the Indians believe (but it seems hardly credible), by some traders with whom the Utes were unwilling to deal. A few Indians having taken the disease from the infected clothing sold them, others were advised to be vaccinated, but were, instead, inoculated with the disease with *malice prepense*—so the terrible story goes—by unprincipled quacks in the towns south of them. The epidemic raged with fearful power, and hundreds of families were exterminated. It is heart-rending to hear the account of it, reminding one too strongly of the Plague of Athens. Their method of treatment was that panacea for all aboriginal ills—the sweat-house.

The sweat-houses are a common object in all villages, and usually are built close to the stream upon which the encampment is placed. A shallow pit is scooped, a low hut of willow-bushes built over it, a small fire kindled, and a number of stones set in the coals to heat. When the stones are red-hot the naked man or woman who is to be treated throws a blanket over the shoulders, pours water upon the hissing stones, and instantly squats over the steam. Perspiration follows as a matter of course, and when it is most profuse the patient bursts forth from the sweat-house and plunges into the cold river. This is very good treatment, perhaps, for light fevers, or even rheumatism; but the result in small-pox is immediate death. Nevertheless, the practice went on; and those who were too weak to try it were tom-tomed to death by the insane noise and conjurings of the medicine-men. The only wonder is that a redskin of them all survived the plague.

The southern neighbors of the Utes are the Navajos, a tribe of restless, spirited people, who, though constantly wandering, and often at war, still possess large herds and carry on certain manufactures, the most noted of which is the production of those peculiarly excellent blankets known as the "Navajo," for which they raise wool, dye, spin, and weave it on looms nowadays furnished by the government, but formerly of their own contrivance. They make a good deal of pottery, too, and seem the most industrial of any nomadic Indians of which I know. The Navajos have seen much of the Spaniards, and have transmitted to the Utes many notions thus imbibed, Navajo-Spanish coloring appearing everywhere in the language, customs, and ideas of the latter. This tradition of the Creation, for example, seems too conformable to the Old Testament account to be received as altogether original with the nation; yet the old men aver that it is a Ute tradition—pure, so far as they know:

The world was created by one Power, they tell us, and existed until it became too densely populated, when the Creator commanded one man to build an ark, and collect in it a pair of every species of animal from all parts of the earth. He did so, and remained safe through the flood which speedily followed and destroyed all other life. "Noah"— the Indian name of this individual I could not obtain—could converse with each animal, and when the waters began to subside he sent out a raven—at that time a white bird—strong of wing, to see whether the storm was fairly over, and discover, if possible, any dry land. The raven went, but delayed his anxiously-looked-for return so long that "Noah" sent out after him a dove, which, quickly returning, brought news that the raven, true to his nature, had forgotten his errand, and was all this time gorging himself from the floating carcasses. Wroth at this neglect, the dove was sent to bring the culprit back, who, for his wickedness, was cursed, and changed from white to black. Soon after this incident the ark rested, and the animals were sent forth. But at this time the earth was almost entirely covered with water, and was everywhere level. So, in order to get rid of it, the Creator commanded the water to make highways for itself by casting up mountain chains and digging valleys and passes through which to run into the general ocean which still remained. In this ocean, which tradition described, Ouray never believed, he explained, until, on his first visit East, he saw the Atlantic. This flood they consider to have been the first and the last which came upon the earth, but that the final destruction of the world will be by fire, after which it will be peopled by the spirits of the present inhabitants. So much exhibits to my mind the result of Jesuit teaching; but as I cannot ascertain that any of these missionaries ever visited the Utes, it must have reached them (so long ago that they have forgotten it) through the Southern Indians, who had frequent communication with the Spanish priests.

Aside from such a tradition as this, their religious belief seems peculiarly their own. They believe in one great ruler of the universe—omnipotent, omniscient, good—a personal God. This spirit is nameless to them. They do not try to represent him to their minds by any concrete form or in any stated condition. But each man seeks some object in nature which shall typify to his mind all that is pure and holy, and exhibit to his best satisfaction the supremest excellence of which he is able to conceive. This natural object, whatever it may be, he does not hold sacred or to be worshipped in any sense as an idol, but only seeks to glorify the Almighty and Good One through his delight in it.

Subordinate to the Good Spirit, they believe, is an evil spirit — a spirit of malignant mischief—Mephistopheles, rather than Satan. Anything human or animal that is red—as red hair—is supposed to belong to him. His chief exertion seems to be to gain possession of the souls of dying ones the instant they escape from the body. His foe and watcher, who must conduct the freed soul safely to heaven, is Sin-ó-wap, the good angel, who is supposed to attend all persons when they die and take charge of their souls. All this, of course, implies a hereafter of rewards for good and evil, and that every one is responsible for his own actions, which they hold. The way to heaven is straight and accessible to all good men. As the Good Spirit can pardon us all sins but wilful murder, and as the evil spirit is never, or rarely, supposed to be successful in his effort to steal souls from the good angel, the inference is that nearly everybody gets there.

The best of them regard the human race as of but one blood, and that all nations will reach heaven alike; but many Indians think that most other races are simply animals of a high order, and not men as they are.

Such is their religious belief, taught them about the lodge-fire, by their fathers and grandfathers, as soon as they can begin to understand, and insisted upon by the medicine-men, but never formulated by priests, for there are none such whatever, or expressed in set phrase of prayer or adoration. Their minds are untrained, unenlightened by any exchange of ideas with better intellects, clouded and dimmed by mists of superstition which it is impossible to clear away from the best of them.

Some of their laws and customs are yet, apparently, untainted, as, for instance, their laws of inheritance. During a man's lifetime, as fast as any children are born to him he sets apart for each one certain property—principally, of course, young live-stock—which grows up and accumulates with his increasing years, until the time comes for him to use it, when it is ready for him. But the father retains whatever he wishes for himself, to which the children have no right whatever. When the old man nears death he can give away such of this, his own property, as he wishes, but all that he does not give away is buried with him, for fear that he may need it in the other world. When a man is dying a constant noise and ceremony is kept up, to frighten away the evil spirit and secure his soul to the good angel's charge. There is always some man, usually the physician, to attend him, who, immediately upon his death, designates several women (never men) who take charge of the corpse, and in the night take it away and bury it secretly in some crevice of rock in a lone cliff, or sometimes in a grave, taking great care that the sepulchre is not accessible to wild beasts, and that no one else knows where the body is buried. His arms, implements, and clothing are buried with him, and his horses and dogs killed; but no food is put in the grave, and no human sacrifice is ever made or permitted. The Indians are not positive that there will be any use for these worldly things beyond the grave, but, for fear there may be, the provision seems never to be neglected.

If a young man falls in love with a young maiden and they agree to marry, they do so without farther ceremony, and go to house-keeping, with or without the assistance of their parents, as happens. This is the case when there is no obstacle. Should the young man's father object to the alliance, the girl's parents consider it etiquette to object also, and matters become complicated. If, however, the young fellow can prevail upon his sweetheart's papa to give the girl up, and can get away with her in spite of his own father, the old gentleman is supposed to give in gracefully and contribute his blessing. Inasmuch as ample provision has been made for him from boyhood, the young buck rarely finds himself in need of assistance to begin his married life. But if through misfortune he is poor, help to start with is given him by both families, unless he has behaved disrespectfully toward them, when he has no right to expect favors. The greatest respect is exacted from one and all toward those older or greater in authority than they.

The Utes are hospitable to strangers. If a poor man comes among them and by his behavior gains their respect, he is furnished with a horse and good outfit, which he is at liberty to use as he pleases so long as he remains with them; and when he chooses to leave he is furnished the means for his journey.

The Utes in 1874 numbered something over three thousand all told. They practise no industries, but are rich in horses and arms. They are tall, straight men, chaste and honest. How brave they are is open to discussion, but we know that they are pretty well scared at the Arapahoes and Cheyennes. I was in their camp one night when an attack by Comanches was apprehended. Scouts were out far and wide, the warriors had their horses saddled, and the whole camp was up all night, beating drums to keep up their courage. But no Comanches came, for which I was rather sorry, but the Utes appeared greatly relieved.

One more incident, and then I leave Los Pinos. One morning, just as we were sitting down to breakfast, a gaunt, white mule staggered into our camp, bearing a man emaciated almost to death, and scarcely able to sit in the saddle. An Indian trail came down the ravine, which was separated from us by a row of thick bushes. Coming through the bushes the man burst upon our camp suddenly. With an almost frightened look in his sunken eyes, the poor fellow threw up his hands and ejaculated, " Thank God !" with a heartfelt fervor rarely accompanying

8

those words. We helped him off his beast and offered him a seat at
our table. But, as though after all he was not safe, he muttered, " No
—I'll chew some mushrooms," taking one from his pocket. It was with
difficulty we prevailed upon him to taste better food, and then learned
his story. He lived sixty miles or so west of there, and had had some
horses stolen from him. He knew the thieves, and started in pursuit,
taking only a little provision and no matches. Following them, he forgot his direction, failed to overtake them, ate up his food, and went
wandering about a desolate country, living wholly on mushrooms (trusting to luck not to get poisoned ones) and a few acorns. He said the
fungi were "good raw, but he wished he'd had a fire to roast 'em, for
then they was bully." After a few days' rest at the Agency he went
back home, but whether he ever got his horses I don't know.

To lose one's way used to be a common occurrence among the
early wanderers in the Rocky Mountains, but now that the country is
better known the danger is proportionately decreased. I shall have a
little story of the sort of my own to tell presently.

XIV.

FROM Los Pinos we followed a trail over the mountains into the edge of Antelope Park — a magnificent valley, watered by the Rio Grande — then cut across a high spur to a point above Wagon Wheel Gap, and followed up the river through two days' journey, past splendid cliffs of soft, volcanic rocks, tinted white and black, yellow, buff, deep blue, light blue, and red. One of the men related a funny story of a tender-foot who passed through here, with some miners, *en route* to the San Juan silver region, where, also, we were then bound. When these deep-blue trachyte walls came in view the tender-foot was told that there was an extensive *indigo lode*, which capitalists had hitherto neglected, because crazy after the silver beyond. He was so impressed with this that he actually made a long *détour* and frightfully difficult climb to examine the "indigo" stratum. He was a fair example of a large portion of the drifting population of the new West, who, when they fail — as, of course, they do — go back home and curse the country, never learning their own ignorance and stupidity.

This trail to Baker's Park, then the centre of the San Juan mountains and mining-district, led directly up the Rio Grande to its very head-waters, on about the loftiest ridge of the Great Divide to be found anywhere, and called for feats like that of Blondin; while the cold was intense, and deep drifts of snow impeded our progress. For the last few miles the river itself was hidden from sight deep down in a mighty cleft between the peaks, where, nevertheless, we could frequently hear its rumbling as it rushed down the precipitous and rocky defile. This was far above timber-line, and not even a bit of soil broke the wide waste of crumbling trachyte which lay in vast slopes on the sides of stupendous summits, or relieved the sternness of the black basaltic cliffs around which the snow-storms beat and the drifts curled in ineffectual rage. There is no possible desolation greater than these lofty peaks show — fastnesses where winter is supreme and chaos retains a foothold upon the earth — fragments of a primeval and Arctic world dotting the fair expanse of tempered nature below.

The Rio Grande del Norte rises here, in a little pocket just under
the very apex of a peak whose name I forget, and the trail passes
around the springs and boggy ground whence it flows. It catches the
drainage of the snow-banks encircling a wide amphitheatre, and so is
well dowered at the start. Then a hundred small streams hasten to
recruit its force before the range—the Sierra Madre, Mother of Mountains, of the old geographies—is left behind, and so it is a sturdy stream

TRAVELLING ABOVE THE SNOW-LINE.

that tears its way through the gates of columnar basalt at Irene cañon,
and has worn down the noble passage through Wagon-wheel Gap. Perhaps I weary you with this rhapsody over a river; but I have a peculiar admiration for this mighty Rio Grande, whose birth I have seen,
whose youth I have followed step by step even down to Santa Fe,
and whose death I have witnessed, in the dignity and solemnity and
slow movement of old age, all its frolics left behind, all its sparkle lost
in the hot deserts, only its depth and weight and solid power sent to
annihilation in the greatness of the Gulf of Mexico.

On this same high ridge, which for all intents and purposes of climate lies within the Arctic circle, and not two hundred yards distant, are the similar sources of the Las Animas. But the sharp little crest which lies between—a favorite play-ground for the lightning—is a part of the Continental Divide, and separates Atlantic from Pacific drainage: for the Las Animas is one of the strongest tributaries of the Rio San Juan, and *that* of the Rio Colorado, which forces its way to the Gulf of California through the tremendous cañons that Major John W. Powell has made us all familiar with. The matter of a few feet one side or another up here, therefore, determines whether a snow-bank shall send its liquid aid to the Gulf Stream or melt into the torrid seas of the equatorial Pacific.

Down the trickling, reckless rill which later broadens and deepens into the Rio Las Animas—River of Spirits—leads a trail almost as tumbling and impetuous as itself, along which none but a trained mountain mule would even look ; and we dismount from our animals, letting them go on alone, and pick our way after as best we can. It is worse than Berthoud Pass. The woods are dense and the rocks high, so that we cannot see out ; but when at last some sort of levelness and bottom appears to be reached we find ourselves in a vast cañon. There is another way in here, by which we afterward crawled out. It was called a wagon-road ; but the only means of using it is to take your wagon to pieces and let it down several steep places by ropes.

The cañon is called Cunningham's Gulch, and is a vast chasm in the mountains, with walls in many places absolutely vertical for eight, twelve, or even fifteen hundred feet in height, on top of which rest peaks that pierce the clouds and gather almost ceaseless snows. From these heights in melting weather, or after storms on the summits, come dozens of little streams, which dash down to the brow of the precipice and then leap off into space. Half of them fly to pieces and are lost in spray before they get half-way down. Others have body enough to hold their shape and paint a long, flashing, silver stripe upon the greenish-gray face of the crag. Others are broken by projecting points and tumble upon shelves and ledges, where they cling ineffectually an instant and then pitch off again with noise and foam, but nourish a few twigs of hardy brush and tufts of herbs by their continual presence. On a cold morning ice enough forms overhead to make little penthouses, from under which they spring on their final leap, and their edges are fringed with icicles. Then, when the wind in the spruces is still, you may hear their sharp and sibilant murmur plainly, and see at once a dozen swollen water-falls, any one of which in height would dwarf Niagara to a mere mill-dam. The most beautiful of them all could be seen to begin far back from the edge of the cañon-wall, seemingly on the very apex of the highest peak of the range, which had been slightly nicked to guide its current.   Of course there were greater

LOOKING FROM A QUARTZITE ROCK.

altitudes behind, and it was our peculiar point of view that gave that strange appearance; but we never could see it otherwise.

At one or two places it is possible to climb up, and there prospectors went.   Was ever any pinnacle too high, any hole too deep, for the silver-seeker when he thought he saw a "prospect" there?   Here their climbing was wise, for good mines were found, and I had curiosity enough to spend half a day in visiting them.   The trail up was like the stairway in Trinity spire; but my little beast climbed it, and landed me on a plateau at last, just at timber-line, where a family of miners lodged, in a sort of niche, and had sunk their shafts and tunnels into the veritable brow of the hoary old mountain.   From their dooryard you had an outlook over masses of chaotic heights which defy words to portray; and

TRAIL TO A HIGH MINE IN THE SIERRA SAN JUAN.

if you fell over the front paling your useless carcass would bump and roll and take flying leaps for a quarter of a mile, and there would not be enough left of it down in the cañon to afford the slimmest pretext for a funeral, much less a eulogy. It makes me shudder now (though not then) when I think how we skipped along those little nicked-out shelves of foot-wide and slippery trails by which these æronautic miners of the "Highland Mary" went back and forth from their cabin to their tunnel. Sometimes the path would lead right across the bed of one of the falling streams I have spoken of. Down below it had appeared only a tiny gutter—a mere thread; now we discovered its width to be fifty feet, and its polished bed inclined at an angle of forty-five degrees or more. The water slid down it as a thunder-bolt slides down a steel rod; and if you lost your footing and started there would be no stopping for five hundred fathoms.

Cunningham Gulch—only one of a great many wild chasms in these great San Juan mountains—leads down into Baker's Park—a little circular valley nestling among lofty walls of trachyte. Through it ran the Las Animas and two creeks, along which are about two thousand acres of available land. The park was named after Colonel "Jim" Baker, who in 1862 brought a large party of gold-seekers in here, expecting to find profitable gulch mining. But, disappointed, they were caught here by winter, half froze to death, and the other half came within an ace of hanging Baker for his pains. After that an occasional camper's fire was the only indication of civilization until 1872, when silver was discovered and a stampede hither occurred.

We did not camp directly down in the park, where the now flourishing town and county seat of Silverton was then a map of squarely-laid-out streets and a few half-built log-cabins, but chose a ledge five miles above, opposite the older mining camp of Howardville. We had, and witnessed, some stirring incidents in life here; for the locality was a good old-fashioned "h—ll of a place," as "the boys" fondly spoke of it. It is too late, and not within my purpose, to discuss the mineral characteristics of the district, and a word or two only must content you in regard to scenery.

The tops of all the mountains in this portion of the Territory are trachytic in their character, and there are five thousand square miles of this rock hereabouts, overlying gneisses and schists, with many intruded quartzite peaks. In this group is included the highest land in the Territory, as a whole, and one can see from almost any of the hoary summits within view a round dozen more—east, west, north, and south—

reaching up to and beyond 14,000 feet. It is the roughest country I
ever saw, and I could go on endlessly with descriptions of scenery, any
single detail of which would be sufficiently astonishing. But the chief
interest to the world of all this is not the unspeakable grandeur which

BAKER'S PARK AND SULTAN MOUNTAIN.

oppresses you by its vastness, nor yet the fact that here is a geological
problem to solve which the student must discard many a cherished
precedent, and anticipate nothing; but rather that here are veins of
crystalline rock, each one full of wealth.

With respect to the ore itself, it is found accompanying lead, zinc,
iron, copper, antimony, etc., and in iron and copper pyrites, and is en-
riched by gray copper and brittle silver. Different mines vary in character and adaptability. Those around Howardville, which is about the
centre of the district, are smelting ores; those in the Uncompahgre
region are fit for chlorodizing, and so on. Nevertheless, little can be
said with confidence beyond the developments already made; but, so
far, there is promise of an almost boundless source of wealth to the
nation for years to come.

XV.

IT used to puzzle me as a boy, when I heard of the marvellous mines of gold and silver found in Australia, Africa, and the western part of our own country, to understand how the discoverers knew when they really had the precious metals. I had seen quartz with flakes and nodules of yellow gold in it, which could not be mistaken; and I knew that on Silver Islet, in Lake Superior, and at a few other places, silver appears in a white metallic shape equally unmistakable. But I was told that "native" gold or silver, as this unmixed metal, recognizable at a glance, is called, was rare; that the usual form in which it occurred was mixed with other metals and earths in a compound called an "ore;" and that this ore often looked as common and worthless to an inexperienced eye as any other rock. How, then, I used to ask myself, do the miners know the rich earth from the poor, the "pay-streak" from the "wall-rock," and how are they able to say exactly how valuable this or that ore is?

Since then I have learned enough to answer my own questions.

The man who digs the gold and silver, as a rule, does not know the value of what he finds, but his experience teaches him that rocks of a certain appearance, found in certain situations, are likely to be valuable. Some gold can be seen in quartz and picked out with a penknife. There is a small class of lazy men in the West who are content to do no better than hunt about the ledges and "coyote" out the yellow specks in this way, and now and then they strike a large nugget embedded in the glistening quartz. But this is not the scientific and profitable way of mining.

Quartz is a white, transparent or translucent rock, made up of crystals. It occupies cracks that have been made in the earth's crust by some of the forces which have acted upon the rocks in their cooling from the state of heat in which all the foundation rocks of the world, such as granite, gneiss, and the like, began their existence. The supposition is that the quartz has gradually been deposited in the cracks by water saturated with silica, of which quartz is composed; and a crack thus filled up is called a quartz "vein." From where I sat writing in my camp, in Baker's Park, I could count perhaps fifty of these whitish veins or "lodes" running up and down the façade of the opposite cliff, and a mile away in any direction I could have counted fifty more, all of them competent to carry gold or silver, or both, which was borne in with the waters that deposited the silica.

When, in the course of the crumbling of a mountain by glaciers or lightning, or the ordinary wear and tear of frost, sunlight, rains, and the rest of the destructive agencies, quartz-veins carrying gold are ground to pieces, the grains of gold are swept down in the beds of the streams along the gulches, and mingle with the drifted pebbles. This golden gravel forms what is known as a "bar," and the operation of washing the gold out of the gravel is "placer-mining." Where a vein appears upon the surface it is said to "outcrop," and it is the outcrop that the prospector first hits upon. To an untrained eye this outcropping rock hardly looks like quartz in many cases; perhaps it was impure to begin with—impregnated with iron or some other foreign material. The once white rock is yellow and rust-colored, and has become honey-combed under the action of the weather, until it is altogether changed in aspect. In such a decomposed quartz gold cannot be seen with the eye, but must be detected by tests which shall cause the gold, if any is there, to separate from the quartz and make an exhibition of itself.

As for silver, it occurs in various different ores. Sometimes it is found, like gold, in veins of quartz and other crystalline rocks; sometimes saturating rocks lying in strata; sometimes, as at Leadville, Colorado, mingled with other minerals in beds which usually occur between stratified rocks underneath and volcanic overflows above, being derived from the latter. Usually the silver is found closely associated with copper or lead, and generally great quantities of iron are also present. These minerals join to make silver ore in some shape or other, and form a rock or earth having the peculiar appearance that attracts the attention of the prospector, who has seen such ores elsewhere, and notes the resemblance.

Judging, therefore, that he has hit upon a deposit of rock containing gold or silver, the miner takes specimens to the one man who can tell him whether he is right in his judgment, and how valuable his specimens are. This man is the assayer.

The assayer, then, is an important man, and among the first to hasten to every new camp is an enterprising graduate from Freiburg or some American school of mines, eager to put his newly acquired learning to practical use. He is a mere boy, perhaps. His hands are soft, his tongue unused to all the rough phrases and quaint slang of the diggings, his frame so slight that one of those brawny pick-swingers could hurl him over a cliff with a single hand; but they are glad to see him, and, however much they may laugh at his greenness in mountain manners, hold in high respect his scientific ability, and wait with ill-suppressed eagerness for his report upon the samples they have brought to him for analysis, impatient to hear the word that shall pronounce them rich men or send them out again, disappointed, to search still longer for the glittering prize the rocks so effectually hide.

Our young assayer builds a rough cabin like the rest, and proceeds at once to make himself a furnace. If he can get bricks, so much the better; but I have seen assayers two hundred miles from a brick, and resorting to stone and mud. His furnace is provided with a good draught, and contains as its central feature an oven (called a "muffle"), where the cupelling and scorifying is done, as I shall explain presently. The muffle is a chamber of fire-clay, about eight inches wide and twenty inches long, much like a section of flat-bottomed drain-pipe. Meanwhile the young man has set some one at making charcoal out of poplar, for his fuel, and by the time he is prepared to go to work this is ready for him.

He has also brought with him a bucking-board or a mortar, upon which to crush his ores; an anvil, several dozens of scorifiers, a mould and die for making cupels; tongs; bottles of acid; several scales of great delicacy, kept under glass cases; and some lesser tools. This is his outfit, and it makes a very small and cheap appearance in its rude quarters. Many assayers in the towns, of course, have very elegant offices and elaborate arrangements; but these nabobs do not come into my story.

Now he is prepared to begin work, and hangs out a shingle. Before long a miner comes in, bringing a salt-bag full of fragments of stone and earth, and asks that its value be tested according to those scientific methods which, when properly managed, admit of no mistake in what they disclose.

The assayer first makes a careful record of the specimen and assures himself that it is perfectly dried. If there is more ore than can well be handled, it is then "sampled" by being sprinkled upon a sort of wide-grooved gridiron, where a portion falls through and part remains. The part remaining is then sprinkled over a smaller gridiron, and so on until a sufficiently small sample is left. This is to make sure that the portion tested is a fair, average sample of the whole lot.

The next step is to reduce the sample to powder. This is done either by pounding it with an iron pestle in an iron bowl or "mortar," or by crushing it under the sliding, back-and-forth movement of a heavy, round-faced "muller" of iron on an iron plate, the surface of which is slightly roughened. The latter process is the favorite one, and is termed "bucking the ore." The verb "to buck," whether of Western origin or not, certainly has a comprehensive and what might be termed a *striking* meaning. It signifies to resist determined opposition, and to resist it with pertinacity. A man bucks against the law when he appeals his case to higher and higher courts; bucks against piety when he is unmoved by a sturdy "revival;" bucks at faro when he sits down and gambles all night; bucks ores when he crushes their tough lumps and hard grains until they slide between his thumb and finger like flour.

Fifteen to twenty minutes will usually suffice to produce a teacupful of dust out of the hardest stones; but not until this dust will pass through an eighty-mesh sieve, which is one almost as finely woven as a lady's handkerchief, is the assayer satisfied to cease his hard labor. The finer the dust, the more fusible or capable of wholly melting it is, and upon its complete fusion depends the success of the assay as an accurate test.

But the amount of ore which has been powdered is far too large to be carried through the furnace, for that is its destination. The sheet of paper that holds it, therefore, is taken to the balance-room, and perhaps a twentieth of the whole, a thimbleful or so, is put into the ore-balance against one-tenth of an assay ton, or two and nine-tenths grammes, the precise weight being ascertained with the greatest care. This final "sample" is now placed in a "scorifier" (a small shallow cup of fire-clay or some other refractory material) and mixed with twenty to thirty grammes, according to the quality of the ore, of chemically pure lead, a portion of this test-lead being saved to be placed as a layer over the surface of the rest, together with a few pieces of borax-glass, useful as a flux. The scorifier is then placed in the arched muffle of his furnace, where it is subjected to red heat, carefully though roughly regulated, and is allowed to remain until a thorough fusion has taken place, part of the test-lead having then become rusted or oxidized, forming of the impurities a slag which covers the whole surface like a cake. In the process which has brought this result about, the test-lead in melting has sunk by its greater weight through the mineral contents of the cup, and has collected all the gold and silver on its way, forming at the bottom a globule or "button" composed of an alloy, or chemical mixture, of lead and precious metals.

Usually the assayer has some idea of the character of the ore he is at work upon, and knows pretty well whether there are both silver and gold or only one in it. As a rule, also, the ores of silver are pretty free from gold ; and if he is searching for silver, all he has to do is to sepa-rate the lead and silver in the button to know what proportion of the latter it contains.

The fusing operation just described having been completed, the sco-rifier is taken out of the muffle and its molten contents poured into a little deep mould. Several of these moulds are cast together into an iron frame, and resemble very closely the house-keeper's "gem" mould, whence issue the russet delights of our breakfast-tables. When the molten material is poured into this mould the button falls to the bot-tom, and is covered by the glassy slag, which when cool is easily de-tached from it by a blow of the hammer on the anvil.

This done the button is ready for "cupellation," and is placed in a cupel, which has previously been heated to redness in the muffle. The "cupels" are flat cups of about an inch diameter and a third of an inch in height, which are pressed out of white bone-ash by means of a brass mould and hand-die, and may thus be made by the assayer himself as fast as required. This cupel and the button having been deposited in the muffle, the action of the heat upon the button causes a rapid change in the character of the lead contained in it, a portion of which passes up the flue in fumes of the most noxious properties ; but the greater part is absorbed by the bone-ash of the cupel, leaving the gold and silver free in the shape of a more or less minute shining globule in the bottom of the cup. A quarter of an hour or so is occupied by this operation, and the instant the last trace of lead is gone (and the assayer knows it by the "blick," or appearance of rainbow colors, over the surface, caused by the rapid alternation of the red and yellow oxides of lead) the cupel is taken from the furnace and is allowed to cool gradually. After this the globule is weighed upon balances of such precision that they will accu-rately determine the tenth of a milligramme, which, in round figures, is about one three-hundred-thousandth of an ounce. Pluck an eye-winker, lay it in one of these pans, and the beam of the scale will sink under its weight!

It remains now to calculate, from the weight of the silver pin-head remaining as the last memento of the ore-sample which had been so thoroughly subdivided, the number of ounces of precious metal to the ton of crude ore represented. This involves a pretty bit of mathematics, which, though intricate, I hope to make plainly understood.

The "assay ton" is the unit of the system of weight in testing for silver and gold. An assay ton is arbitrarily assumed to be 29,166 grammes, which is the number of troy ounces in a ton of 2000 pounds avoirdupois. Therefore one milligramme has the same relation to an assay ton as one troy ounce has to the avoirdupois ton. Consequently, having found by weight how many milligrammes of silver remain from the assay (the sample having been determined before the test, you remember, to be exactly one-tenth of an assay ton), you know just how many ounces of silver there are to the ton of ore, since the two exactly correspond. The tenth of an assay ton of a certain ore, for instance, is put through the furnace, and yields six milligrammes, which is sixty milligrammes to the assay ton. As the relation of the milligramme to the assay ton is precisely that of the relation of the troy ounce to the avoirdupois ton, a simple proportion shows that the ore carries an average of sixty ounces of precious metal in every ton mined.

Should any gold be suspected to exist in the button, the "parting" of it from the silver is accomplished by the process of "inquartation." This consists in adding a considerable quantity of silver and re-fusing in a cupel, in order to separate the particles of gold, so that the silver can be acted upon by nitric acid, which is used because it is powerful enough to dissolve all the silver away. The fusing having been finished, the metal is placed in a little porcelain pan filled with nitric acid, and cautiously heated over a spirit-lamp until all the silver has disappeared. Then the acid is thrown away, and the gold is saved by decantation, as the chemists say, which amounts to a miniature "panning out." The gold remaining in the little pan seems like a black dust—black because the grains are so minute that the eye is unable to perceive that any light is reflected from them, for it is the reflection of the light that causes gold in larger quantities to gleam yellow. If you put it under the microscope you will find that this dust of gold is not really dust in separate grains, but a connected, lace-like net-work of gold wires, finer than any gossamer, and exceedingly beautiful. It is the golden skeleton of the button left behind by the acid, which has dissolved all the silver away from it. The last step of the work is to anneal this gold-lace into a little lump, when it is weighed, and its amount, and the value of the ore it represents, is announced.

Most of the tests, however, are of ores known to be valuable, but the exact worth of which it is desired to ascertain. When ore is to be smelted, also, in order to be cast into bullion, the assayer must first determine the proportions of the different minerals it contains in order to know how much lime and iron and coke to mix with it, that the operation may succeed.

There is plenty of use for the scientific man and his furnace in a prosperous mining camp, therefore, and his business is a profitable, pleasant, and healthy one, so long as he preserves himself against inhaling the lead fumes that his fire-tests set free from the metals.

SEEN FROM AN ASSAYER'S WINDOW.

XVI.

IT happened that everybody went off on a side-trip the next morning after our arrival, except Dr. F. M. Endlich and myself. With us remained a young Cheyenne packer, as general servant, and our little French cook. Ugly rumors were abroad, and daily growing thicker, that the Indians south of us were on the war-path—had burnt ranches, driven in herdsmen, hunters, and prospectors, and were intending to raid this very valley and camp. Each report confirmed these sanguinary rumors, and everybody began to believe that they must at least be partly true. Discussing the matter about our camp-fire, it appeared that Bob, the packer, was extremely anxious that the redskins should appear, and that he had vowed to perform miracles of valor in resistance and vengeance. His courage and cunning in Indian warfare, he assured us, were boundless. The cook, on the other hand, frankly said he was afraid ; and though he thought he should feel obliged to defend his pots and pans, if it came to "the scratch," yet he hadn't lost any Indians, consequently searching for none, and would rather they stayed on the other side of the mountains.

Well, that night, as usual, we went to bed at nine o'clock or so. The camp, as I have mentioned, was fixed on a wooded bluff or terrace about a hundred feet higher than the level of the narrow valley, where stood the miscellaneous assemblage of houses, huts, tents, and half-buried kennels called Howardville. To get up and down from the village to our camp was only practicable by a winding sort of road, narrow and steep. Almost on the edge of the bluff, near the top of this roadway, Endlich and I made down our beds, while Bob and Charley slept some distance away at the cargo.

I suppose I had been soundly asleep for two hours, when I heard the most diabolical shrieking and yelling, with a rattling and popping of rifles and revolvers, as though I had suddenly been dropped into the heart of the battle of Gettysburg or Chancellorsville, *minus* the artillery. At the same instant I opened my eyes, and there stood Bob, half-dressed, his face so blanched with fear that I could detect its paleness in the wan starlight. Trembling so that he could scarcely articulate, he stammered out, "They've come! They're killing 'em all down there! Oh-h-h!" and with that he disappeared into the bushes.

Well, it did look that way. A most infernal racket came up out of that gulch, which was hidden from our sight, and volley after volley assailed our ears. Endlich and I got our arms, and hastened to the brow of the bluff, where we could command the approach; but there before us was the little Frenchman, with his old carbine, as polite and unobtrusive as ever, about as much disturbed as he would have been to find a chipmunk in his bag of hominy. Then, all at once, the noise ceased—not a yell nor a pistol-shot reached our ears. It was remarkable how suddenly the whole massacre, or whatever the thing was, had been put a stop to; and we really felt the dead silence to be more ominous than the noise had been, for we could form no idea of its import. Was everybody stone-dead? After an hour or so of perfectly quiet vigil, however, we became tired of this midnight masquerading as warriors, went back to our blankets, and compared notes. He had stopped in dressing to lace and tie completely a pair of high-ankled shoes (over the nuisance of which he had wasted expletives every morning), but was quite unconscious that he had done so till he proceeded to take them off. As for myself, I had carefully spread out my blankets before going away, for I had said to myself, "After this scrimmage is over I shall want a warm nest to come back to for my morning's nap." But poor Bob—the valiant, the boastful, the Falstaff of the party— shivered the night away in the bushes, far up the side of the mountain, and didn't sleep at all.

Next day came the explanation, disclosing a typical phase of Rocky Mountain life. It appeared that, a fortnight before, a gentleman had brought to the camp several thousands of dollars in cash, for the purpose of buying interests in the mines. Ready money was very scarce in this district at that time, and greatly needed to develop valuable property. The coming of this capitalist was, therefore, hailed with joy, and undoubtedly good bargains were at once offered. But day after day he held off and would not buy. This over-cautious course disgusted the miners, and they made up their mind to free the community of so objectionable a person. He and his money (which they might easily have stolen) were safe enough from harm, only he must "go." Hints failing, they sent some good talkers to fill the old man's ears full of Indian rumors, and then a lot of them disguised themselves as Indians, and made a sham attack upon his half-tent, half-hut of a house, with all the yelling and firing that we had heard. The scare was effect. ual. The old man was frightened nearly out of his wits, and fled to the woods. Then, having got their hand in, the boys continued the fun till everybody was roused out. Next a raid upon us was proposed, but, fortunately, was not carried out. If we had seen blanketed forms climbing the road to our camp there would certainly have been *one* dead mock-Indian; and after that, probably, there would have been three dead surveyors.

With the exception of our rapid run southward, when Mr. Jackson and myself photographed and brought to light, for the first time,* the wonderful ruins of the Cliff-dwellers of the Mancos, Hovenweep, and neighboring cañons (the story of which cannot well be told here), we had no other adventures of note before or during our speedy return to civilization, except one, down on the Mésa Verde, personal to myself, which is related in a subsequent chapter.

---

* The first publication of this matter was my letter to the *New York Tribune*, printed November 3, 1874.

XVII.

TIME was when a traveller must begin his tale by an account, at the very least, of the parting with his lachrymose relatives at the farm-house, and then continue through several chapters with the small incidents of his journey, however long or well travelled. Readers now won't stand such dallying. Behold me, therefore, at Rawlins, Wyoming, a station on the Union Pacific Railway half-way between the terrors of Cheyenne and the horrors of Ogden. This was in 1877, when I was attached to the division of the United States Geological Survey for Primary Triangulation, in charge of Mr. A. D. Wilson—may the fates be kind to him!

Rawlins stands upon the edge of the infamous Bitter Root* country—a spot without a rival for miserableness until you come to Death Valley or the Sand Hills of Idaho. Nevertheless, here is where we rendezvoused for an excursion up into the almost wholly unknown region lying south of the Sweetwater river. The less said concerning Rawlins the better. I need not describe the outfit of a camping party, with a pack-train of mules; and so we are quickly ready to mount and be off to where (we hope) sage-brush will be less abundant, and rattle-snakes farther between.

Moreover, I shall make this part of the tale an itinerary, although such a journal is only one step higher than a diary, and a diary is every sensible man's abomination. Yet I think I must try the itinerary for once, because the fact is, I am sending to the printer almost unchanged the identical manuscript of my note-book. It was written on the spot, in the roughest of libraries, when the mules were hobbled, supper was over, and the brier-wood was glowing. If it is a topsy-turvy sort of a record, you must remember that, like other Topsys, it wasn't *made*, but

---

* Colonel Fremont (" Narrative," p. 163) says this name was given to this stream by the Shoshonée and Utah (Ute) Indians, "from a great abundance in its valley of a plant which affords them one of their favorite roots."

grew as we marched along, making our triangles and collecting our information.

June 11.—Twelve miles from Rawlins to-day, and the present writing is being done under an enormous cottonwood, in deadly fear that
the mosquitoes may find the scribe out. An insignificant little rill purls
along over black sand in a crevice three feet wide and ten feet deep,
and a dense growth of shrubbery lines its edges. The valley is known
as Brown's Hole, and it is said—but I cannot vouch for the truth—that
Smith's Hill and Jones's Creek are within neighborly distance. Whether
or not *Robinson* is mentioned in the illustrious nomenclature of this district I am not informed.

Leaving Rawlins on our march northward, the road led us at once
up into the bluffs and over an extensive grazing region, the absence
of sage-brush being gratefully noticeable. The soil is made up of small
angular fragments of broken sandstone, and the surface of all this region (outside of the lofty ranges) consists of a series of grassy slopes,
from one to five miles long, rising smoothly toward the west, and terminating in a precipitous cliff of exposed sandstone, at the bottom of
which, perhaps, is a rill of water, and then begins the slope of another
grassy hill-side. The faces of the cliff have been worn more or less into
dry fiords and promontories, and in some places have been quite cut
through. But for many miles, frequently, the rock rises perpendicularly
one or two hundred feet, nowhere affording a chance for a horse to get
up or down, unless he be endowed with the volatility of Don Quixote's
steed. It usually happens, too, that some of the strata in the face of
the bluff will be harder than the rest. These will withstand longest
the wear and tear of the "elements," and the result is that the cliff will
have a series of horizontal shelves running in and out of all its sinuosi-
ties of front along the entire length.

Seen from a commanding point the landscape fashioned by this
geology is very peculiar. If you are standing on the dividing ridge, so
as to look at both the Atlantic and Pacific slopes, you will perceive at
once that all the cliffs face you, and behind each recedes a grassy slope.
This is true on both sides of the Divide. The reason is patent. After
the sandstones had been laid down the mountains were slowly elevated,
carrying the sandstones resting against their sides and over their lower
portions up with them. Then the edges of the uplifted strata were
eroded away little by little, until now you see in the cliffs only the worn
edges of the ancient beds. Sometimes there is only a slight outcrop,
appearing like a stone fence running across the bluish plain; and often

the cliffs show thick red sandstones, and resemble vast brick walls going to ruin.

There is very little life on these uplands. I saw several antelopes
as they hurried away from the approach of our noisy pack-train, and
watched them as they paused on the edge of a distant cliff, alert and
graceful, silhouetted against the soft sky. A few birds—not many—
were seen, and our mules shied once at a rattlesnake that glided out
of our path in a hurry, his tail sounding the rasping alarm as he went.
The mules are terribly afraid of these reptiles, which are abundant all
through here, giving their name to a range of rocky hills a few miles
east of this point. Marvellous stories are told of their abundance about
Fort Steele, and we killed some at our last camp, where we lived in
constant dread of their coming to sleep with us. The natives, nevertheless, affect a great " despige," as Mrs. Gamp would say, for them, and
seem rarely to suffer from their presence. The species is that known as
Crotalus durissus.

Half-way to this Brown's Hole, where we are encamped, and which
is the first water, we crossed a little ridge, and could look back. The
foreground was a grayish-green plain, intersected by ridges of yellowish
rock, dappled with the moving shadows of clouds, and dotted here and
there with herds of cattle. In the middle distance were higher hills
and broken bluffs, and the horizon was full of far-away mountains, the
Medicine Bow range on the left, and the Grand Encampment group on
the right. Except the broad dome of Elk mountain all were simply
masses of blue, details of form being lost in the distance; and over the
serrated outline of the lesser front ranges gleamed the solid snows of
the crowning heights behind. Looking forward we saw spread below
us a broad alkali plain, with many zinc-colored ponds and glistening
white patches of soda; and, on the other side of it, the short range of
the Seminole mountains, very noble at this distance of twenty miles.

Coming into camp this afternoon I had my first adventure. My
riding animal is Texas Jack, a big, black, obstinate mule, with a passion
for kicking. I wanted he should go a certain way, and he refused, for
no good reason that I could see. I spurred him. He jumped, struck
on a loose bank, and fell heavily. I managed to kick free from the
stirrup, and get some sort of control over my flight, as I was hurled
from the saddle into the briers and sage-brush, but could not get out of
the way before he stepped on my foot. It made me cry out lustily;
but the steel shank of my spur had borne the weight, and my foot was
only a little lamed. I got out of that with commendable agility. I am

sorry. I have labored with that mule, have tried to persuade him of
the errors of his ways and correct his manners, and this is the result.
I am about discouraged, and I sometimes have dreary suspicions that
there is not enough moral character in a mule to pay for the expendi-
ture of much missionary labor. *Quien sabe?*

The camp to-night, as I have said, is in a grove of ancient cotton-
wood-trees, under which grows a dense underbrush, hiding the ravine
along the bottom of which a trickling rill of pure water secretes itself.
Close up to this long, narrow line of miniature woodland, crowding and
elbowing it almost over the very brink of the ravine, presses the gaunt,
vagabondish sage-brush; and we have hard work to grub away a sufficient space to pitch our tents and pile our cargo. After tea we cross
the ravine and search a high plateau on the other side for moss agates
and tinted pink-and-white flints. Of the former we get no first-class
specimens, but an abundance of beautiful flakes of the latter, and plenty
of a poor kind of opal. Some antelopes come pretty close, but we fail
to get one, which is no matter, since we have brought down a fine buck

THE CARGO AND ITS CARRIERS.

during the day, and have plenty of its flesh. I try to shoot an owl, also,
that excites my curiosity; but in the twilight he flies briskly away. At
last we make up our beds on the ground, down by the cargo, and sleep
soundly under the chilly stars.

June 12.—Twenty-five miles to-day—and hard ones, too; but the
dreaded plain foreseen yesterday is passed, and we are at the foot of
the mountains. Sunrise saw us entering upon our march over a trail

dry and dusty with the saline exudation from the soil, that parched our lips and irritated our eyes under the blazing sun. Through the marvellously clear air it seemed only a pleasant before-breakfast walk across this heated valley to the bald bluffs on the other side. But at noon these landmarks seemed hardly nearer, and the sun was well down the west before we stood in their shadow. Even then our work was by no means done—the mountains were still " on the other side." The sandy valley we had crossed was level, and supported a slim growth of sage-brush, buffalo-grass, cacti, and some gaudy flowers—two sorts of poppy, a mustard, many different wild peas, sunflowers, white asters, and curious blossoms I did not know. Dozens of antelopes had crossed our path during the morning; sage-hens and jack-rabbits had whirled and scudded from before us continually; here, on the very top of the crag, were a group of mountain sheep, colorless statues against the sky; and a deer bounded away as we came around the foot of the hill.

They were fine fellows, those seven sheep! The bluff was, perhaps, four hundred feet high, with a vertical face, and they stood upon its very edge, motionless, an old ram in the front, with immense coiled horns that doubled the size of his head. They were out of range; but we watched them with our field-glasses until, alarmed, they took themselves out of sight. In the remoter portions of the Rocky Mountains this splendid animal, which used always to be called the " big-horn," is still found in considerable numbers; and it is so retiring in its habits, loves such inaccessible places, and is so well fitted by its endurance and agility to escape from its enemies among the cliffs and cañons of its native heights, that it is not likely soon to suffer extermination. At the same time, places which knew it once know it no more, and civilization is gradually circumscribing its range and reducing its numbers. It is a sheep in anatomy and appearance, but its habits are more those of a goat, for it will climb to points where wolves even dare not follow, and make leaps from pinnacle to pinnacle, or gallop away over the loose rock on the side of a mountain, with an ease that might well make a chamois envious. This seems very wonderful when we look at their ovine, heavy form, great weight (for the rams sometimes weigh three hundred pounds), and the enormous horns coiled at the side of the head. It was these that gave the sheep the appropriate common name, " big-horn;" and it used to be believed that they could throw themselves down from tremendous heights, alighting on their horns without injury. This was a fable, of course, arising from an account of the marvellous leaps they really do make, alighting on their feet. In early sum-

mer the old hair is yellowish brown, but their new coats in fall and winter are bluish white, and they are then very noble-looking game. In
early morning and about sunset they descend to the grassy plateaus to
graze, but during the middle of the day keep among the snow-banks, in
small flocks, when they are exceedingly wary. The day you kill one is
a good day to date from.

Leaving this bluff, the rest of our way lay through a sea of loose
sand—drifting dunes and ridges formed by the wind—sometimes brown
with the scant grass of the region, often for a mile at a time perfectly
naked, and ribbed by the wind as a shelving beach is ripple-marked
under the waves. The horses sank to their knees, and the rays of the
afternoon sun were reflected with a painful glare.

But in forsaking the sheep-crags we by no means left the game behind us. Just as we turned, an old buck blacktail got up far ahead and
made off. Antelopes became more abundant and less shy than ever;
hares were started every few rods, and sage-hens lifted their little heads
above the brush to gaze at us, entirely fearless of harm.

Approaching, finally, the foot of the much-desired mountains, we
came upon some little duck-ponds of blue water, fed by springs whose
soft banks were pitted with fresh hoof-prints of elks. An elk's track
looks very much like that of a cow, except that it is considerably smaller, more pointed, and neater. Thus put upon the *qui vive*, we quickly
caught sight of a troop of them, far away over the white ridges, trotting
slowly away like a party of mounted Indians. It was too late, and they
were too far distant, to think of following. Had we not felt so confident
of meeting many more of them, we might have been more zealous; but
we knew they were abundant in the region to which we were bound.
Later, indeed, we did get a shot at a stupid old cow, whose curiosity
got the better of her discretion. But the whistle of a rifle-ball past her
ears put a *flee* into them, and she acted on the suggestion at a pace
which defied pursuit from our jaded animals.

This was at the farther edge of the desert, and we were soon rising
out of the level of the old lake-bed up toward its rocky and ancient
shores, now scantily clothed with long coarse grass and groves of poplar and willow shrubs. The line of dense timber showed where a stream
came down from the mountains, and thither we made our way just as
the sun was setting. Turning from the open plain into the grove, as
we approached the spot selected for our camp a crash occurred in the
underbrush, and the huge form of an elk appeared for an instant to our
startled eyes, and was gone before anybody could shoot. A few rods

SHOOTING THE BIGHORNS.

beyond we camped in a dense grove of tall white-barked poplars, by a little stream whose channel was so sunken in mossy and fern-clothed banks as to make it almost subterranean. The bright water was soon set boiling, and our bacon and antelope steaks were greedily disposed of, even though unaccompanied by the elk-flesh we had hoped for.

This grove was the home of a colony of Swainson's buzzards—hawks not very different in habits and appearance from our common Eastern "redtail" or "hen-hawk." They had built their rude nests of sticks, in the tops of the trees, from ten to thirty feet above the ground, and kept up a continual cawing and screaming of fright and protest at our incursion into their domain. The females that were sitting stood it out and preserved the warmth of their eggs, but the males were shy of coming near. The eggs were splashed with bright brown and yellowish tints like our redtail's; but they varied considerably. I saw bluish-white, entirely unspotted ones in the same nest with those plentifully blotched with deep reddish brown. Considering the number of hawks there, the absence of all other birds except some blackbirds was not surprising.

But I found another specimen of natural history in the shape of an elk calf only a few days old, which I nearly stepped on in wandering about through the brush, looking for snails. It was crouching in perfect quiet, and made little resistance when I picked it up in my arms and carried it to our fireside. Of course it was ungainly and awkward on its legs. Its bright bay coat was spotted all over like that of a young deer-fawn, and it was the stupidest animal I have seen in a long time. By-the-way, when everybody knows and acknowledges the elk as a deer, why apply a different set of words? Couldn't we say *buck* elk as well as "bull" elk, and *doe* instead of "cow, in speaking of this species as well as another? Then the young would be *fawns*, not "calves," which is not only needless but wrong, for calf and cow and bull are bovine, not cervine, terms.

This youngster was all instinct and no training. He well knew that if anything came near, his cue was to lie perfectly quiet. He copied the traditional ostrich whenever any one approached where he was tied and buried his head in the grass. Now and then, however, his longing to see his mother (probably the same elk we had startled as we came in) got the better of his prudence, and he began to bleat and squeal lustily, crouching hastily down after each outcry as though frightened at his own noise. In half an hour he grew very tame, and we watched him with amusement until bed-time, when Harry and I took him back to his lair, whence his mother led him away during the night.

XVIII.

June 13.—To-day has been one of climbing, for we ascended the highest peak of the group of mountains at whose foot we are camped. It is a range about a dozen miles in length and 10,000 feet in greatest height, thus rising only about twenty-five hundred feet above the plain. It lies in an east and west direction, directly north of Rawlins, from which it is about thirty-five miles distant. The name is said to commemorate a visit made by a delegation of Florida Indians (Seminoles) searching for a home. We know that the Cherokees once came out here, and a few Seminoles, who are neighbors and kinsmen of the Cherokees, might have been with them. Although holding quartz veins, this range does not seem to show any prospect of containing reasonably paying gold mines. A spur from the eastern end, however, is the scene of small diggings which are said to have proved highly satisfactory.

The ascent of the mountain was very difficult. We packed the theodolite, etc., on a strong little mule named Molly, and rode up as far as we could—perhaps two-thirds of the way—through birch and pine trees that had been extensively killed by fires. A cloud, dense and well defined, hid the summit, and, after we rose into it, shut out from our view everything except the near foreground. But as we got higher the sun rose sufficiently to look over into the cañon, when suddenly the heavy fog was luminous with yellow light, and began to break away from the tree-tops and roll out over the plain. As it slowly moved away there loomed up right beside us, as though advancing to our overwhelming, a mighty perpendicular wall of rock that towered into pinnacles painted by the sun, and shining hundreds of feet over our heads. Opposite this side of the mountain rose a steep, wooded slope, ending aloft in black and broken ledges of granite, which glistened with dew and gleamed like polished bronze. They looked very beautiful; but when we had tied our mules, distributed Molly's load among us, and had begun to trudge a mile up, and up, and up over those black and jagged ledges, and through the soft snow-banks which lay between, the delight gradu-

ally subsided, and we were very sincerely glad to get to the top. It did
seem as though we should never attain it! Peak after peak was scaled,
only to find another beyond. Mountain-climbing is no fun. It attacks
your endurance, your wind — tests your "bottom," as turfmen would
say—in a way that nothing else I know of equals. This is particularly
true of high mountains, where the thinness of the air makes it doubly
difficult to fill your lungs, and you cannot run ten steps without painful
panting. The coming down was about as bad in this case, and, under
our cumbrous loads, was somewhat dangerous, since we had to keep on
the high granite crests, because of the depth of the snow below, where
ordinarily it would be smooth travelling.

"A STRONG LITTLE MULE NAMED MOLLY."

The view from the top of the mountain, where the theodolite was
placed on a cap-stone of glistening green granite (orthoclase, I believe,
it is termed), was very extended. At first the fog, swinging out from
the mountain, hung like a curtain below us; but the sun pierced through
the masses of white fleece, the wind tore them asunder, and the whole
drapery of the mist speedily vanished. Then we sighted eastward to
the Elk mountains, sixty-five miles away; to the massive, snowy Medicine Bow, behind it; to the Elkhead range, in Colorado, south of Snake

10

river ;—sighted southward to Pilot Butte, and Yellow Butte, and Black Butte, scores of miles distant from us. North of these, on our western horizon, a hundred and twenty-five miles westward, we gazed toward where rose up the magnificent wall of the Wind River range, capped with unblemished snow, and studded with peaks whose summits towered two miles and a half above the sea.

A glimpse northward was caught of the far-away, indistinct Bighorn mountains, and north-eastward lofty hills showed themselves, isolated and cone-shaped, "like solid stacks of hay;" but these were all on the horizon. From the flanks of the pile of mossy and ancient rocks that formed our pedestal (and lay like some sleepy leviathan, with roughened, barnacle-grown back half-submerged) on every side stretched away the green and rolling plains. Here and there in this level expanse rose little island-like "bumps" of ragged, primeval rocks, where the pines grew thick, and the elk and mountain sheep hid. It was easy to see that all the dusty plain, with its heated sand-dunes, that we crossed the day before yesterday, was only the bed of an old lake ; but beyond its ancient banks, looking northward, lay the fertile valley of the Sweetwater ; and yet beyond this stretched the unmeasurable plains of Wyoming. Here are the future pastures for millions of cattle, and they are sure to be occupied. Here are water, grass, shelter, and natural boundaries serving to restrict the wandering of the cattle to join the herds of the Atlantic slope. No better ranges could be found anywhere than these plains afford.

Coming down from the mountains, after three hours of successful triangulation—where we were alternately broiled in a burning sun and chilled by a freezing wind—we aroused two or three herds of elks, the last within a hundred yards of the camp-fire ; but we were not prepared for the chase. When we got into camp, however, Harry was found to be skinning one that he had just shot, and the venison was quickly frying. Its "sizzle" seemed the sweetest sound, and its odor the most elk-cellent savor, that ever saluted the senses of weary travellers.

June 14.—Breakfasting at sunrise, the frost still glittering on the grass, we were packed up within an hour, and marching westward over the foot-hills. For ten miles we tramped across these ridges through the most beautiful grazing region I have yet seen. The grass was thick and tall, and some of it headed out. Every depression had its little stream of pure cold water. At the foot of the range, which was protected from northern winds, were plenty of trees for shade to cattle and for building-timber. Out on the plain were the sand-ridges (always free from snow), and the "soda" lakes offering pure salt ; while every valley was a jewel of a site for a ranch. This fine country extends all through northern Wyoming, and it would, no doubt, have been of far greater advantage to the Union Pacific Railroad had it followed up the North Platte to the Sweetwater river, and down it to South Pass, instead of running the line through the desolate tract occupied, simply because along that route it could be finished a few months earlier. Perhaps it is better as it is, however, since the fertile grass-region is now open to immigration, untrammelled by railway claims. Fear of Indians has kept back occupation thus far, but now this has passed away.

It was a constant delight to ride across the green ridges at the foot of the mountains. They were dotted with gaudy flowers, growing in such profusion as to throw great patches of color upon the hill-side, and a faint sweet smell of tender grasses and myriads of wild blossoms was wafted to us upon each breeze. Then we were entertained by the unceasing company of big game. Antelopes were always in sight, and we might easily have shot a score. They would stand in twos and threes, gaze at us a little while, and then trot off, pausing every now and then to look back; or, frightened, would arch their necks and prance away in that swift, stiff-legged gait peculiar to them. Many were fawns. Every now and then we would start small bands of elk, or an elk cow and her calf, out of the bushes of some little valley as we came over the hill, and these would make no haste to get out of harm's way, seeming not to understand that we were to be feared. Many others were seen at a distance, for the gulches leading up into the mountains were full of them, as also of deer; but we did not fire a shot, not needing the flesh.

Several of the small willow-embowered creeks we forded were obstructed at frequent intervals by beaver-dams ; and in one valley we surprised two large yellow wildcats that cantered off to some thickets near by, where the crows began to plague them, cawing vociferously. No buffaloes were seen, although they occasionally wander near the spot where we are now encamped, nor any signs of the presence of bears, which is something to be wondered at. Small game—sage-fowl (and their broods), hares, etc.—were as abundant as ever ; and of course that sneaking bag of bones, the coyote, who, when he runs, simply makes a streak along the ground, was lurking about all the bluffs.

The last half of the twenty-mile march was rather hard and monotonous. There was no trail—better than that made by elks—and we had to pick our way over a long series of barren hills of marl, up a narrow gulch where the sage-brush was so dense and tall as to be difficult to ride through, then over the wind-swept top of a high bluff, and up again to our camp in a willow-grove near the summit of Whiskey Peak.

We have got "high" on whiskey, so to speak; but we had water in it. Just as all the mules were unpacked the mountain became enveloped in heavy clouds, and we had only time to protect our goods with canvas when the snow and hail burst upon us. Dinner was cooking, and the process went on to a successful end; but the sleet drove between our teeth with every mouthful, and one couldn't keep his coffee hot long enough to drink it, except when the coals from the fire were driven into the cup by some eddy of the storm. Nevertheless we ate our fill, and enjoyed it too. All this time the sun was shining, for through the white veil of snow we could see the blue sky out over the valley; but the mountain was dark as ink; and when an especially fierce blast would smite us we would look at the battered summit and say, "Supposing—?" for we knew we were getting only the switching of the storm's tail.

The Seminole mountains are separated from contiguous groups at their western extremity by a deep valley called Whiskey Gap. This is one of the passes from the Atlantic to the Pacific slope, but it has never been much in favor. A wagon-road from Rawlins to the Sweetwater mining-camps passes through it, and some ox-teams went by to-day. The western wall of the Gap rises into a shapely peak of glacier drift, grass-mantled to its very apex, close to which we have our bivouac. An icy wind still sweeps across, and we retain our cavalry overcoats, albeit the sun shines, and a rainbow dyes the western heaven; but rain is falling all around the horizon, as though a deluge were pouring over the eaves of the sky. Seminole Peak, where we had our hard climb yesterday, stands out blue and beautiful, but its allurement for me is gone. I have been there, and fully appreciate

> "'T is *distance* lends enchantment to the view,
> And robes the mountain in its azure hue."

XIX.

June 15.—The night was wet and cold, but the morning broke clear and frosty, and, after an early breakfast, some of us rode up to the top of Whiskey Peak, to make a topographical station. It was an excellent point for the purpose, because of its isolation, although not as high as timber-line even. It generally happens that from a summit you can

TOPOGRAPHERS AT WORK.

look at most in only three directions, because of neighboring heights cutting off the view, but the whole horizon was open from this station, and on every side the country lay spread out before us like a map in an area two hundred miles in diameter. We were thus enabled to take the bearings of Seminole Peak, Rattlesnake Peak, Elk Mountain, Mount Steele, Mount Rawlins, Hart's Peak, Separation Peak, the Grand

10*

Encampment group, Black, Pilot, and Yellow buttes; the whole magnificent Wind River range, with its snowy, resplendent peaks; the hills
along Owl creek and those along Powder river; behind them the hoary
heads of the far-away Bighorns; and, lastly—for I began in the east
and have followed around the circle—Laramie Peak, away on the other
side of Laramie plains. Channing could not have enjoyed a better
occasion than this for his line:

> "Sierras long
> In archipelagoes of mountain sky."

On a clear day the whole visible earth is mapped out before the
observer who stands on such a mountain-top. All the features of the
landscape take their proper place, and their true relations to each other
are perceived. You see at once how closely these apparently isolated
ridges are connected into systems, broken now, but perfectly apparent
ages ago, could you have looked upon them then. It suggests the
slow modifications that the surface of the earth is constantly undergo-
ing. You comprehend at a glance that the winding creeks *must* run
just the way they do, inexplicable though it seems as you follow their
gorges, because the hills are placed in a manner that precludes any
other channels. Indeed, a skilful man can tell where the great rivers
run, and construct a copy of the whole drainage scheme of the country,
without seeing a single drop of water. Tracing your late pathway
across the previously unknown region, you can easily suggest improve-
ments. This hill might have been ascended so much more easily a
little farther to the eastward; that miry spot avoided by going over
the low ridge just west of it; that plain crossed in a far straighter line,
if only you had known just what to steer for. The bluff that hid the
mountain so long, as you marched past, is a very small affair now, sur-
passed by many other insignificant hills; and the weary circle of the
lake you thought so large hardly makes a spot in the broad picture.
You profit by the opportunity to look ahead, and take a sketch, or
a mental memorandum of to-morrow's course. To gaze from a high
mountain is to travel, and it tends to rid a man of his egotism.

The finest weather is in October. Then the air is still, the dry
ground gives up no mists, and the mountains on the very edge of the
world stand in serene and leisurely content, with cool and freshly-blue
brows. At that season only are clear days, for in summer there is
ever a purplish haze upon the horizon, as ethereal as the scenery of
dreams, obliterating all features except the outline of the crests of the
ranges, and even those broad contours are bereft of all jutting points,

and toned down to great smooth lines. On the horizon, in a bright, cloudless day, the sky is white, or faintly tinted like the inside of a shell; but as there is an imperceptible gradation in the atmosphere from the hazy purple of the horizon's dark mountain-wall to the radiant air next you, so is there a fine opposite deepening of tint from the opalescent white behind the peaks up to a depth of perfect azure overhead that is beyond all dreams of sky-color. It is such solid, opaque blue—yet luminous to ineffable depths—as I have never seen from the lowlands. It is an all-day study to note the varying effects of the sunlight, changing, reflected, and refracted, upon the world viewed from a mountain's summit. Snow is visible at an enormous distance, no matter what its background. Tennyson knew this when he wrote that perfect bit of Alpine description:

> "Some blue peaks in the distance rose,
> And white against the cold white sky
> Shone out their crowning snows."

June 17.—Our camp at Whiskey Peak was just east of the Continental Divide—the backbone of the continent, or water-shed between the two oceans. We crossed it through a grassy depression, hardly noticing the fact, but a very large part of the Rocky Mountains were in view. It is hardly decided as yet among geographers, by-the-way, what ultimately shall be defined as the main range, and what shall be considered subsidiary groups and spurs; that is, it remains to be determined just where the sinuous dividing ridge between the Atlantic and Pacific shall be drawn. Considerations of geography and geology are both to be looked at; and it is quite possible that there may arise irreconcilable differences between these two sets of facts; so that two " divides " may result—a geologic and also a geographic one—just as the true north and south line fails to coincide with the magnetic meridian. In that case it will probably happen that the divergence will be greatest north of Colorado, the geologists holding that their divide trends eastward, while the geographers will claim the actual water-shed here at the west.

Unlike the Andes, the Rocky Mountains are broken into a series of groups, ranges, and cross-ranges of about equal altitude, and connected by high plateaus. It is only in a few places that they present the orderly rank seen in the front range in Colorado, between Pike's Peak and the Wyoming line, where they face the plains. Elsewhere they stand in confused masses, for the most part.

The origin of the name, also, is a matter of inquiry. The first approach to the term Rocky Mountains is said to be found in Bellion's Map of North America, published in Charlevoix's "History of New France," in 1743, where they are called *Montagnes des Pierres Brillants*. The word *Rocky* Mountains first appears on a map in "Morse's American Geography," dated 1794; while in the text of the edition of 1789 they are still called the Shining Mountains. The name, however, seems to have been firmly established in the time of Lewis and Clarke, whose trail, by-the-bye, we are almost following through this portion of the country. It is probable that both "Rocky" and "Shining" are translations of Indian words learned by the early map-makers from trappers. Most of the names of the lesser ranges have this origin, or, at least, were named by the old trappers employed by the fur companies years and years ago. Witness Saguache, Uncompahgre, Uinta, Wahsatch, Medicine Bow, Shoshonée, Wyoming, for Indian terms. The early trappers and explorers at the North were mostly Frenchmen, while those at the South were Spaniards. Both left their language in designating the geography of the new regions they visited. Every town in New Mexico, Arizona, and Southern California begins with a *San;* every old fort north of the fortieth parallel was called after some *Saint*.

Some of these primitive names we have since translated. Powder river, so often mentioned of late in despatches from the Indian fighters, was first known as Cache la Poudre. Half the Indian tribes have lost their own names under the titles given them by the French traders or Spanish priests. Such cases are the Gros Ventre and Nez Perce tribes of the North-west, and the Pimas and Cocopas of the Gila valley, in Arizona. The early appellations almost always had some special significance, and are worthy of respect, but when the gold-miners began to overrun the mountains and tack a name to every spot where they camped, their designations became frivolous and inadequate. We shall be sorry and ashamed, some of these days, that the most glorious spots on the American continent are demeaned by names so trivial. Who would be willing to change Yosemite to Smith's Hole? Yet equally shocking christenings have taken place everywhere. The largest rivers on the Western Slope, draining all these mountains, are simply the Green, Blue, White, Snake, and Grand; and the great artery they go to swell is only the Red river—Rio Colorado. In the North you find worse names— Stinking-water river, Bad river, Crazy-woman's fork, No-Wood creek, Bitter creek, Horse, and Goose, and Wolf, and so on, for beautiful, plenteous streams. But worst of all is the habit lately introduced of naming noble mountains, reaching up into an ever-living purity, after politicians whose schemings and tricks a coyote would scorn to avail himself of. Is there such a paucity of adjectives in our language? The Chinese go to the opposite extreme in their flowery nomenclature; but that is better than calling a peak, whence your eye may take in ten thousand square miles of unexcelled scenery, after a dram of whiskey!

THE SWEETWATER PLAINS.

From Camp 4 to 5 the road led over sage-grown ridges along the southern foot of the Sweetwater hills, the direction being westward, and the distance about fifteen miles. Elk in small bands, several accompanied by young calves, were visible all along, and antelopes were constantly in sight, so unconcerned that they would not even get upon their feet as we rode by. On one of the hills an old buffalo bull was grazing all alone, and our hunters started after him. But our hopes of seeing a chase were baffled, for the old fellow carried his heavy mop and long goatee up the bluff and over its top at such a rate as made the catching of him highly unprofitable labor. He was one that might have sustained a noble part in such a head-to-head struggle with an elk as Mr. William Cary has so graphically depicted in his well-known paintings.

The camp that evening was made toward sunset in a little grassy glade on the bank of a creek hidden in bushes, by a path where the deer come down to drink of the pure cold water. The willow branches were all rubbed bare and the new twigs gnawed off by elks. Just above us was a beaver dam, and there were small trout in the stream; but our luck in catching them was limited.

I do not know when I have seen so many small birds in one place since I left the States, particularly warblers and fly-catchers. As I lay idly under one of the bushes a tiny warbler, all lemon-yellow, except some reddish streaks on the sides and breast, alighted on the branches within reach of my arm, not seeing me, and began to warble its delicate song. It was an old acquaintance, the common summer yellow-bird that builds its nest in your lilac-bush; it did not seem to recognize me at first, but, a moment later, espying me, stopped in the middle of a bar and darted off. Other birds came, many of them strangers, with sweet music and soft *phit* of pretty wings; and at last I saw a dandy of a sparrow (the white-crowned, *Zonotrichia leucophrys*), whose plumage is bright chestnut-brown above, marked with black and ash-color, and a satiny white below, and whose black cap is set off by heavy zigzag bars of white from the base of the pink bill back over the head, and above each eye—I saw this gay fellow enter an archway of dead grass by the side of the brook. I knew it was its home, and, creeping near, almost caught the bird on its nest; but it eluded my hand and flew to a branch near by, chirping loudly, like the clicking of a stiff gun-lock. That was its alarm-call, and its mate was soon by its side, full of anxiety. The nest was carefully woven of grass — coarse stalks outside, and fine blades within, and was warmly lined with elk's hair. It was sunk in among the grass-roots, and so snugly concealed in the long nodding tufts*—for the bird had made a sort of tunnel underneath the grass by which to enter—that hardly a weasel, much less a hawk, would have discovered it. There was one egg, greenish-white, dotted—profusely at the great end, and thinly at the sharper end—with a pepper-and-salt of brown and red. This single egg was all the nest contained; but when I looked again at sunrise the next morning a second one was by it — the mother-bird had done her day's work early.

How circumspect the birds are! I had my eye on the sparrow, as it flitted about the bush in well-affected unconcern, uttering a simple refrain and seeming not to mind me, for half an hour before it got courage to slip into its nest, to see if all was safe. Try to force a secret from

---

* See p. 38.

THE FIGHT.

THE RESULT.

a bird, and you are sure of failure: have patience to keep perfectly still, and he will show you his inmost heart. There was no end of them about that day, mainly sparrows—sweet singers; but the golden-mouthed leader of the choir was the mountain mockingbird (*Oreoscoptes montanus*), whose versatile fluting is heard morning and evening on these plains as he rejoices over his happy home in the sage-bush. He is a relative of the Southern mockingbird, and also of the brown thrasher of Northern orchards. Probably his melody is not equal to that given by either of those musicians, but it has a wild sweetness in it, as he readily runs the scale of all the other bird-songs of the plains, and his music is so varied that you never tire of it. I hear this pleasant voice, like a vesper hymn, long after the twilight has melted into darkness and the performer is hidden from view; and now that moonlight has come again I shall hope that it may mingle with my dreams, attuning them to its tender melody.

There is something new and peculiar about each successive camp which stamps it individually upon the memory. I shall always remember Camp No. 1 as our starting-point; No. 2, because there my mule fell and stepped on me; No. 3 was the scene of the climb to Seminole Peak, and the place where we caught the calf-elk; Camp 4, for the storm and the wide outlook; Camp 5, on account of the fire and the stampede of the mules; Camp No. 6, because of the lack of water; Camp 7, bad lands, coyotes, and the patching of my trousers—a spectacle for gods and men!

The fire at Camp 5 caught in the sage-brush and bushes along the creek from the cook's fire, while our backs were turned, and spread with such extraordinary rapidity that we had an hour's hard fight to save our goods. Many and many a camp outfit has been burned on these plains in the same way. The sage-brush is as inflammable as tinder, the living shoots burning as readily as the dead stems, and with surprising heat, making most excellent fuel.

Between the Seminole and Rattlesnake mountains and Camp Stambaugh, and from the rugged hills south of the Sweetwater river (which takes its source at the southern end of the Wind River mountains, and flows easterly to the North Platte), southward to the Union Pacific Railroad, stretches an expanse of rolling plain, interrupted by no mountains deserving the name, covered with good grass, and tolerably well watered. It is through this country that we have been passing for the last week.

As we marched westward from the Continental Divide the soil became more dry, the country more rough, many of the valleys taking the form of great basins surrounded by precipitous hills of glacial drift, sandstone, or marl, which showed steep cliffs of rock or earth, and gave rise to very few springs. For three days before reaching here it was with difficulty we found good water to camp by at night, and what we did find was scant in quantity. The grass, however, is good for cattle, and in the driest portion there are large lakes here and there, which have been supplied by springs. This area, a tract about one hundred and seventy-five miles long by one hundred wide, contains no settlements, those northward being the little mining-camps of St. Mary's, Atlantic City, and others on the Sweetwater; South Pass City, in South Pass; and Camp Stambaugh; and those on the south being the sparse stations along the railway. Our route took us to this place by the way of Yellow Butte, a prominent point twenty-five miles south, whence we came directly hither in one day's hide. At Yellow Butte we struck "bad lands," by which is meant hills of marl or clay, carved into cubic, isolated bluffs, or worn into fantastic ridges and pinnacles, by running water and frost. They are utterly destitute of any vegetation, except some sage-brush along the plains scattered among them, and the neighborhood is cut into miniature cañons, with perpendicular walls of mud, by the torrents which the violent spring storms cause. The earth is gullied by rains and cracked by the baking sun; worn full of sink-holes, whence the drainage of the plains finds its way to the streams (dry threefourths of the year) through subterranean passages; and abounds in excavations made by water in the sides of the bluffs. These holes and crannies are the chosen haunts of wolves, whose long-drawn and lugubrious howls resounded in our ears all night, more to our disgust than terror. There were both coyotes and big gray wolves, and they subsisted mainly upon the fawns of antelopes; but the coyotes often have a hard tussle to get the little one, for the mother will fight fearlessly. We witnessed one coyote doing his level best to get away from the sharp fore-hoofs of a doe whose fawn he had been after. How effectually these sharp hoofs may be used as weapons against another enemy —the rattlesnake—the opposite woodcut well portrays.

These bad lands are rather picturesque in their desolation. The bluffs are abrupt, and generally domed; some, however, are perfectly square and flat on top; while one near our camp was a perfect mansard-roofed cottage, dormer-windows and all, and another was round, flaring above, and concave on the summit. The earth, as I mentioned, is cretaceous marl, in differently colored layers—yellowish-white, blue,

PRONGHORN ANTELOPES KILLING A RATTLESNAKE.

lead-color, and red—so that some of the round, pillar-like bluffs look like a huge—I was going to say lady's stocking; but I won't. "Huge" is a wrong adjective in such a simile.

All this time the beckoning heights of the grand Wind River range, "hull-down" in the northern horizon, showed us mighty spars and splendid breadths of snowy canvas cutting their way steadily through the clouds—

> "Like some vast fleet,
> Sailing through rain and sleet;
> Through winter's cold and summer's heat.
>
> "Ships of the line, each one,
> Ye to the westward run,
> Always before the gale,
> Under a press of sail,
> With weight of metal all untold."

XX.

THOUGH it had been in sight for many days, our introduction to the range at last was abrupt, since only one day's long march (on the last of June) carried us out clear of the dusty plains, past vast gateways of water-worn granite, up through the rough foot-hills, and fairly toward the summit. The mountain was nameless then, but now it figures on the maps as Wind River Peak, and it is the southernmost, and almost the highest, mountain of the whole magnificent series.

Every one who has spent long periods of time in the wilderness understands, notwithstanding a halting-ground may become dirty and bedraggled, so that a change is agreeable, how a strange familiarity yet attaches even to a bit of brook and mountain side; and, knowing there is no better representation of *home* within many hundred miles, how easily it is given that name. "Let us wander where we will," says Thoreau, "the universe is built round about us, and we are central still." Nowhere did this home-like feeling assert itself more (and with less good reason) than to this first mountain camp high up at the very sources of the great Sweetwater—perhaps because we invaded angry solitudes, and boldly held our own in spite of every effort on the part of the well-roused spirits of the place. The trees there were all pines, and stood thickly, but were not of great size, though straight and tall. Many lay at full length upon the ground, for they had but shallow roothold among the bowlders; and the very first night the forest treated us to an exhibition of its power to injure—a hint, perhaps, that we would better not violate its sacred shades by our presence and consume its royal timber in our paltry camp-fire. "When I want fire," the forest seemed to say, "I rub my limbs together, and the flames sweep for miles through my oily cones and dry tops, that love the blaze!" The trunks began to fall all around us—dozens at a time—while the air was full of tremendous sounds of concussion and the screams of rending fibres. But not one of those mighty bolts harmed us, beyond the crushing of a single tent; and when the hurricane was over we found our fire-wood close at hand, ready cut, so profiting by the anger of the resentful gods.

The object of making this camp just here—the most elevated point to which the mule-train could be led—was to ascend the peak and make topographical observations from its summit.

This peak, as I have said, had long been our guiding-point—a perfect cone with apex as sharp as a pencil-point, and of such unblemished shining white that even the telescope failed to show any bare ground. It was therefore with some doubts of the success of the morrow's venture that we gathered round the fire the night before, where chilling winds, freighted with snow, swept down from the frosty heights around us, and even the splashing of the water in the tumbling torrent, struggling on its way to the peaceful plains, had an icy ring.

But when we unrolled from our stiffened blankets in the gray of the next dawning the sky was clear, giving deceitful promise of a fair day. A solid breakfast soon eaten, Mr. Wilson, Harry, and myself were early in the saddle, with a sure-footed little mule to carry the instruments.

It had been observed when approaching the range that a deep depression separated the peaks here, and at its head we hoped to discover the easiest place of access. How soon it would be necessary to dismount and take to our legs was entirely problematic; but resolving not to do so until absolutely necessary, the animals were pushed on over the most discouraging region that ever a mule bore a man, among rocks, and woods, and bogs, over ridges and through gullies, always upward, until at the end of about seven miles we came out above timber and square against an enormous wall of broken blocks of stone, which threw an impassable barrier across the cañon into which the valley had here contracted.

Here, then, we unsaddled, and, tying the animals, distributed the pack-mule's load between us, as at Seminole Peak, one taking the theodolite, another the folding tripod upon which it is mounted, the third the tripod-head, and so began our climb, the character or limit of which we could only conjecture.

At first there was little trouble. We turned westward up a long cañon filled with snow for the most part, and after a hundred yards of fallen rocks were crept over we walked easily for a mile or more upon an ice-bridge, hearing underneath the gurgling of the torrent which flowed out to make the Sweetwater river. The air was not uncomfortable, the ascent gradual, and our eyes, not yet pained by the glare, were delighted with the scene. On the right towered white heights, thousands of feet in altitude; on the left were cliffs of granite, from whose top you might drop a stone almost as far as you could fire a pistol-ball up Fifth Avenue. In the full light of the sun the face of this prodigious precipice shone salmon-white, dappled with the shadows that its protuberances cast, streaked with black lines of dripping water and glistening with icicles; but its chief and marvellous beauty was the manner in which the pinnacles of its crest struck up into the lambent azure—no! not azure, something deeper, more intense, and pathetic. If indigo could be rid of its hardness and made to look like a bluebird's back; that would be nearer the hue of this wondrous sky.

So we plodded on over the crisp snow, one behind the other, wasting no breath in talking, up through the great spruces, up among the dwarfed trees and bushes that were beaten close to the ground by incessant tempests, out beyond these and over successive ridges till we were far above all vegetation except the mosses and grasses hidden under the heaps of hard snow. We had come a mile and a half, had climbed fifteen hundred feet, and had only just caught sight of our destination. It stood on the opposite side of a great basin, rimmed by ragged ridges, and by snowy summits whose bases sloped to a common centre where a patch of black ice concealed a Stygian lake. There was no help for it but to go down as deep as the level from which we had first started into the bottom of this devil's punch-bowl, and begin the ascent anew from the lake. I thought of *facilis descensus Averni* (and fitter circumstances for its verification could not be found in the upper world), but it failed to prove itself true. What with hard falls on the ice and missteps among the sharp rocks, the *descensus* was decidedly *difficilis*, yet it was play compared to what came afterward. The lake was traversed at last, however, and we struck across a long slope of snow studded with trees whose trunks were thick and gnarled, but of no great height. The drifts of snow were here from ten to twenty feet deep, yet they all must speedily melt and be carried away. We had been asking whence the Sweetwater, Popo-Agie, and other rivers that seemed to have no tributaries, received their large volumes of water. We wondered no longer. Millions of cubic yards of snow remained to be melted, though it was now the beginning of July, the Sweetwater feeding upon great banks at the head of the cañon we first came up. The Popo-Agie (pronounced Popóshia) drains this circular valley into the Wind river, which itself flows into the Bighorn, and thence into the Missouri.

The groves being passed, and the vast snow-fields on the side of the mountain stretching ahead, the real work begins, for the sun now soft-

ens the snow so that sometimes you will sink to the waist or crush
through a treacherous ice-bridge into the cold water of a mountain
brook. The previous exertions begin to be felt, the load you carry
weighs you down, the wind blows steadily, and the air seems charged
with spicules of ice piercing the skin like needles. But you walk on—
head down—teeth clenched—saving every step—never stopping. It is
three hours since you left the mules, and you have walked four miles
through the snow and over jagged and slippery rocks. At the last
clump of stunted trees rooted in a sheltered nook you halt three minutes to build a fire by a prostrate log, and thus provide a hospice for
your return.

Then you start in for the last mile to the summit, which seems
scarcely nearer through the transparent air than when you first saw it.
Mechanically your eye receives the pictures that successively present
themselves: the walls of granite rising on each side in grim uprightness
and frowning at your intrusion; the long dark cañon, cutting the eastern wall, through which the snow-banks drain away; the alabaster peaks,
lifting their heads to the sky in silent grandeur—eternal thrones of repose; the cerulean canopy; the flocks of little clouds that seem to have
been frightened from the crags, as sea-gulls are startled into the air at
one's coming. You do not strive to see these things, or record them in
your mind, as you struggle on; only afterward you remember them.

Now you are all lungs and feet. The "ever-living purity of the air"
is becoming a terror. You gasp instead of breathe; your tortured eyes
are painting dancing rainbows on the snow; your ears are singing with
the rush of the cold wind—but stop not! The slope grows steeper—
dig your toes in and go on! Your legs are becoming brittle and your
knees unjointed—stand firm! You slip and fall on the glazed surface—
scramble up, and take a firmer hold! Your breath grows short; your
mouth and throat are parched until your tongue protrudes; your stomach rebels; your nerves are failing to direct your muscles; your head
swims and a pall of darkness settles upon your mind—rouse yourself!
A few more steps—a last leap—you fall—but on the summit!

This is mountain climbing.

After all this labor it was hard to find that nothing could be done.
The wind that day blew a gale; the cold was so intense that fingers
would freeze in ten minutes; and a heavy snow-storm came up the
mountain with us to hide the landscape under its thick veil. It was
capricious polar weather, and back we ran, slid or tumbled through snow
and ice, like traversing Arctic floes with Kane or Franklin, and ate our

(very) cold lunch by the big fire we had built at our hospice, while the thick gale howled about the strong, dark, desolate mountain overhead, and drove a flock of stiffened snow-birds to the warmth of our smoke. We were in a frigid zone, and I fancy the Arctic regions have little worse to offer a man, except their wearying continuity. The mile of up-hill work, where we had descended from the "rim" of the "punch-bowl" to the lake, still remained—a very hard tug for tired legs and toes, weary of prehensile service—and after that another mile and a half of tramping through the snow to the mules.

Now those precious beings, anticipating our coming, had prepared a fine joke; but, to add hypocrisy to treason, they welcomed us with so-norous brayings of joy. Then waiting until we were close by, and could well see the fun of it, those facetious mules started off on a run, having broken their ropes, pulled them away from the fastenings, or bitten them in two. Their sense of humor, however, made them wait a little too long, so that we caught all but one and trounced them well; the hunter walked the seven miles to camp.

There was some of the hardest work done in the history of the Survey from the head-quarters of this camp; but one night, when the snow drifted steadily down on our beds as we lay in quiet, I was not so tired but that I lay awake for hours, stowing away in the coffers of my memory the fast-crowding impressions; and perhaps it was those hours of reflection that fixed all the details of the wild timber-line camp so firmly in my mind.

What a sombre world that of the pine-woods is! None of the cheerfulness of the ash and maple groves—the alternation of sunlight and changing shadow, rustling leaves and fragrant shrubbery under-neath, variety of foliage and bark on which to rest the jaded eye, exciting curiosity and delight: only the straight, upright trunks; the colorless, dusty ground; the dense masses of dead green, each mass a repetition of another; the scraggy skeletons of dead trees, all their bare limbs drooping in lamentation. The sound of the wind in the pines is equally grewsome. If the breeze be light, you hear a low, melan-choly monody; if stronger, a hushed kind of sighing; when the hur-ricane lays his hand upon them the groaning trees wail out in awful agony, and, racked beyond endurance, cast themselves headlong to the stony ground. At such times each particular fibre of the pine's body seems resonant with pain, and the straining branches literally shriek. This is not mere fancy, but something quite different from anything to be observed in hard-wood forests. There the tempest roars; here it howls. I do not think the idea of the Banshee spirits could have arisen elsewhere than among the pines; nor that any mythology growing up among people inhabiting these forests could have omitted such supernatural beings from its theogony.

But do not conclude that the gloom of the pine-woods clouded our spirits. So many trees had fallen where our tents were pitched that the sunshine peered down there, and at night the moon looked in upon us, rising weirdly over a vista of dead and lonely tree-tops. Then, too, the brook was always singing in our ears — absolutely singing! The sound of the incessant tumble of the water and boiling of the eddies made a heavy undertone, like the surf of the sea; but the breaking of the current over the higher rocks and the leaping of the foam down the cataracts produced a distinctly musical sound—a mystical ringing of sweet-toned bells. There is no mistaking this metallic melody, this clashing of tiny cymbals, and it must be this miniature blithe harmony that fine ears have heard on the beach in summer where the surf breaks gently.

But these are drowsy fancies, and one night of such sleepless dreaming is about all a healthy man can afford out of a whole trip; and if he is not a healthy man he ought not to go into the Wind River mountains at all.

XXI.

OUR next objective point was Fremont's Peak, about fifteen miles northward in an air-line. As we were not provided with balloons, however, we had to take a circuitous route on *terra firma* along the base of the range, and found it a three days' journey. It would be idle to detail all the particulars of those marches. The snow and sleet in which we started gave place to rain as we got lower down, and by the time the groves of quaking-asp that fill all the slopes between the outer foot-hills were left behind this also ceased, leaving us only a cold wind to contend with. Our way led us northward over sage-brush plains, part of the time following a wagon-road almost as old as the emigrant trail, and called "Lander's cut-off;" but it is said that, like most of the attempted short-cuts along the overland route, it saves nothing "in the long run." It was a very dim road, but the marks of wagon-wheels last a long time in this region; and, besides, occasional hunters and prospectors take their teams over it, thus keeping it visible. Did it ever occur to you, reader, how these roads are made? Certainly they are not laid out by engineers. They all follow old Indian trails, and the Indians simply straightened out the paths made by the game in their seasonal movements from one district to another. Fremont gets the credit of the "discovery" of the South Pass, and that old trapper and hero, Jim Bridger, has a pass named after him down by the rail-road; but, in truth, the buffaloes guided both of them there and were the real finders.

The next day we left the road, it turning too far eastward to suit us on its way across the settlements in the lower part of Idaho and on to Salt Lake City, but were helped in travelling by striking a poor trail, which saved us some dodging about among the sage.

A trail is not a road; it is not even a path sometimes. As the word indicates, it is the mark left on the ground by something dragged, as lodge-poles, which the Indians fasten to the saddles of the horses their squaws ride when travelling, allowing the ends to drag on the ground. Having picked out a road once, they will naturally follow the scratching or trails of the poles the next time they go that way, to avoid the trouble of exploring a new road, and so a route will become fixed. In an open country like this, where one can see for a hundred miles, and steer by sky-cutting peaks, there is little need of trails, and thus few exist. But in such a mountainous region as Colorado the best ways about the rugged backs of the ridges have been learned from the elks and marked by Indian trails from time immemorial, and the Survey has found it exceedingly convenient to follow them. Some are very plain, but the best marked of any are those which wind up and down the declivities of those Alpine peaks in the San Juan region of Colorado, and south of it across that plateau called the Mésa Verde. There water is so scarce, and the country is so cut up by cañons utterly impassable, that it is unsafe to leave the trail; and some of these paths, by thousands of years of constant use, have been worn deep into the rock. But this plainness of trail is rare. Ordinarily it is a mere direction, an assurance to the mind that you are going somewhere, if only over into the next valley. Yet it is fascinating to follow the slender, wavering line winding between the rocks or among the trees; and if you set spurs to your fancy you may ride round the world on a mountain trail.

Anent this matter, the reader will, perhaps, pardon a digression which carries him southward into the dry table-lands on the border of New Mexico.

If any one proposes to himself a tour of observation of the very worst portions of these United States, let him not neglect the Mésa Verde. It lies in the extreme south-western corner of Colorado, among the few streams that struggle down from the splendid Sierra de la Plata to feed the Rio San Juan. As the traveller marches down one of these sunken water-courses he sees that the Indian trail takes that particular route because it is impracticable for it to go elsewhere; and he finds himself descending an incline into the earth, as it were, the walls of a seemingly interminable cañon rising higher and higher on each side of him as he advances. Nor is this impression very wide of the truth; only after a time one finds that he has reached the end of his incline, and for fifty miles or more rides in the bottom of a remarkable gorge.

The Mésa Verde—which is Spanish for "green table," and a name, no doubt, given by some one who saw it in early spring, for at no other time does it appear verdant—is a somewhat irregular table-land, comprising an area of about seven hundred square miles, and formed of an extensive series of nearly horizontal sedimentary (cretaceous) rocks, of which the surrounding country has been denuded. These beds are sandstones and shales of varying degrees of hardness, generally with the softer shales underneath. When the erosive agent — a mountain stream, for example—reaches these underlying soft beds, they are carried away far faster than the firmer rocks above, which are thus undermined and fall in large fragments, leaving vertical exposures. The cañons have in this way worn to a great depth, and are all of the same sort—V-shaped at the bottom, where the slopes of crumbling *débris* have formed steep taluses, crowned by perpendicular cliffs, sometimes many hundreds of feet in height. Such cañons—dry, except at the time of the spring freshets, when vast volumes of water tear their way through the yielding soil—intersect the Mésa in all directions; and, as almost invariably it is out of the question to get down into or up out of the gorges with a horse, and nearly as impossible for a man on foot, while there is the utmost scarcity of water, it becomes of the greatest importance to adhere carefully to the Indian trails, some of which have been travelled for thousands of years, and are worn deep into the sandstone. The southern boundary of the Mésa is defined quite as sharply as the borders of the cañons by a sinuous scarp of vertical white cliffs, whose bases are buried in steep slopes of fallen fragments, overgrown with scattered gray shrubbery. And south and west of it stretch repulsive plains of dry and thirsty sand, whose dreary waste is diversified only by jagged buttes and the splintered remains of volcanic dikes. Through it all ramifies an endless labyrinth of cañons and arroyas, with scarcely a living stream.

However interesting or uninteresting this geographical description may have proved, it is important as preface to the adventure I am about to relate, in order that you may appreciate the peculiar discomfort of the situation. We had been travelling for over a fortnight across this desert, and were then returning by a new route. We had circled about rapidly, and one day our guide drew on a leaf of my note-book a rude little map in explanation of our devious track. On the morning of one of our last day's marches, before reaching the coveted mountains and green woods, I decided to stop behind to examine some ruined pueblos of the ancient inhabitants of the region—in whose history I was much interested, and which lay somewhat off our trail, adjoining a fountain called Aztec Springs — expecting to overtake the party before they encamped some twenty-five miles eastward. I was told that another trail crossed the one I was to return to, not far from where I should strike it, upon which I was to turn off; and I understood that this was much the plainer trail of the two at their forking.

It was perhaps eight o'clock when I started back from the ruins, finding the old trail without difficulty, and looking for the branch road. A ride of two or three miles brought me to a stagnant pool in a rocky

A CAÑON IN THE MÉSA VERDE.

basin, where both my horse and myself were very glad of a drink, and where I filled my pint flask with the warm, muddy water. This done, we went on at a jog-trot. The trail seemed to bear rather too far to the north, and I kept my eyes fixed upon the ground, expecting every moment to see a path diverge to the eastward; but none appeared, and after a while I got down and examined the trail. It was evident that a

large number of animals had been over it recently, though the ground
was too hard to give much information about them. But I made up
my mind that the tracks must be those of our train, and went on across
the table-land—for the top of the plateau had now been reached—
where the coarse grass and herbage were scorched and withered under
the fervid summer sun, and the harsh foliage of the scrubby junipers
and piñon pines had become almost copper-colored through drought
and dust. Enduring the heat as well as I was able, and observing every
little incident, in order to derive therefrom any comfort or encouragement possible, I jogged on alone across the arid plateau, somewhat un-
easy at the steady northward trend of the trail, but scarcely suspecting
that the footprints I was following so confidently were those of Indian
ponies, and that long before I came to the pool in the rocks (now left
miles behind) the path of my companions had branched off, making little show in the shifting sand of the yellow plain. About noon I halted
in a grove of thick cedars, and ate a small luncheon, saved from my
"break-o'-day" breakfast, while my horse nibbled for an hour.

I had travelled on again only a short distance when the trail suddenly brought me out of a chapparal jungle upon the edge of an exceedingly steep and long hill-side, densely grown with currant and berry bushes,
dwarf oaks, and various shrubs. At the foot spread a beautiful valley,
where the tall fresh grass waved in the cooling breeze, and a sparkling
river wound its way with swift and noisy current. Beyond the river
stretched a landscape of hill and dale, deliciously green to my strained
eyes, and dotted with groves of patriarchal spruces, outcropping crags
of inky basalt, and pretty thickets where birds congregated. It was an
attractive contrast to the lava-blasted deserts behind; yet I was not
wholly glad to see it, for the pleasant vale, with the strange blue mountains, snow-peaked, beyond, admonished me that I was astray. From
this lofty point I commanded a wide view, and paused to study the to-
pography and fix upon my memory the shape of the prominent summits.
One point only I thought I recognized as being in the direction where I
supposed my comrades to be. It was my single landmark : and fixing
the bearings well in my mind, I descended the zigzag path to the river,
where horse and rider hastened to plunge their lips into the grateful
flood. Then picketing my tired animal in the midst of sweet grass,
and stretching myself in the shade, I applied myself to severe practice
in the art of making correct deductions from doubtful premises.

It was certain that I had wandered out of my way, and probably had
travelled twenty-five miles that morning. This was one side of a trian-

gle; the right trail was another side; the length and direction of the third side thus became the problem. This warm and fertile river-bottom, where fuel was abundant, pure snow-water inexhaustible, and game and fish in plenty, seemed to be a central point for Indians. The remains of many of their bivouacs were scattered here and there among the tall cottonwoods, and one of their long, straight race-courses was plainly marked on a level flat, where the grass was not allowed a chance to grow. Four trails diverged nearly to the cardinal points, and the question was, which one of them to take. Of course, I might go back to Aztec Springs, my starting-point of the morning, and make a more careful scrutiny for the right trail, but I disliked doing this until driven by grim necessity.

Before my half-hour's rest was over I had determined to take the trail that crossed the river and led toward the mountains, and I did so. It was a beautiful district—picturesque, home-like, and sunny. I spurred into a short, fierce gallop, swung my hat, and shouted with the exhilaration of the scene. Then misgivings seized me. From a little eminence I had caught sight of rocks ahead that made me fear that the lovely park would soon come to an end, and I should find myself toiling among the jagged fragments of one of those old volcanic eruptions so frequently met with throughout this region. I therefore turned my horse's head slowly round, conscious, by a sort of intuition, that I was again wrong, and that danger lay in that direction. Afterward I learned that that path would have taken me to the Rio Dolores—River of Sadness!

It was not a particularly pleasant predicament to be in. I had no food, or gun to shoot it with. My only protection in a country full of grizzlies, mountain lions, and wolves was the revolver and knife in my belt. Moreover, I knew that if ever I left that river there was small chance of finding a drop of water nearer than the mountains scores and scores of miles away, with a horse already jaded to carry me. I almost decided to toss up a cent between going clear back where I started from—which argued thirty-six hours more of hard and, at best, doubtful work, with no better food than piñon-nuts—and the other alternative of following hard after the band of Indians whose tracks had beguiled me; for now I readily perceived, by the almost warm ashes of the fires scattered all about, and by a dozen other signs, that it was a wandering company of Southern Utes that I had been unconsciously pursuing with such eagerness. I could travel faster than they would be likely to; yet overtaking them was not an agreeable prospect, leaving out of view any distasteful features of association with Indians, since they were then on the verge of open hostility; and, if they did not choose to take my life, I was tolerably certain they would assume proprietary rights over my horse and personal effects, none of which I had yet grown tired of possessing.

Thus, with more seriousness than before, I stood halting between the horns of this evil dilemma, when I bethought me of the rough little map in my note-book—I have it yet.   It required much ingenuity and hard thinking to get at my probable position and the assumed position of the train, for neither of those points nor any trails were indicated; but the meagre sketch hinted at the existence of a stream somewhere in the vicinity of the one I was then resting beside, and convinced me, with the aid of what woodcraft I could bring to bear on the subject, that my true plan of escape was to follow the trail that led up the river.

Before I started I wrote a brief epistle on a leaf of my note-book, setting forth who the writer was, his business and destination, his present situation, and the course he was about to take, with a word of remembrance to friends at home on the far-away shore of New England.   This inscription was pinned up against the bark of a prominent cottonwood, where it would be most likely to be seen, should any of my party come in search of me after a few days.   I wonder what wandering trapper or prospector has found that letter, and what he thought; or whether Indians tore it down in wanton destructivenes, as is their wont; or whether it was snatched from its fastening by some breeze and wafted into the river!   At any rate, I never heard from it.   Then I pulled up a hole or two in my belt, as a compromise with an empty stomach, tightened my steed's girths, and swung myself into the saddle.

It was fully three o'clock in the afternoon now; and, feeling the need of urgent haste, I kept my horse upon the lope wherever the ground permitted, and before long found myself leaving behind the clear current of the stream, the green shrubs, soft sward, and willow thickets, and slowly mounting again to the table-land, where the medicinal scent of the sage-brush came to my nostrils instead of the sweetness of flowers, and the prickly leaves of cedar and piñon scratched my face as I dashed by.   I realized that the delightful valley was a sort of oasis. supported by the constant river, and it was no marvel that it was a favorite resort of the nomadic aborigines.

Now came into view again some of the heights sighted before; and I felt so strongly that they were trustworthy guides, that I resolved to steer by them, abandoning the trail, should it materially diverge from its present eastward direction. This would be really a serious thing to do. Even if I had felt perfectly safe in undertaking to travel across this wretched country—sure that impassable chasms would not yawn unexpectedly at my feet, forbidding farther progress—I still should forsake much comfort in abandoning the path; for, as I said before, even though it be scarcely more than a suggestion, a trail is a happy promise to the anxious heart that you are going *somewhere*, and are not aimlessly wandering in a circle. Therefore I devoutly hoped my present slender and wavering guide would not fail to lead toward the desired point.

The farther I advanced the worse the road became. Instead of a level plain ahead, overgrown with a continuous low thicket of sage-brush and grease-wood, there now appeared a range of rough hills, whose declivities bristled with little, dead, scrubby trees, blackened and maimed by a fire which recently had swept through and killed them. The sun was setting by this time, and the first of these hills was not surmounted before the gloom had become so thick as to render invisible the trail already much obliterated by the conflagration.

Fearful of losing it irretrievably, I saw that I must stop and save the remaining moments of twilight for gathering fuel.

A large stock of wood was collected with no little pains, and when it became too dark to collect more I built my fire, using as kindling some bits of cloth, corn-husks, and so forth, from the old Indian camp at the river, and lighting the mass with a shot from my revolver. Then I spread my thick Navajo saddle-blanket in the light of the fire; and, throwing my army coat across my shoulders, lounged down, with the saddle for a pillow. I wasn't sleepy, so rested, watching acorns roasting upon the coals; but they proved not good. Buckskin, poor fellow! hadn't a blade of grass to solace himself, and soon tired of browsing oak-brush.

The darkness became intense—a solid wall around my fire—and occasional gusts of wind rattled the dry branches. Once a far-away coyote sent to my ears very faintly his "yip-yip-yuea-h;" and a moment afterward an owl called musically from the next ridge. I do not remember that I occupied myself with any particular thoughts. This thing and that flitted through my brain in an inconsequential manner, for my head was resting as well as my body, and I was too old a camper 'to feel any special dread of the loneliness, or the objectless fear that sometimes troubles inexperienced persons.

I was a little hungry, but, all things considered, might have found it hard to complain, had I not been tormented by thirst.

The soil in these burnt woods had been reduced to ashes, and rose in a cloud at every step. The breathing of this was bad enough after my long abstinence and fatigue; but add to it the swallowing of much hot smoke in kindling my fire, and you have cause for misery almost unendurable.

I had the pint of water in my saddle-bags, but more than one sweet swallow dared not take; for when I should find another flaskful was something I hesitated to think about. I chewed some bitter oak leaves as an effort at relief, whittled a bullet out of a pistol-cartridge to roll about in my mouth, and pretty soon fell asleep.

Suddenly there seemed to penetrate my slumbers a shrill, wavering echo, as of a long-drawn, distressful cry. It brought me to my feet, wide-awake in an instant, for I knew very well what it was—the scream of the puma! But a more present danger threatened—the tree, against which was built the fire, had burnt nearly through and was toppling, ready to fall upon me. The mountain lion at once became, to my mind, a guardian angel sent with warning of my peril; and it was none too soon, for I had only time to snatch my saddle away, when the tree came down with a tremendous crash and burst of sparks directly upon the spot where I had been soundly sleeping an instant before. Yet, now that no harm was done, I found a blessing even in the fall of the tree, for here was plenty of wood at hand. Raking up the fire, I listened for a repetition of the puma's mournful voice; but it did not come, and finally I got drowsy and went to sleep again.

The next thing that interrupted my slumber was the plunging of Buckskin. Sitting up quickly, I heard a scurrying in the bushes, and caught sight of two green eyes. That meant wolves; not sneaking little coyotes, no worse than Indian dogs, but the great gray fellows you read about—wolves as big as a mastiff, hunting in packs, and as fierce as the utmost development of a savage lupine nature can make them. To secure my terrified horse was my first concern. I ran with all haste across the little space that intervened, but had not reached him when a wolf leaped out, and the horse gave a great jump, which I thought must surely break his lariat. But fortunately the rope held, and, snatching my revolver from my belt, I broke the brute's leg and sent him off to the somewhat abashed pack limping and howling. Quieting my horse as well as I could, I brought him close to the fire' and tied him firmly, whereupon he approached as near to me as his tether would allow. He was badly frightened and very lonesome. It occurred to me to put the saddle on his back, but I concluded it was

hardly worth while, fancying that the greatest danger had been avert-
ed in escaping the loss of my horse, which would have been an irrep-
arable disaster, and that so long as the blaze could be kept up I might
feel at ease; however, I did choose a convenient tree as a house of
refuge if worst came to worst. Then I heaped high upon my watch-
fire the crackling and redolent limbs of cedar, lighting up the dead forest until all the scarred old trees held out their gaunt, dismantled arms
and bony hands to warm them at the blaze. How the wolves gave
tongue at that! I could see them moving spectrally here and there
as the arrows of light shot far into the circle of darkness, and judged
there might be ten or a dozen; but their lugubrious, reverberating,
angry howls multiplied themselves until it seemed as though a regiment
of wolfish fiends had corralled me and were yelling their triumph. It
banished sleep, and I sat there wondering whether they would dare
charge while the red cedar kept consuming with such fragrance and
lively scintillation, thanking my stars that I had had sense enough to
collect a good supply of fuel, and finally the wolves went off in full
cry and all together. Then, wrapped in my Navajo, for the third time
I sought "tired nature's sweet restorer."

In an instant I was in San Francisco with a party of jovial friends,
each free-handed. We entered a restaurant where fountains were leaping among the emerald fronds of tropical plants, the rainbows in their
spray reflected from services of costly silver and rare porcelain. We
seated ourselves at a sumptuous table, and one called out gayly, "Well,
gentlemen, what will you choose as appetizers before our feast?" Some
said hock, others champagne; a dark-faced man, aguardiente; a lucky
miner, cognac. I answered, "Oh! please, please give me a cup of water!" Aroused by my own piteous cry, I opened my eyes upon the
faint new light of a dawning day.

Little remains to tell. By the time the saddle was fastened on my
horse—who looked as though he had made a worse night of it than I
had—it was light enough to hunt for the trail; but the search proved
utterly fruitless, and I was obliged to trust to my previous calculations
and strike straight across the country, steering eastward, not by a star,
but the nearest thing to it—a snow-crested mountain-top, where rested
now the golden slipper of "jocund day." Mile after mile did we climb
those rugged hills blasted by the breath of fire, and cross those deceitful valleys, where a dozen times I dug deep holes for water in the sandy
"wash" at the bottom; for though I still had resolution enough to save
the supply in my flask, my throat was parched till I could scarcely speak

to my horse, and did not know how much longer I could resist. It was always hot and dusty and rough; but after a while the country became more open and grassy, and little by little we got out of the burnt district and could go faster. A rolling, tree-dotted park came now, and I think nothing ever discouraged me more than to rise to the crest of each of those rapidly succeeding waves of land only to see another ridge ahead. But toward noon the glad surprise of the last one was reached, and beyond it we saw the glancing wavelets of a clear, cold brook. "Did we run?" Wouldn't you? And when he had drunk his fill my horse held up his head and uttered a shrill neigh. I took it to be his way of giving thanks, until speedily there came back an answer —an equine welcome; for camp and home were not a hundred yards away.

Curiously enough, the pleasant valley I had strayed into had long ago been named by trappers Lost Cañon.

XXII.

HAVING reached the southern branch of the Sandy river, one of the main tributaries of the Green, and which consists of three branches originating in the Wind River mountains, we camped opposite some great meadows, through which the river wound in a tortuous course nourishing dense thickets of willows. The river was deep, cold, and rapid, but not more than fifty feet wide. It was inhabited by beavers, and we saw a few trout. The bottoms embraced several thousand acres of the best grass, and if the willows were burned enormous quantities of good hay might be harvested. The adjacent hills furnished fine timber, and it cannot be long before cattle ranches will be scattered all over these broad valleys. Indeed, we saw one herd of cattle feeding, which we supposed to belong to some ranchmen living down near the mouth of the stream.

The mules having been unpacked, Harry took his gun and sauntered out after game, for we were eating our last elk steaks. I suppose he had not gone a hundred yards before we heard the crack of his rifle, and then his voice calling for help to bring in his capture, a fine young doe blacktail, or mule-deer (*Cervus macrotis*), as some of my friends will tell me is the proper name, reserving "black-tail" to the north-western variety—*C. columbianus*. The evening was chilly, and we made a big fire of that best of wood, dead quaking-asp, around which we sat as darkness gathered close, watching the deer-ribs roast to the right turn, and listening to Harry Yount's tales of hunter-life as he had experienced it in this very region.

From May to September, as everybody knows, it is not possible to do profitable hunting, or "shooting," as my English friends would insist was the right word—but I use Harry's phrase and in the American sense. The hair is being shed and replaced on all the game, so that the coats of the valuable fur-bearers are useless; the females of the deer are isolated, caring for their young, and the males are hidden, renewing their horns; while the flesh of all animals is in a lean and

12*

inferior condition.   During these months, therefore, Yount would go
"prospecting," work in the silver-mines, become an amateur "bull-
whacker" on some freight-train of ox-teams, or enlist as hunter and
muleteer for one or the other of the parties of the Survey.   But as
soon as the September frosts begin, when the first flurries of snow
whiten for a day or two the far-away gleaming summits, then Harry
prepares to bid good-bye to civilization.

These autumnal weeks are the most beautiful of the whole year
in the Rocky Mountains.   The air is clear and bracing, without the
warmth of July noondays or the dampness of August nights.   The
flies are gone, the streams are fordable, and the snow has disappeared,
leaving the upland bogs firm.   Young grouse and sage-hens are full-
grown and whirring, the fawns are able to keep pace with their parents,
and the fattening deer are aggregating into herds and slowly moving to
their winter resorts.   The elk and blacktail bucks now strut out upon
some projecting crag, or move into the centre of a valley, calling in
loud, clear greeting an invitation to the does to flock to their standard,
and a challenge to rival bucks to meet in deadly tournament.

"Ah," says Harry, "it's finer music to listen to that old bull-elk
squealing up at the head of the cañon than to hear the Prussian band!"

It *is* better music.   It arouses all the poetry of the hunter's nature
—and he possesses not a little.   Then he will creep up within range,
perhaps cleverly imitating the sonorous whistle to draw the foolishly
proud buck on, drop on one knee, and fire, planting his bullet behind
the fore-shoulder.   Harry always carries two light rods, tied together
near one end, in the fork of which he rests his heavy rifle.   His misses
are rare; but I think that his general success in shooting is due less to
his accurate marksmanship than to his perfect knowledge of the ways
of the game.   He is a student of the science of hunting.   He has
learned, for instance, how to impose upon the confidence of the timid
pronghorn, by exciting its curiosity; knows that the white-tailed deer
must be sought in their runways low down among the watercourses
(whence they are sometimes called "willow-deer"), and the blacktail
higher up among the aspen-groves; watches the "black brush" to see
whether deer have been browsing upon it lately; tells you that wapiti
have been there that morning, because he sees that the plaintain-leaves
have been nibbled; judges by the half-emptied pine-cones that grouse
have been picking at them, and therefore may be looked for.   These
evidences of the presence of animals are classed as "signs" and "doin's,"
and it is a hunter's business to know how to interpret them properly.

THE MULE-DEER.

In the early autumn Yount will shoot a wagon-load of game at a time, camping for a few days not far from market, and bringing his venison into Laramie, Cheyenne, or Sydney, for sale; but when winter seriously threatens, Harry puts into his wagon a small tent, some buffalo-robes and blankets, a bake-oven, frying-pan, coffee-mill and kettle, some copper pails, plates, etc.; his score or so of steel traps, axe, some boards to do his skinning on, half a box of candles, plenty of fixed ammunition for his breech-loading rifles, and, with Texas led behind, starts off to the mountains alone for six months of winter residence.

His provisions consist of flour and coffee (browned and ground by himself), a little bacon, some beans and hominy, sugar, salt, pepper, and a few pounds of dried fruit, or perhaps some cans of preserved vegetables and sauce. This is not bad fare, and is luxury beside his larder of twenty years ago, when for weeks and weeks he would have nothing but meat and dried berries to eat, with sage-tea, camas-root, and spruce-gum for variety. He takes also a little whiskey for emergencies, and a vast quantity of tobacco, to be the solace of his solitary hours.

Thus, all alone generally, though sometimes a chum joins him, Harry drives off to the chosen spot in the foot-hills, where he counts upon the game centring during the winter, or where there seems to be an opportunity for profitably setting his traps; and, fixing his camp in some sheltered spot, with wood plenty and water accessible, he lives a hermit's life through the " long and dreary winter." The weather allows him to tramp about most of the time, and what he shoots too far away, or too late to get to camp, he can bury in the snow, sure against decay.

Thrilling tales could be recited of the adventures of these mountain men, who are abroad at this season almost as regularly as in the summer. Some, like Harry, are hunting in the foot-hill valleys, where the game hides until the spring grass sprouts; some are driving freight-wagons between frontier towns and military posts; others working in army pack-trains; many herding on elevated plains, where the snow does not lie long enough on the grass to starve the cattle. Most of them are ignorant of how to take proper care of themselves, and, secure in the pride of their toughness, are reckless of exposure. It happens too frequently, therefore, that they are crushed in snow-slides, starved by being weather-bound far from help, or are frozen to death. Not a year ago a company of freighters were stopped on their way from Fort Laramie to Cheyenne by a hurricane of snow. They wrapped themselves up as well as they could, and built fires in the wagons unavailingly, since the bottoms of the boxes would burn through before the men could get warm. When the storm was over they were all found dead, with the horses frozen stiff in the traces. If a prospector conceives an idea that at a certain locality in the mountains gold will be found, often he will become so eager to realize his dream that he will not wait for spring to clear the trails, but in the dead of winter will start alone into the heart of the range, carrying the whole furniture of his camp, his tools, and his provisions, on a single pack-mule. Very likely he is never heard of again; and when, a year or two afterward, some hunter finds a skeleton with a skillet, pick, and shovel beside it, he discovers all any one will ever know of the prospector's "strike." Perhaps he became snow-blind, and starved to death; or was snowed-in in some cañon until his scant supply of flour and bacon was exhausted. It may be Indians murdered him; possibly he slipped over a cliff, or broke through some treacherous snow-bridge into a crevasse—at any rate, the wolves pick his bones, and the last claim staked for him is six feet long by two feet wide!

Our hero—a very cautious man—told us at the camp-fire one night how narrowly he escaped being smothered in a snow-storm in April a few years ago. He was trapping beavers along one of the tributaries of the Platte, flowing through bluffs about sixty miles east of Cheyenne. April is always an extremely disagreeable and dangerous month on the plains, but it is not often that heavy falls of snow occur. Yount established his camp upon the edge of a small stream frequented by these animals, and placed his tent a little way up the bank in a steep gully, since it was almost the only spot free from snow, and at the same time out of reach of freshets. He had provisions for some days, a shovel, etc., and plenty of bedding. One evening it began to snow pretty hard, but he went to sleep without any special apprehension. In the morning he found a gale blowing, and the snow falling in blinding fury. All that day it continued, through that night, and until almost noon of the second day—forty hours. He had no chance to cook any food, and so ate nothing; but he and his dog lay in the blankets, and kept as warm as they could. The prospect of being entirely drifted under and smothered to death was so imminent during the second night that Harry once wrapped his legs in blankets, and started to fight his way out with a board as his weapon, but decided to wait a little longer, and managed to live until the gale ceased. Then he cut his way out at the top of the tent, climbed over to the bare ground above, dug his kitchen out of another drift, and lighted a fire. His next move was to cut loose his tent from the frozen earth and take it to the high ground, preferring the chances of an Indian attack to risking another burial.

The previous winter—1874, I think—was an extraordinarily cold one. Harry was hunting through the hills near Fort Laramie, and had fixed his camp in a cañon called Goshen's Hole. Heavy snow came, with intense cold, and for forty-five days the hardy hunter was weather-bound, but this time he was in the timber and otherwise sheltered, so that he did not seriously suffer. Near his camp was a round, flat-topped butte, where the wind blew the snow off the grass as fast as it fell. Here there was always an abun-dance of black-tailed deer and other game,

A HUNTER'S BLOCKADE.

rendered tame by privation, so that he had plenty of meat. At first Harry shot many of these, burying their bodies in the snow, but the wolves speedily found his *caches*, melted the snow by some means, and dug out all the carcasses; so he gave it up, and killed only enough deer for his own use. Wolves were exceedingly plenty, and had hard work to live, while large numbers of white men and Indians were

frozen to death during that "cold spell," which has rarely been equalled there.

Our next day's march was a long one, and the wind was very cold.
We were passing over a rolling, sage-brush country and sandy soil, with
bowlders dispersed throughout it; and an incessant cloud of dust was
kicked up by the mules. Three or four times we descended deep valleys and crossed considerable streams flowing from the mountains that
were not at all easy to ford. Their sunken course was defined for miles
by the rows of tall hemlocks that lined their banks, and whose topmost
twigs were about level with the surrounding country.

It was on this morning that we met a couple of trappers going into
the settlements with their peltries. They carried their "plunder" on
four or five ponies, all of which began to make friends with our mules,
and were received with kicks and squeals innumerable. Nevertheless,
it was hard to part the two sets of animals and make each train go its
own way. These roughly dressed, bearded men, with their Indian
ponies loaded down with uncouth materials lashed on in uncivilized
fashion, made a picture very much in keeping with the wild landscape
and ever to be remembered. They had been camping in the mountains
all winter, and were now going in to sell the products of their hunt,
and probably to spend all their hard earnings in a series of sprees. We
gave them letters to mail at Camp Stambaugh, offering compensation
for the trouble; but they refused to accept anything, resenting it almost as an indignity, with the explanation that they were "neither
wealthy nor hard up."

The sage-brush thinned out somewhat as we approached New Fork,
another large affluent of the Green, and the goodness of the grass and
rapidity of its growth excited the attention of every one. It was already curing into hay as it stood, though half buried in snow. Flowers
were blooming in profusion everywhere, birds were singing gayly to their
mates sitting at home in the bushes, and yet all about us glistened the
glacial fields of the uplands, and the wind made us shiver under our
overcoats, as though it were January instead of June.

It being impracticable to carry a pack train farther into the mountains toward Fremont's Peak than the outlet of a large stream, tributary to the New Fork of the Green river, the camp was fixed there to
wait while a small and unencumbered party made the ascent. Fremont's Peak being in the very heart of the Wind River range, having often been sighted from every side except the north, and com-

manding a view of a wide extent of country, was considered one of the most useful geodetic points in Wyoming, and it was therefore especially desirable to get good observations from it. Accordingly, on the morning of July 2, water having frozen thickly in all the little pools the night before, Mr. Wilson, Harry Yount, and the writer started on a side-trip to the summit, taking two pack-mules—one to carry the theodolite and other instruments, and a second for the bedding and "grub," which latter is the corner-stone of all scientific work in this country. We particularly observed the features of the landscape as we went along, for a peculiar interest attaches to this mountain, by name one of the most widely known in the West, and yet perhaps at that time the most utterly unknown of any. Even its position has been confused, and the latest map of this part of the world (that accompanying "Captain Jones's Reconnoissance of North-western Wyoming"), made in 1873, puts Fremont's name upon the peak several miles south of here, which we ascended the other day, and which the people near here have called Wind River Peak; or possibly Captain Jones meant another high point still farther south—ascended the day after the former, and named Atlantic Peak, from the fact that it gives all its waters to the Atlantic ocean, while the other heights of the range contribute to the Pacific, on the west, as well as to the Atlantic, on the east. This latter is the southernmost peak of the range. At any rate, whichever of the snowy tops was meant, the existing maps are wrong in putting the name "Fremont" upon any other mountain than this one in the centre of the range; and it is difficult to understand how the mistake could have been made, had the map-makers taken the trouble to read General Fremont's own description of his explorations here thirty-five years ago, when, in 1842, he conducted a governmental expedition from the Missouri river to Oregon. Fremont says he marched from the South pass to the Sandy river and camped, and thence to the New Fork, and camped, and thence two days up the New Fork, beyond a lake, when he camped as near to the mountain as he could get, and thence climbed it on foot, enduring immense hardships, and being justly proud of the undertaking ever since. Somebody has told me (whether his book says so, I am not sure) that, either by accident or design, the brass cover of his telescope was left there, and remained as a monument "even unto this day." It is doubtful, however, whether, if really he did leave such an article there, it could be found after the storms and thunder-bolts of thirty-five wintry years had striven to obliterate it; at least we could find nothing of the kind.

A TRIBUTARY OF THE GREEN RIVER.

Getting above the thickets of the ravine where the camp was, we followed—always upward and north-eastward in general direction—a ridge of granite bowlders which had been shoved out and heaped there by glaciers, and was covered with sage-brush. From it we could look southward over the wide plain of the Green River basin, and westward across to the blue wall of the Wahsatch, capped and streaked and spotted with snow. Northward the crests of Mount Leidy, and one or two more of the higher summits of the Gros Ventre mountains, were just visible above the wooded foot-hills which in other directions limited the outlook. Right and left of us, wherever we could look down into a valley, there in the bottom would be a lake—sometimes round, like a blue eye; sometimes long and straight, with regular edges; sometimes winding in and out between the hills like a long, still river. The water was deep, and reflected the light in different and varying ultramarine; or if it was shaded, receiving only reflected light, the glassy surface seemed like polished iron, and suggested some Titan's shield—under which who knows but the giant may be buried?

Once our course—for we followed no track—led us for half a mile along the sinuous crest of a high narrow ridge connecting two hill-tops as by a causeway, where we could at once look out upon the world of plains below and up to the old white heads so far above us, where the clouds were playing hide-and-seek among the crags. On one hand our ridge-side dipped into a deep valley filled with immense quaking-asp groves and thickets of birch and good grass; on the other, to a lake fed from the snow-banks above, through half a dozen turbulent torrents, as we could see by gleams of white foam through the black spruces.

This lake overflowed into that next below it, and so on through a narrow stream filled with beaver-dams; and the dams were so close together that the river was terraced, as it were, into a series of circular ponds, framed in vivid green, and touching one another like a chain of gems. The beaver is still abundant here, and trappers are beginning to find it out; and now that the Indians are no longer troublesome, every one of these lakes will soon float their canoes and echo to the crack of their rifles. Beaver will not be their only game. Most of the other fur-bearing animals are to be found in good numbers, and there is any quantity of elks, deer, bears, and possibly an occasional buffalo and moose, with ducks and trout for the kitchen.

But the mules had been jogging on, and, catching a last glimpse of an inky lake past an eagle whose broad back is scarcely blacker than the water as he sails smoothly below us, we entered the forest. At first we rode at a canter between the trees over a firm pavement of pine-needles; but after a mile or so, all the time ascending, the trunks began to stand closer together, and blocks of granite to obstruct the way, with boggy hollows between, so that we must slowly wind about. This increased until the wet spots became ponds, with mounds of soft snow about their edges, while the bowlders grew into cliffs to be climbed, and the defiles between them were choked with fallen timber. After that there was no fun. We jumped trees and struggled through bogs and floundered in snow, and scrambled up and down piles of broken rocks, until we were ready to give up again and again. But, wriggling on, after a while we came to what seemed almost the last gorge, and, getting down to this with a great deal of labor through the deep rotten snow and fallen timber, we skirted the border of a lake, stepping gingerly on the half-frozen ground, and found a fine camping-place on a little bluff, where there was a decent amount of grass for the plucky mules. We were eight hours on the road, and perhaps a dozen miles from the main camp in a straight line, but had probably tramped twice that distance in getting to our present point.

The sky was lowering, and the chilly wind blew as though it presaged a storm. We built our fire quickly between two great pines, whose thick tops joined overhead, and hurried our dinner, which consisted of two loaves of very nice crisp bread, moulded in a small milk-pan, then hardened a little by being held over the fire in the frying-pan, and finally baked equally on both sides by being propped up in front of the fire on a bit of stick. Then we had two elk-steaks apiece and a rasher of breakfast bacon for relish, together with coffee (no milk) and stewed plums from California. After dinner we heated some water in the frying-pan, washed our dishes, hobbled the mules, put more fruit a-stewing for breakfast, baked some new bread, smoked our pipes, and fell to talking about bears, since signs of their frequent presence were very observable everywhere in this neighborhood.

" Harry, did you ever actually see a grizzly bear?"

Preposterous question! Much like tossing a red rag to a bull. He is lying with length and breadth full unfolded in the ease of well-earned rest, his broad sombrero pushed back until the yellow blaze lights up his brown face with strong and ruddy light, like some portrait by Rubens. There is grief and astonishment in his eye as he repeats,

" *Did I ever see a grizzly!* Well, I allow it was only two year ago my horse Tex and me was corralled by seven of 'em in Colorado! It was on White river, in September. I'd been out and shot a blacktail, and was a-bringin' the quarters into camp tied behind the saddle, an' I spose the bears smelt 'em ; for all at wunst there was the damnedest rustlin' round! and I knowed what it was. But we couldn't stir a step —was just stuck in them bushes, an' had to fight. Texas stood still, and I says to myself, ' Just you come out where I can see, and I'll give one dose anyhow!' But they got scared, or suthin', and went off up the hill. There was seven of 'em, young and old, and all right up on end. Well, I didn't fool away no time gettin' out o' that, now, you may bet your life!

"It was that same trip," Harry continued, "when we was down in the Grand River cañon, that we had some fun with a bear; but he was a cinnamon—not so big as a reg'lar grizzly, but big enough for me. . I was skinnin' a mountain sheep right in camp, when the nigger cook, George, hollered out, 'Jee-rusalem! see dat ba'!' An' I looked round, and here come a cinnamon pitchin' down the mountain right on top of us. 'Oh! what shall I do? what shall I do?' yells Shep Madeira, and runs and jumps on the old Preacher bell-horse and gits, while George picks up the shovel—first thing he could catch—and runs and jumps into Grand river. My gun wasn't close by me, but I got it purty quick and pecked the bear a couple o' times, and he was the deadest cinnamon I about ever seen. But Shep and the Preacher horse was a devil of a time gettin' back!"

"That reminds me," laughed Mr. Wilson, "of a funny thing that happened once in Nevada. Coming back from a mountain one day, we surprised a bear and shot at him, but missed him, and he ran off very lively. We followed along and chased him right through camp. There were only a Mexican and the cook there, and they, seeing the bear run by, started after—the Mexican on the horse with an old army pistol, and the cook on foot with nothing but his rolling-pin. The bear got away, but what the fellow proposed to do with the rolling-pin was more than I or he could tell. Emmons and I did run a bear down on the plains once, though, and killed him with our revolvers."

That called to Harry's memory an outfit he was with once, where a Mexican saw a bear not far from camp, and having shot at it, started after on a mule. Now a mule will nearly jump out of his skin at sight or smell of Bruin, and the Mexican must have known it; but he rode hotly after the grizzly all the same, along the steep side of the mountain. It was supposed he must have met him, for when the mule rushed back to camp riderless and they went to look for the Mexican, they found him down in the cañon, where his mule had probably thrown him, with his brains dashed out against a rock.

"Well," rejoined Harry—for none of the rest of us offered any farther experiences, though our chief might have detailed many—"I've seen lots of fellers terrible anxious to shoot a grizzly—till they seed one. There was a little feller from California named Charlie Millen. Charlie was crazy to slay a bear, and one day one of the men came in and said that a terrible big grizzly was down in the cañon. So Millen

13

he gets his gun and starts after that bear red-hot. He got on his trail,
and followed along till he come to some bushes, and was a-goin' through
'em, when all at wunst he come right on the grizzly lying down right in
the trail, with his head on a log. He wasn't more'n ten feet away, and
Charlie just gave one look, and then he lit out for camp. He'd had
enough grizzly just seein' them eyes.

"Then there was another feller I knowed—a sailor. He thought
he was the devil at shootin' bears, and was spilin' for a chance to try.
Well, one day I saw some signs, and told him I 'lowed if he'd go down
in the willows he'd get a shot. So off he goes, and pretty soon we
heerd a devil of a hollerin', and there was that sailor up a tree! He'd
wounded a cinnamon, and she came for him, and before he could shin
up the little cottonwood damned if she didn't claw the whole seat out
o' that snoozer's breeches. He didn't want any more grizzly in his'n
neither!"

So the stories go on, as easily as the smoke rises upward and drifts
away across the face of the moon. Finally the coffee is well browned,
the pipes are out, the camp-fire sinks into embers and then into ashes;
darkness and stillness reign in the mountains, and each story teller and
story listener is only a gray mound of blankets and fur.

The gray of the morning found our camp awake, and the smoke of
our fire warmed the wings of the earliest birds—and there were plenty
to be warmed around this frozen lake, with tuneful throats, too. Before
sunrise, therefore, in order to get the clear morning light on the landscape and take advantage of the unmelted crust of the snow, the long
climb was begun.

First there was a tedious tramp of three miles over the roughest of
rocks, where living timber grew thick and dead logs lay thicker, with
snow and bogs between. This was enough to tire a strong man out,
yet it was only the preface. Above the last tree stretched two thousand five hundred feet (half a mile) of snow, lying at as steep an angle
as gravitation would allow, and relieved only by black ridges of rough
rock; nevertheless the climb was not a perilous one, requiring only
steady, muscle - straining, breath - exhausting work, and three hours of
this did it.

The summit proved to be a ridge two or three hundred feet long,
on which lay a deep bank of snow. On what seemed the most advan-
tageous part of this ridge the instrument was planted, and, the weather
being favorable, although naturally cold and windy, a good set of observations were secured with speed. No traces of General Fremont's visit were

to be found; but had there been any—which is uncertain—the deep snow would have hidden them. All material being buried, the building of a monument was out of the question; and the return, although not by any means easy, was so much more quickly accomplished that the camp was reached by noon. Then the furniture of our house—for a night's lodging-place in this utter wilderness has the semblance and re-ceives the regard of a house—was packed on our mules and in our sad-dle-pockets, our hot and hasty lunch was eaten, and the march taken up for the main camp in the valley by one o'clock. The snow we had driven our mules over the day before was too soft to hold them now, and they floundered so in the very first drift, actually rolling over and over in the slush, that we had to go ahead and tramp a road through for long distances. But this was ended at last; and, following our trail back with less difficulty than we had made it, the main camp was reached in the early evening, and we sat down to our supper of fried trout with eminent satisfaction.

This ends our special exploration of the Wind River range, and I wish to give some general facts ascertained about it before going far-ther, for these magnificent elevations are almost entirely unknown, or misunderstood, and are attracting much attention and inquiry at pres-ent throughout the West. Beginning at the Sweetwater river, in longi-tude 109° and latitude 42° 15′, approximately, the range extends north-ward to Union pass, the whole length being about seventy-five miles in a straight line. Although well defined on each side it is the greatest mass of mountains in Wyoming Territory, and contains the highest peaks, unless the Bighorn mountains should prove far more imposing than they look. The Wind River is really a double range of peaks side by side for the whole distance, but at frequent intervals a mountain or lofty "saddle" will stand between the two ranges, connecting them into a series of circles of peaks. I know of no range which might so properly be termed a chain as this, whose mighty links are defined by walls of towering rock and hollowed into tremendous depths. To look from a summit into one of these amphitheatres scattered from end to end of the interior of the range is to pause in amazement at the thought of the immensity and power of the agencies that have worked together to shape these masses. By what inconceivable fires was this adamant forged, and with what unspeakable throes of nature was it cast up, and through what patient labor of winter and summer, glacier and lightning, was it fashioned into its present form? Conjecture long may busy it-self, and science ponder well, before the history of these monuments

of the infancy of the globe is made plain to us. To try to think of
when these rocks were new is to begin to understand in what very
ancient times we live.

But, to resume a more literal treatment of my theme, it is enough
to say that these interior, cliff-hemmed valleys are very grand. Each
one is a vast hole, the bottom occupied by a lake, frozen during four-
fifths of the year, and having no apparent outlet or draining through a
narrow cleft to form a river below. Seen from above these lakes look
black, except when covered with snow, and from them the land ascends
in masses of solid rock and slopes of splintered *débris* to the high peaks
or to the top of the talus, or the boundary wall, which often has a vertical face of a thousand, fifteen hundred, or two thousand feet. Within
these cañons some trees may grow, perhaps, along the edge of the lake,
but scraggily, and showing that they have a hard time of it, and you
may creep down into most of the basins and creep out again, but having done it once you will not care to repeat the feat. I know this from
experience.

The inside walls of all the mountains, as I have already indicated,
are for the most part nearly vertical from immense heights, but their
outsides show a series of slopes divided into great ridges and buttresses
by glacier-cut cañons, and propped up by foot-hills of unusually rough
aspect. Nowhere in the West is the prodigious effect of ice in shaping
mountain ranges more manifest than in this chain. The paths of old
glaciers, and the gigantic furrows they have ploughed, are visible all the
way to the desolation-scarred summits, while rank behind rank of the
outer foot-hills, and the plains far beyond them, are moraines of gravel
shoved up under the prows of the glaciers, deposited along their sides,
or rolled out from beneath their blue arches by the rivers which their
melting fed. In many cases these banks of gravel and bowlders remain
as they were heaped up by ice, but more often they are changed from
their original form, and owe their present appearance to the action of
water subsequent not only to the retreat of the great continental ice-
sheet at the close of the glacial epoch, but also after the disappearance
of the local glaciers which remained for thousands of years, no doubt,
in this stronghold of cold, but gradually succumbed to the increasing
warmth of the air as the progress toward the present continued. What
now are cañons these local glaciers filled full of slowly but steadily
moving ice, thousands of feet thick, whose under surfaces, shod with a
rasp of granite blocks frozen in, filed deeper and deeper the vast grooves
in which they slid, pushing the chips out ahead of their advancing front,

and spreading them far and wide by torrents of water poured from beneath them. Each year, as the change from the frigid to a warmer
climate went on, the winters would be shorter and less severe, the snow
less and less in amount, affording the glaciers less nourishment and cur-
tailing their growth. Each summer, therefore, the ridge pushed up by the
advance of the ice during the previous winter would be a little behind
the ridge made by the larger growth of the previous year; and thus
a succession of ridges of rolled fragments and soil would be left lying
across the valleys from the outermost edge of the mountains up toward
the summits. The cañons, vacated by the glaciers when at last the
milder climate would no longer allow of their formation, would then
become the channels for the drainage of the vast depths of snow which
at that time covered the range; and how broad those great streams
of melted snow were, is plain from these wide beds cut down the side of
every mountain. But the warmth of the climate of this latitude continued to increase, less snow to fall annually, and the volume of water
to decrease in proportion, until now the largest outlets of the greatest
snow-banks are mere rills meandering among the pebbles of ancient
channels far within the terraced margins of the old flood. The Green
river of to-day, compared with the Green river ten thousand years ago
—and the general course is the same now as then—is as a scratch of
my pen down the page on which I write.

Viewed from the west, and I fancy equally from the plains which
spread from its eastern base, the Wind River range fills the horizon
with a tumult of lofty mountains. I am warned by the fate of many
before me not to attempt any set description of this chaos. There are
domes and pyramids, cones and pinnacles, and mighty slabs on edge
like the curbing of a continent, nowhere standing in orderly rank, one
behind the other, but everywhere between the eastern and western
foot-hills tossed in white crests and ridges irregularly, like the foaming and curling tops of the bewildered waves in a chopped sea. They
seem ready at any instant to break into new combinations of dome and
peak, yet stand forever the same. It is what Thoreau called "tumultu-
ous silence." They seem ever stormy. Our experience among them
I have detailed—it was like February all the time, though our almanacs
pointed to midsummer. Since we have left these cañons we have seen
the tempests marching among them back and forth, mustering upon the
high summits and charging down the valleys. This stormy climate, the
quantity of snow they hold, the lateness of the season before it begins
to melt, the new appearance of the cliffs, the scantiness of the soil and

size of the rivers, the young look of the forests, all point to the conclusion that, geologically speaking, it was only a short time ago when the ice held full sway among these remarkable mountains, and when winter was never absent from their fastnesses.   Old Boreas even now is loath to leave this castle.

THE WIND RIVERS.

There is no range of mountains in this country, and perhaps none in the world, that support so large a drainage.   From the southern slope flows the Sweetwater, a river two hundred and fifty miles long, and the largest affluent of the Platte.   Near it half a dozen large streams find their way out of the cañons and unite to form the Wind river, which empties into the Bighorn river one hundred and fifty miles north, receiving many small streams by the way, while the Bighorn itself takes its origin there.   Then the western slope feeds, through innumerable creeks, the Green river, which heads at the northern end of the range and gets water enough to flow two thousand miles to the Gulf of California.   But this is not all.   Rising at Union Peak, the northernmost of the Wind River mountains, and divided from the Green by a line of hills, the Snake river starts on its long voyage southward through Wyoming and Idaho, and thence flows north-westward into Oregon to make the Columbia. Clark's Fork of the Columbia, the Yellowstone, the Gros Ventre, and innumerable minor watercourses also owe their strength to these generous reservoirs. The amount of snow that is stored up here, to be slowly dealt out, can be appreciated when it is considered how many thousands of miles its meltings run; and it is not difficult to understand why the neighborhood of such an abode of cold, in the midst of wide and heated plains, should be a scene of almost perpetual storm. It is the head-quarters of meteorology on this side of the world, and this single group of mountains saves Wyoming from being what old geographers used to have it—a great American desert.

The mountains of this chain consist altogether of granite, this primeval rock being manifested in all its forms, with more or less gneiss. At the northern end high bluffs of sandstone and limestone are tipped up against the granite overlying it. Of course, veins of quartz intersect the granite in every direction, and in endless variety of character, shape, and condition. Our men, familiar with the appearance of all sorts of American auriferous quartz, could duplicate every kind they had ever seen in the specimens chipped from the leads or found in the "washes" of rolled gravel. There were veins of pure shining crystals, adhering sharply to their granite walls, or lying between granite on one side and gneiss on the other; veins of opaque green quartz; veins of decomposed quartz, red as cinnabar; veins dark brown; veins ochre-yellow; veins of all manner of mineral-bearing rock, with the coarser metals sticking out of them.

XXIII.

IT was the morning of the Fourth of July when we struck our tents at the base of Fremont's Peak and bid good-bye to the Wind Rivers—those haughty Highland chieftains, impassive as their granite thrones, bonneted with cloud and kilted with snow, awaking one another with clan-cries of thunder and flashing claymores of lightning about their wrinkled brows—leaving them with little regret, for they have not been gracious, but rather have sought to oppress with their majesty and power. So we clattered gayly through the bright river, scaring shoals of young trout precipitately to their deep holes, and wound our way out to the plains or gravel-hills, which latter gradually became less and less in height, dwindled into the terraces that mark the lessening of the Green river from its ancient breadth, and finally were lost in the level of the sage-brush plain, where, in the bottoms, there was much alkali and spots of soft ground. But for the most part, for mile after mile, the surface was as firm and level and smooth as a lawn; nor was there any sage to trip over, but short, tough marsh-grass, among which black-birds bred, clamorous curlews circled, whistling to one another in clear, loud signals, and snipe peeped as they scuttled away from our approach. This was too good to last, and we had plenty of worse before we encamped that night on a branch of the river and smoked our *very* last cigar in commemoration of Independence Day. The weather seemed delightfully warm after the Arctic experiences of the previous month; and not only did we not put up our tents, preferring, like Coriolanus, to make our beds under the canopy, but took a refreshing bath in the rapid brook. Among the willow-bushes here innumerable birds nestled in happy confidence—among the rest several fish-hawks, whose huge domiciles were within reach of my hand, and our ornithological man was kept busy.

This is the upper extremity of the Green River basin, which may properly be said to extend southward as far as Southern Utah, being bounded on the east by the Wind River mountains, the Sweetwater hills, the buttes south of Yellow Butte, and the Uintah mountains, in Colorado and Eastern Utah. Its western drainage is from the Wahsatch mountains, dividing it from the waters of Snake river and from the Salt Lake basin. At this latitude the valley varies from ten to fifty miles wide, and is barricaded at the north by the Gros Ventre

THE FIELD-LABORATORY OF AN ORNITHOLOGIST.

hills, among which the Green river rises, finding exit close beside the Snake river, through Union Pass. But the Green river flows fifteen hundred miles to make the Rio Colorado, while the Snake finds its way far to the north and pours through the cañons of the Columbia into the North Pacific, enclosing between them a triangle having all California and Oregon for its base.

It is too cold up here to raise any crops, but there is magnificent grass for cattle; and if the sage-brush were burnt off there would be ten times as much more. Still it would be hard to winter herds here, although a hundred miles lower down it could be done on sheltered ranges. Nothing but the usurpation of the ground by dwarf willows prevents thousands of acres of good hay from growing naturally on all these bottoms. The willows are easily eradicated, nevertheless, and the hay will follow. Perhaps oats and barley could be made to ripen also.

Starting almost at sunrise on the morning of the 5th, we continued our northward march over the same plains-country and under a cloudless sky. It was warm, truly, but not sultry. The temperature often rises as high here in midsummer as in New York, but you do not feel the heat so much. The direct rays of the sun are scorching, but the air is not murky; and if you get in the shade you are comfortable in a very short time. No one is ever sunstruck here, and "hardly ever" in California, where the thermometer sometimes indicates 120 degrees. We carried canteens of water, but those who drank scarcely once from morning till night suffered the least from thirst. The mountains toward which we were wending our way were the Gros Ventre hills, a range of no great altitude, stretching east and west from the upper end of the Wind Rivers over to the Snake river—forty miles or more. Few of the summits reach above timber-line, yet all bore considerable snow and were clothed with forests. First entering groves of aspen-trees of unusually large size, and abounding in underbrush of various shrubs and plants, with high grass in all the glades, we soon passed them, and began to climb ridges of quartz-gravel, wooded to the top, sometimes finding a game-trail to follow, but oftener working our way through as best we might.

Everything showed a rapid and luxuriant growth. The foliage was all green, weeds were high, flowers in a profusion of bloom. Many species which are small out on the plains grow taller and larger here; the ground was sodden, and where we had to cross depressions there was danger of miring. Meantime we kept getting higher and higher, and at last could see over, and behold! north and west of us stretched a great park, fenced in by snowy mountains, embroidered with streams, and diversified by low hills and green valleys, groups of light quaking-asp, dense groves of pine and spruce, purple patches of sage-brush, and sunny bits of prairie where antelopes were disporting. Yet the entrance to this happy valley so eluded our grasp that we were all day wandering about in a dense spruce forest, and only got down at night in time to startle two sand-hill cranes from the fen in which they lived, setting them flying in a crazy manner about our heads, croaking in a guttural, rattling cry like a hoarse frog, and to camp on the opposite hill-side among hosts of mosquitoes that preyed upon us incessantly, in spite both of pitchy smudges and of the midnight chill.

The following morning we were glad to get away, but had little respite from the mosquitoes and flies.   We steered for the highest promontory ahead, called Wyoming Peak, and went down some terrible hills at the foot of it.   We could not ride down, or at least we would not risk it, and at home would have thought it almost impossible to *walk* where the loaded mules picked their way after Mr. Wilson through the unbroken woods, jumping trees, crushing through bushes, squeezing between trees, and pushing the gravel ahead of them at every descending step.   Even the insects deserted us here.   They couldn't stick on the mules' backs at such an angle.   This done, and a number of other difficulties surmounted without accident, we crossed a torrent of sudsy water, and began to climb through the woods, where fallen timber was thick, up to the open plateaus above, and at last camped at the limit of tree growth—perhaps 10,500 feet above the sea—in the last grove of dwarf spruces.   Enough of the day remained to make the topographical sightings wished for from the peak, and this was done satisfactorily. These hills consist of upheaved edges and gullied-out ridges of sandstone and limestone strata, the latter being above.   From their northern slope the Green river originates and flows out to the south, around their eastern end, instead of rising east of Union Peak, among the Wind River mountains, as had been supposed.   Near the head of the Green are the springs of the Gros Ventre river, which flows westward a hundred miles or so, and becomes one of the largest tributaries of the Snake.   This river and the hills, which do not rise more than 12,500 feet at the highest, are named after the Gros Ventre Indians, a tribe that once inhabited the Upper Missouri, and were famous in the time of Lewis and Clarke.   They were gradually driven back and killed off, until the remnant is now in Dakota.   Beyond the Gros Ventre a very mountainous country extends to the Yellowstone Park, which itself is by no means small.   From the western termination of the Gros Ventre hills there stretches southward an unnamed range of mountains, whose summits rise far above timber-line and hold much snow.   It is really a continuation of the Wahsatch, and perhaps ought not to receive any separate name; nevertheless it is well isolated from the rest of that chain, which is ill-defined at best.   It is this range that makes the western wall of the Green River valley, and toward a high point near its northern end we directed our next day's long and tiresome march.

But one word about our camping-place on the mountain. The site was a ledge, or hill-top, just under the edge of the crowning bluff, and the easily crumbling sandstone had formed a deep soil. Wherever the snow was gone we saw that this soil was thrown up into innumerable ridges by the moles, which had tunnelled under the snow in every direction. Instead of "making a mountain out of a mole-hill," these little miners had been making mole-hills out of the mountain. The least current of water running from the drifts carried away this loosened earth, and thus the soil to a depth of several inches is yearly stripped off the height and contributed to the valley. Blind moles are levelling the Rocky Mountains! Getting down without extraordinary difficulty into the gulch, through which a fair-sized stream, called Fall river by the trappers, made its way out into the park we had seen on the previous day, we rode along its banks. It was full to the brim of muddy water, for the unusual warmth of the past two days had produced a freshet.

In almost any stream in the mountainous parts of the Territory you may find more or less beavers and beaver dams. But this stream, and this whole region, surpasses any place I know of as a resort for these animals, now so scarce east of the Mississippi. In the rocky cañon higher up, this creek was thirty or forty yards across, nor would it have been much wider in the more open valley below, had it not been impeded; but for a dozen miles the beavers had so dammed it and choked it with their houses that the water spread out to a mile or more in width, and hundreds of dead and living trees, once far back from the margin, were now standing equally far out in the water. Some of the dams measured a hundred or more feet in length, and were built on a curve, with the hollow of the curve up stream, yet so substantially that they were standing the beating of this freshet with slight damage. All along the bank of the stream the hill-side was bare of aspens, and their stumps, cut off close to the ground, showed what had destroyed them. Some of the stumps were of trees ten or twelve inches in diameter, and seventy-five yards from the water, yet there was no doubt that these rodents had felled those trees, trimmed off the branches, peeled away the bark, and then dragged the logs all the way to the water, to put into a new dam or repair an old one. Indeed, we surprised some of them at work. Most of the dams were shorter than I have mentioned, and ran from one to another, so that there was a net-work of them supporting a growth of willows, and each enclosing a little basin of deep, still water, in which would rise like an island the domed top of their home.   But the houses of many were under the

IN THE GROS VENTRE HILLS.

bank, and of others beneath the dams, as we could see by the paths to them, which showed plainly through the water.   Wherever the willows grew closely to the water's edge for some distance, there would be roads through them at frequent intervals, the stems gnawed off, and the weeds trodden down smooth.   "Busy as a beaver" acquires a new force when we think how ceaselessly he must work to get his daily food, collect winter stores, keep his house in order, repair his dam, and guard against enemies.   We saw none of the animals themselves.   They are rarely seen by any one who does not secretly watch, being able to detect your approach by the jar of the ground, if not otherwise, and hide themselves.

A good trapper ought to secure a thousand dollars' worth of beaver skins on this one stream in a single winter, and there are other great communities within a short distance.   He would find the place an excellent one to spend the winter in, too.   Besides the beaver he would get not a few otters, whose skins are worth seven or eight dollars apiece, and martens, minks, and fishers in the marshes; but he must go away from the big beaver colonies for the others, none of these animals, and particularly the otter, consorting well with the trowel-tailed gentry. In the mountains and woods, to which the hunter wintering in the Fall River valley would have access, he would be able to shoot and trap bears, both grizzlies and the cinnamons, wolves (both gray and the prairie), wild-cats, lynxes, and foxes. All these furs would be valuable, and he could get plenty of venison and "small deer" for his larder, not to speak of skunks to bait his traps with, and the feathers of the sage-hen as a lure to his mink and marten snares.

It was at the lower end of this stream that we started a band of elks (consisting of a young buck with half-developed horns, and several does) from the shallows, where they were pawing in the water to escape the flies. They did not notice us till we were right upon them, and no less than three Nimrods banged away, only breaking the leg of one doe, which ran away, the injured limb swinging like a rope's end. A second shot mercifully killed her. She had a small calf—a circumstance not known when the first shot was fired—and this calf, in its bewilderment, came right toward us, bleating pitifully. It would have starved to death, and so we shot it, and the veal proved to be very good. The abundance of game which I have chronicled in my notes on the Sweetwater country, has continued, but we have not seen quite so many individuals, because the regions we have traversed of late have been less open, affording more hiding-places; because the mosquitoes and flies have driven them up above the timber or into the dense brush; and lastly, because the Indians have been hunting through here for some weeks, and have made the animals wary. We noticed this at once after getting into the Green River basin, before which the elks and deer regarded us with an unconcern equal to that Selkirk complained of on his lone island:

> "The beasts that roam over the plain
>   My form with indifference see;
> They are so unacquainted with man,
>   Their tameness is shocking to me."

I can't say that the tameness of these "beasts" shocked us particularly; but we were so loath to impose upon their confidence that I know of but one that has been shot uselessly. Lately the antelope have fled at our approach, and the larger game have made themselves scarce. Our hunting propensities consequently have been excited, but somewhat fruitlessly, not having time to hunt systematically; yet we have not been a single day since the beginning of the trip without at least two varieties of venison in camp. "Sow-belly" has not been in lively demand, therefore, although a few bites, nicely cooked, season a meal well.

Latterly we have struck the bighorns, which we had not seen since leaving the Seminole mountains. They are the noblest of game, after all. Much like the chamois or ibex, the man who would get them, even though they never saw the human form before, must have the strength and agility to climb to the loftiest ledges and skill to shoot at long range. Even then he may lose his dead game, its body often tumbling over some precipice utterly out of his reach. The mountains west of Green river are full of them, and in making stations upon their summits the topographer has a good chance at them. Once or twice we have had bands in sight for two or three hours at a time, feeding upon the green hill-tops below us, where scattering clumps of dwarf spruces furnished shelter when they cared to rest, and the young grass afforded the best of pasture. It was very interesting to watch them. An old ram or two, easily distinguished by the immense horns from ewes, whose horns are small and light, would lead the flock, and there would be from ten to fifty younger rams, ewes, and kids following. How they can run! Let the ground be rough or smooth, level or inclined, it seems to make no difference, and the kids will race up and down the steep snow-banks just for fun. The hair of these mountain sheep is coarse and slightly crinkey, and when the bluish winter-coat comes out, displacing gradually the brown summer pelt, you may find everywhere between the hairs a shorter coat—a sort of undershirt—of the finest silky wool. The flesh of the bighorn is tender and juicy in the autumn, when the animals become fat, and has a taste between mutton and antelope, partaking of both. We have seen one small company of buffaloes west of Green river, and their skulls are scattered over all these hills up to timber-line. This plenitude of animal life and wealth of all such vegetation as the climate will permit (for the valleys are eight thousand feet in height) is due both to the sheltered position of the district among the mountains and to the constant moisture supplied by the melting snow-banks. These very circumstances are productive of two great disadvantages, without which the Green River basin would be a paradise for travellers. One of these is the increase of the streams by the raising of the water in the beaver dams, causing them to be boggy and unfordable for long distances.

Another disadvantage, springing from the amount of still water lying everywhere, are the hordes and hosts and legions and myriads of mosquitoes and flies—flies large and small, all sizes and shapes and colors, but with a single eye to blood, and no compunction as to what they puncture. Mule and man alike were attacked, and with equal ferocity. We did nothing but fight flies day and night, decking our riding-animals with boughs till they looked like the duck-batteries gunners use along the New Jersey coast, and slashing about our heads with

A LEISURE AFTERNOON.

other branches till our arms ached. There were the black flies of the Adirondacks, the 'skeeters of Jersey, the blunderheads of the Catskills, the buffalo gnats of the plains, and a giant of a horse-fly peculiar to these mountains. Nor when we got out of the timber and camped away above on a bald ledge, hoping to get rid of them, did the flies "let up," but swarmed about us as we ate, buzzing in our ears, getting into our food, and running red-hot needles into every exposed part of our bodies. At dark they all disappeared, but were relieved by the mosquitoes, who kept the battle up till midnight froze them out.

XXIV.

SEVERAL days were spent in hard climbing about these precipitous, untracked hills, and in wading through the slushy snow on their high crests. Their tops were all covered with fragments of stone quarried out by the frosts, and on the edges of the cliffs huge masses are separated and just ready to topple. In the season of melting, therefore, it is unsafe to go to the brink of a sharp bluff, lest your weight may send the whole crumbling edge headlong. But we found some slopes, and had good fun rolling stones; just as they got well started they had to bound off a cliff and then "scoot" over a thousand feet of steep snow, racing beyond this across a frozen lake and broad valley. No one can resist the fascination of setting rocks a-rolling from the top of a mountain. You turn loose a tremendous amount of force, and feel like a giant as your hard-headed missile crushes its way among snow and loose rocks, opening lanes through the bushes, snapping off trees like pipe-stems (if the bowlders be large and tough), and bounding on till they are lost to view. You have made a catapult of yourself, and you enjoy it.

Coming down a mountain two or three thousand feet is quick work, but it makes your knees ache; and if the slope consists of large, angular fragments of rock, as many of these summits do, there is about as much hard work in it as in the climbing. But if the slope is loose soil you may step twenty feet at a time, and thus leap down swiftly, taking caution not to trip and fall on your nose. When the snow-banks are hard, you have simply to make use of that portion of your anatomy which a beneficent Providence designed you should employ for this purpose, and slide to the bottom like a shot.

Having completed our work among these rough ridges and turned southward, there was great pleasure in riding down long valleys, across the foot-hills and out through the park-like country. The woods showed an excellence of growth far ahead of anything we had seen before. In the high mountains there was nothing but small-sized white pine and

14

THE CARSON SINK.

slender quaking-asps, gnarled and weather twisted. On the hills crossed
three days before the spruces and pines, though standing thickly, were
not large, and while making good house-logs, would be useless to saw
up or trim for spars.   Here the valleys were full of mighty yellow and
white and pitch pines, ragged spruces three and four feet through, and
giants of red firs, straight as arrows, with shapely spires more than a
hundred feet high.   The poplars and cottonwoods grew to their utmost,
and between them were dwarf maples and sumachs, wild plums, and
many other shrubs new to us.   The crop of grass was dense and heavy
everywhere, proving true the old quatrain:

> "A foot deep of rain
> Will kill hay and grain;
> But three feet of snow
> Will make them come mo'."

Sometimes signs of previous occupancy added to the attractions of a camp, when it was made near some trail, and we speculated on the kind of man who had been there before us. How long before? What was his object? And whither was he bound? In a region so wild and utterly untenanted as this anything pertaining to humanity is invested with extraordinary interest. From these foundation-sticks we could tell the size and kind of tent he had; from the tracks could decide that his one animal was a horse, not a mule (which makes a smaller, narrower track), and knew that at this stake he picketed him at night, and by that path led him to the water; from this stump we guessed the sharpness of his axe; that wadding told the size of his rifle; here was his fire; there, where the grass is trampled, he piled his night's wood. Where this hunter or beaver-trapper has camped and left his history on a few chips there remains a civilized aspect which Nature must work long to efface.

After they are weary of the majesty of mountain walls, here will wander the painters making studies. I commend to them some of those lakelets set in a wall of evergreen-tangled rock, or spreading gently over the green herbage as the melting snow trickles into them and swells their flood; lakes which, in the sunlight, reflect their margins like mirrors, and in the shadow, as you look down upon them, take precisely that opaque, dead, sap-green hue of the pools of heavy oil I have seen in the muddy ravines of West Virginia. Ride along under the brow of some moss-grown cliff, and you are sure to find hidden in a bunch of greenery a spring, seething quietly with gentle hissing of small bubbles. Camp there, and call it champagne; its bead is perpetual.

All day we had caught glimpses of the Green River plains, like a misty gray sea, and in the afternoon got out upon them, and rested at night on a creek bottom where Indians seemed to have camped for generations. It was a pretty place, but disfigured by dirty *débris* and the remains of old wicky-ups, as the Indians call the bough lodges they build when on hunting trips. Angwinam, a prominent man among the Shoshonées, was camped, with his family, two miles distant, and came to see us, happening in, as if by accident, just as dinner was called. He was trapping beaver, or, more exactly, trying to, for he could show none of the skins of this animal among his collection of peltries.

There was a heavy shower that night, but the next morning was clear, and, saddling early, I started up to the top of a neighboring bluff to see the grave, or rather the corpse, of a child, supposed to be Angwinam's, discovered by our cook the evening before. He described it as being wrapped up in bark and skins and cloth, and lashed to a frame of osiers shaped like a snow-shoe. This was lying upon a sheltered ledge. In the morning I found the osier-rack, but no body. It had evidently been taken away and secreted. The reader would have been amused could he have witnessed the exceedingly dignified, circumspect, and conciliatory manner with which I made my examinations there. My restless mule let me know plainly enough, though I could not see them, that Indians were close by; and I had a vivid impression that more than one Winchester rifle was waiting a pretext to send some bullets into my sacrilegious body.

Meanwhile the train had "packed away," and I could see it like a string of black dots far away on the prairie. Trying to make a short cut across the beaver-dammed creek, I steered my mule into a likely-looking shallow, and was half-way over, when she suddenly went clear under and had to swim for it. I stuck to the saddle, and we reached the opposite bank; but it was too steep to climb out, and Mouse had to turn round and swim back against the swift current, well-nigh exhausted when she attained the bank, and looking like a drowned rat. She recovered her breath by the time I had poured the water out of my boots and saddle-bags, and then we went down to the ford, as we ought to have done at first.

Fording a river, where the current is deep and rapid, is a dangerous experience for a pack-train. The attendants must ride on the lower side and keep the mules from drifting down-stream. They are very sure-footed and plucky under their loads so long as they keep up; but let one fall down, and there is not an instant to be lost, if you would save him and his cargo. Leap into the water and help him up without an instant's delay, for if he gets any water in those big, furry ears of his he will do nothing to save himself, but will lie there and drown without a struggle. Mules can swim very well, however, if they are willing to try, as I have just shown. I had presence of mind, in the case mentioned above, though the ducking was startlingly sudden, not to pull in the least on the bridle-reins—a thing which should never be done in swimming a horse or mule.

All mules are very particular and fastidious about their ears. They won't allow them to be touched or interfered with. These long and mobile members are very expressive in their various positions, but I could never learn satisfactorily what each position signified, unless it was that the next movement would be precisely the opposite of what was apparently intended. The paradox is this brute's model of mental action. Never was a mule more innocent in appearance than one which Mr. Wilson was riding just ahead of me one afternoon. I was half asleep, when I felt a smart blow on my stirrup. I thought a stone had been kicked up. A moment after the *tapadero* was struck, and I was just beginning to guess at the truth, when I saw the heels of that mule fly up. Probably nothing but a quick movement of my leg saved it from being broken. What caused that beast to kick at me three times without provocation?—anything but "pure cussedness?"

Their tails, too, being very horse-like, are objects of great pride with them, and they decidedly resent any fooling with them. The worst spell of kicking I ever saw, I think, was once when I accidentally struck backward with my three-lashed Indian *quirt* and got one thong entangled in Darby's caudal extremity. Such a frightened and thoroughly indignant beast I never bestrode and hope never to again; but, in the expressive phrase of that hard-riding region, I "stayed by him."

The first ten miles that morning was across rolling, grassy hills, where thousands of cattle will ere long find plentiful summer pasturage, and whence the eye could take in a wide view of plains and mountains, savannas and woodland. The whole length of the majestic Wind River range stood out behind us, blue-black as far up as the timber grew, and above that all white with snow, many of the peaks showing not a spot to mar their perfect cones. Before noon we could see the storm clouds chasing each other through the mountains, and puffs of cloud drifted away from the peaks, like the smoke from the mouth of a cannon. Listening to the low growling of the far thunder, it was easy to imagine a genuine "war of the elements" taking place among those tempest-breeding heights.

Turning in from the plains to the entrance of the long east and west valley, affording a passage-way through the range, we happily struck an Indian trail, and followed the well-trodden path up a long ravine beside an exceedingly picturesque brook, where the trout were gliding through sunny shallows or leaping miniature cascades, and the willows that arched over the blue beaver ponds were full of singing birds. We scarcely knew when we reached the "Divide," and wound about through open groves of evergreen timber with an ease that was luxury after our experience of the tangled, log-obstructed forests

encountered the week before.*   In the middle of the range the trail
forked at a diamond-shaped prairie, where some herds of Indian horses
were feeding, and there was a log-house, called Bad Man's Ranch—for
what reason I do not know.   Skirting this prairie and ascending the
bed of a torrent through a narrow, tortuous ravine, where black-tailed
deer were common, we stopped in a spruce grove, and made us beds
of springy boughs.

Of all the lovely camping-places in my recollection I think this one
over in Western Wyoming, among the nameless heights between the
Green and the Snake rivers, bears the palm.   A ravine diverged from
the valley we had been travelling through, one side of which was a'
high, grassy bank, and the other was wooded; but in the woods opened
a little glade, down which came an icy rill, tumbling and foaming between banks of moss solid to the water's edge.   All about were gigantic, yellow-barked spruces, among which this level spot had remained
clear, just capacious enough for our tents.   It was a place for perfect
repose.   The eye, weary with incessant far-seeing, rested content on
the verdant slope that cut off the rest of the world.   As, after the tur-
moil and noise of the city, the business man pulls the blinds close together and drops the curtain, shutting out the turbulent scenes of his
daily struggle, and shutting in the peace and love of his home, so we
were thankful that we could not see even the loftiest summits, and
gladly gathered round our cosy hearth-stones, where the spruce boughs
crackled like salt, and coils of black smoke writhed up from the resinous logs.

The night "effect," as painters phrase it, of such a bivouac as this
is weirdly curious.   One need not be afraid to walk away from it into
the gloom: the Prince of Darkness is said to be a gentleman.   And, in
fact, it is not dark out there in the open air; for under the lamps of the
constellations, and in that strange light from the north, even midnight
in the high mountains is only gray.   But beneath the star-proof trees
there is the blackness of plagued Egypt—a darkness which may be felt
in thrusts from a thousand needle-pointed leaves and rough cones, if
one pushes too heedlessly into the recesses of the woods.   The blaze is
orange-colored, the smoke heavy and black, illumined redly underneath.
The pillars of the smooth fir trunks within reach of the firelight stand
like a stockade about the camp, but the shifting light penetrates between them and summons from the darkness new boles, that step out

---

* See frontispiece.

and retreat again as the capricious flame is wafted by the wind toward or away from that side.

While the centres of the great, gummy logs are eaten by the blaze, and while we sit on their ends and smoke our pipes, what soul-inspiring talk is heard! The stories flow as naturally as the sparks explore the dark arch overhead, but it is no more possible to communicate the point and living fun of these narratives, told with the Western freedom of language and usually *àpropos* of some previous tale, than it is to tickle your senses with the sizzle and delectable flavor of the deer's juicy ribs roasting in those ashes. Shut in by the shadowy forest, we seem to inhabit a little world all by ourselves, with sky, sun, moon, and stars of our own; and we converse of you in New York as Proctor does of the inhabitants of other planets, and speculate upon the movements of armies and governments as the Greeks discussed the life of souls across the Styx. The affairs of the outside world have lost interest for us, since we are no longer spurred by the heel of the morning newspaper. In simplifying our life to a primitive measure we have ceased to trouble ourselves about problems of politics or social economy, and are beginning to discover that the universe is less complex than we had made it. Thus we conduct a sort of mental exploration parallel with the geodetic survey.

Early the next morning two of us, with a burden-mule, were off "to make a peak." It was just at sunrise that we rode through the woods, startling a splendid elk from under a big tree where he was sunning his almost mature antlers, and we got out above the timber by eight o'clock. Here the snow was gone, and we rode easily to the base of the crest. This we had to climb; and although the distance was not more than half a mile to the summit, we were well-nigh exhausted, for the whole way was over loose rock that slid from under our feet at every step. It was almost advisable to take the school-boy's plan in the old story: An urchin started for school one snowy morning, but reached there after it had been "called." "Why were you tardy, sir?" shouted the master, birch in hand. "'Cause 'twas so slippery I slipped two steps back for every one ahead," whimpered the boy. "Then how did you get here at all?" "Turned round and walked backward," replied the little fellow, and saved his hide.

Once at the top your breath comes back, and as long as you keep still you suffer no inconvenience. But going up you have dismal thoughts about the cold grave, etc.

This mountain was in the southern portion of the hills ranging north and south, along whose bases we had been travelling for the previous ten days, and around whose foot we had passed the day before. It was of red sandstone, capped with drab, crumbling limestone. Everywhere the view was veiled in purple haze, through which the red and yellow of bare ridge-tops in the plains gave a faint color. The lesser hills about the mountain were of every shape, with wooded valleys between, but their heads were bald, and bare of snow, which lingered only in banks on shaded slopes, melting slowly into hollows of the surface, which, overflowing, drained into larger hollows, and the surplus of these collecting into ponds formed the fountains of rills, whose united waters were gathered into creeks and carried to the river channels, whose courses we could mark across the far purple heather of the plains. Let the sun beat down for a day with unusual fervor and the clear brooks are turbid little floods, carving deep cañons in the mountain's side, and scattering its substance far beyond its base. Thus the surface of the plain and that of the mountain top are slowly approaching one another, and the universal effort of Nature to re-adjust the disturbed levelness of the globe is being accomplished.

However interesting it might prove, time forbids even to suggest all that meets the eye and is implanted in the memory while one is sitting for two or three hours on a peak of the Rocky Mountains—the surprising clearness of the air, so that your vision penetrates a hundred and fifty miles; the steady gale of wind sucked up from the heated valleys; the frost and lightning shattered fragments of rock incrusted with lichens, orange and green and drab and white; the miniature mountains and scheme of drainage spread before you; the bright blue and yellow mats of moss-blossoms; the herds of big-horned sheep, unconscious of your watching; the hawks leisurely sailing their vast aerial circles level with your eye; the shadows of the clouds chasing each other across the landscape; the clouds and the azure dome itself; the purple, snow-embroidered horizon of mountains, "upholding heaven, holding down earth." I can no more express with leaden types the ineffable, intangible ghost and grace of such an experience than I can weigh out to you the ozone that empurples the dust raised by the play of the antelopes in yonder amethyst valley. Moses need have chosen no particular mountain whereon to receive his inspiration. The divine Heaven approaches very near all these peaks.

From our lofty station the smoke of our camp-fire could be seen; and as we could thus lay our course there was little difficulty in getting back home. But in work of this kind it frequently occurs that the topographer must send his camp on indefinitely, and it is not always that he can see their signal-smoke from his station. The finding of camp—frequently reached after dark—then becomes a matter of woodcraft and skill, and some persons never can find it.

A few years ago a young man was attached to one of these Territorial Surveys—a graduate of Yale College—who knew how *not* to do it to perfection. He was forever getting lost, and had some experiences fearful to contemplate. One day the party with which he travelled were on a hill within a mile of Cañon City, Colorado, in plain view of the town, and between two well-travelled roads. On their way to the town a strip of timber was passed through, and when they got past this and into the village the Yale man wasn't there; nor did he come in that night. The next day some of the men started to look for him, and met him coming back—his eyes big with a story to tell. He had fallen a few feet behind the party, which passed just out of his view, when in some curious way he got himself turned about and started in precisely the wrong direction, wandering and twisting and turning to no purpose. He experienced all the doleful sensations of a lost man, and at last built him a little fire and lay down to sleep, when, lo! there stood on its hind legs before him a mountain lion! Color indistinct, ears long, small pointed head, big body, and a short white tail—he didn't wait to see any more, but fled precipitately until out of breath. And that graduate of Yale does not believe to this day that it was an astonished jack-rabbit that scared him!

Another member of the same expedition, the next year, who soon found that he had mistaken his calling in seeking to be an explorer, and wished himself back on Boston Common long before he got there, started to make the ascent of one of those fearful quartzite peaks in the Uncompahgre range one morning, in company with two geologists who were born mountaineers. Seeing his inability to keep up, they pointed out to him where the Indian trail lay, along which, some miles ahead, the evening's camp would be fixed. Poor Mr. G.'s breath soon gave out, and he thought he would stop, then concluded he would go down to where the riding animals were picketed and wait, but, growing impatient, saddled his own mule and started for camp. He recovered the trail and trotted along merrily, but just as he was expecting to reach the camp-train he found himself at the deserted site of their morning's bivouac. To retrace his steps in the right direction took him until twilight, when, just as dusk was coming on, he heard guns fired a little way ahead and thought he saw a fire. Instantly he was frightened—though there wasn't an unfriendly Indian in the whole region—and took to his heels. A moment's sensible reflection would have shown him that these were signals meant for his guidance, but his fears and his greenness together made a fool of him, and he stayed out all night, supperless, fireless, and quaking with imaginary fright.

Of another expedition in Nevada, where some soldiers were acting as escort, an equal stupidity is related. Coming to a halt early one evening, a soldier obtained permission to go and hunt near camp. Darkness came on, and as he had not returned shots were fired and a great blaze made to guide his return. Before long those in camp heard his shouts, and hallooed in reply. This howling dialogue was kept up at intervals until bed-time, but poor Johnny hadn't wit enough to follow the sounds, and so slept far from his blankets until daylight—if he slept at all—and got well laughed at, as he deserved, in the morning.

But such stupidity and absence of woodcraft are the exception; the finding of their way correctly under the most adverse circumstances is the rule with these explorers and native mountaineers, and many astonishing incidents illustrating skill in this respect are to be related.

XXV.

PERHAPS I remember the camping-place described in the last chapter, and from which I have only *seemed* to have wandered, so pleasantly, because of the jolly anecdotes lingering in my memory first heard there.

After sunset the air in these high, Western regions grows rapidly cool, and a chill air from the snow-banks seems to settle down and take possession of the warm nooks where the sunbeams have been playing all day. Now the long-caped, blue cavalry overcoats (bought in Denver or Cheyenne for three dollars apiece) are unstrapped from behind the saddles, fresh wood is piled upon the fire, the pipes are newly filled, and the circling smoke, exploring the recesses of the dark tree-tops, looks down on an exceedingly contented company.

Then, as the fragrant herb glows in the pipe-bowl, and the darkness shuts in the fire and the little circle about it from the great Without, tongues are unloosed, and the treasures of memory are drawn upon to enliven the hour. All these mountain-men are great talkers, and most of them tell a story in a very vivid way—a way purely their own, sounding barbarous to other ears, so full is it of slang, local phrases, and profanity, but in a language perfectly understood and with a wit keenly appreciated by kindred listeners. Tales of Indian warfare and border ruffianism in the old days of the emigrant trail, the founding of the Mormon settlements, the track-laying of the Pacific railway, and the gold discoveries; stories of the road agents—robbers of the mails and expresses—who never let a man out of the country with any money, and of the scarcely preferable vigilantes who sought to rid the mountains of these human wolves, only to learn that the persons most trusted in their councils were the ringleaders of crime. Between the road agents and the vigilantes no man was safe: the former might kill him to get him out of the way, the latter might hang him on the single charge that the ruffians let him alone. But the theme of all themes which is never neglected, and which lasts clear through the trip, is *the mule.*

The mountain mule is a perpetual study. No animal in the world possesses so much individuality and will develop in a given time so many distinct phases of character. His sagacity in some directions is balanced by most desperate stupidity in others. A herd shows a wide range of variation in tractability and in other traits among its members. You cannot fail to note this in their different countenances, to which the long ears lend so much expression; but all their characteristics are positive, and are asserted in the most startling manner. They are

A SENSATION.

crotchety, too, and it is often impossible to overcome their prejudices. One I knew who would never allow himself to be caught to have his pack put on or re-adjusted until all the rest had been attended to; then he was quite ready and docile. Another was a good, gentle riding animal, and had no objection to your pipe, but you must get off to light it; strike a match in the saddle, and Satan entered into his breast on the instant. The same fellow had an insuperable objection to entering water—an unfortunate trait, for before crossing an unknown stream with a pack-train it is desirable to know what sort of a ford it is, and the man who rode this mule was the one whose duty it generally was to make the test. The animal would walk straight down to the margin, then rear upon his hind-legs and spin round like a flash.

I had a mule once that would bray ferociously and incessantly whenever it was out of hearing of the train's bell. It was an excessively annoying habit, and, persuasion failing, I one day dug my spurs into its ribs, and hammered its head first with a strap, then with the butt of my pistol, every time the hideous voice was raised. I felt that there was no sense in the absurd practice, and I was bound to break it. But after an hour or two it was hard to keep my seat, for about once a minute the beast would duck its head and jump as though propelled from a cannon, uttering a terrible bray, apparently just to invite punishment. So I changed my tactics, and paid no attention whatever to the habit, and in a couple of days had no farther annoyance. Mules know what disturbs you, and malignantly do that one thing regardless of pain to themselves. Another mule I had was an exemplar of this trait. He had a trick of swelling himself out when I put the saddle on, so that it was impossible to make the girth tight ; I might as well have tried to draw in the waist of a steamboat boiler ; and to secure the saddle properly I always had to catch him unawares, after we had got started.

It is not easy to gain a mule's confidence, and, on the other hand, he rarely merits yours. I have known one to carry his rider in the most exemplary manner for hundreds of miles, and then one morning begin a series of antics and develop an unruliness as uncomfortable as it was unexpected. Sometimes you can train them with considerable satisfaction, but you never feel quite sure of them. They are forever doing something surprising, heroically pulling through real difficulties to give up tamely before some sham obstacle. This is partly owing to their absurd timidity. If one scares, all the rest are panic-stricken. A piece of black wood, like the embers of an old fire, will cause almost any mule to shy. A bowlder of a certain shape was invariably regarded with distrust by one I used to ride. Rattlesnakes they hold in just abhorrence ; bears paralyze them with terror ; Indians they cannot be spurred to approach. This excessive timidity is the result of their social habits. A mule cannot bear to be left alone ; and although he knows he can go straight back from wherever you may take him, following the trail like a hound, yet he considers himself hopelessly lost and forlorn when he can no longer hear the bell. It is his use and habit to go with it. It means everything which makes life happy for him, and he will endure very much punishment before forsaking it. However, two or three travelling together all day by themselves, keep one another company and get along very well.

This attachment to the train, while it has been the salvation of many an outfit, becomes a great nuisance on the march. Mile after mile you plod along in the rear at a right-foot, left-foot, right-foot, left-foot jog, which in the course of seven or eight hours wears out muscles and patience. The sun beats down, the dust rises up, and your only entertainment is the cow-bell hung on the neck of the leader. The first hour you do not mind it much ; the second, it grows wearisome ; the third, painful, and you hold your ears to shut out the monotonous clangor ; the fourth hour you go crazy. All life centres about that tireless hammering and endless conning, till, in unison with the ceaseless copper-clatter of that ding-dong bell, your mind loses itself in

> " Hokey pokey winkey wang,
> Linkum lankum muscodang;
> The Injun swore that he would hang
> The man that couldn't keep warm."

You cannot get away from it. What is misery to you is melody to the mule; and if you try to ride him outside of the music of the bell, he may, perhaps, be made to go, but it will be in such a protesting, halting, lame and blind way, with such "uncertain steps and slow," turnings of reproachful eye and brayings of uplifted voice, that you will find it better to endure the evils of the pack-train than to attempt to escape from it. Of course, if you go clear away, out of sight and sound, the beast is obliged to content himself; but on the march this is not always pleasant or practicable.

But a diversion awaits. It is afternoon. Everybody is dozing. The distant line of trees which marks the day's destination is in sight, and the mules have been well-behaved all day. Plodding along in front of you at a rapid walk, very demurely, heads down, eyes half closed, ears monotonously wagging, you think they have forgotten all their pranks, abandoned all intentions of wickedness concocted in the restful leisure of the early morning, and you fall into admiring contemplation of their exceeding docility and sweetness. Meanwhile the aparejo and load of a certain little buckskin-hued Cayuse mule have been slipping backward, and he, knowing it, has made no sign, but has quietly wriggled and swelled himself until he has got far enough through the sinch to try his experiment. With the suddenness and agility of a grasshopper he now gives a tremendous leap toward one side, bucks high in the air a dozen times in as many seconds, dancing about and kicking, stands straight up on his hind-legs, and falls over backward; next he squirms rapidly through the loosened girths until he can bring his heels to bear, and kicks boxes, bags, and bundles until the saddle slips down over his legs and confines them like a handcuff. Then he rolls over and quietly nibbles the grass within reach, waiting, in the most exasperating unconcern, until you shall come and release him.

It will readily be understood that an Eastern man finds the tricks and treachery, lively heels, and diabolical disposition of the mule a constant check upon the enjoyment of Western work and wandering. The mule-packers are the most desperately profane men I have ever met;

they exhibit a real genius in "good mouth-filling oaths." Considering the vexation to which they are subjected, and which they must not otherwise retaliate, lest they should injure the precious endurance and carrying power upon which their lives depend, and which make mules far more valuable than horses for mountain service, it is not surprising. And though these strong and agile animals will stand for hours when the bridle-rein of one is merely thrown over the ear of his neighbor, under the delusion that they are securely fastened, they are very wise and cunning, and can doubtless talk among themselves; but it is an unfort-

CONTENTED VICTIMS OF A DELUSION.

unate fact that their wisdom is all exerted for wickedness, and their conversation used chiefly in plotting combined mischief. And it is my honest and serious opinion, founded upon much observation, that so long as any considerable numbers of mules are employed there, it is utterly useless for missionaries to go to the Rocky Mountains.

The last pipe smoked, the longest story heard out, such slumber follows as defies any ordinary disturbance to break in upon. With complete composure you sleep through a steady rain falling on the piece of canvas laid over your face, or in momentary expectation of being surprised by Indians. I have heard of a few camps in the old days having been run over by a stampede of buffaloes now and then; but this, fortunately, was rare. Now few worse interruptions of this sort occur to rest than the tramping among the sleepers of mules, in their attempt to make some felonious attack upon the edible portion of the cargo; and this only occurs where pasturage is scant. Once, camping near a Mexican pack-train of donkeys, we were thus greatly annoyed by those little brutes.

Now and then, on the plains, coyotes venture close to camp, and, if they are very hungry, even come to the fireside in search of meat, and perhaps attempt to gnaw the straps off the saddle or boots your weary head reclines upon. Foiled in this, they adjourn to a respectful distance and set up prolonged and lugubrious howls, which either keep you awake altogether or attune your dreams to some horrible theme. Perhaps I ought not to use the plural, since one coyote's voice is capable of noise enough to simulate a whole pack. No doubt it often happens that when a score seem howling in shrill concert there is really but a single wolf raining his quick-repeated and varied cries upon our unwilling ears. These small wolves are justly despised by all Western men; but the big gray wolves are a different matter.

While cougars and wolves and coyotes, and even Mexican *burros*, are rare infringers on the sacred privacy of your sleep, numerous " small deer" come to investigate the curious stranger who has stretched himself out in their domain. Rattlesnakes are extremely numerous over many parts of the West, and we used to fear that, with their love of warmth, they would seek the shelter of our bedding to escape the chill of the night; but I do not know of any such an unpleasant bedfellow having been found by any of the Survey people. I myself came pretty near to it, however, over on Cochetopa creek, in Colorado, one night, when I unwittingly spread my blankets over a small hole in the ground. I snoozed on, unmindful of danger; but when I moved my bed in the morning out from the hole crawled a huge rattler, whose door-way I had stopped up all night! He would better have stayed in, for big John of Oregon caught him by the tail and broke his stupid neck before he had time to throw himself into a coil of vantage for the strike.

If you camp in the woods you are certain of late visitors in the shape of mice and the ubiquitous and squeaky ground-squirrels, whose nocturnal rambles lead them all over your bed-covers; often, indeed, their rapid, sharp-toed little feet scud across your cheek, and their furry tails trail athwart the bridge of your nose, brushing the dew from your sealed eyelids. To the thousand insects rustling in the grass we never gave attention; and not even the most home-bred tender-foot ever *thought* of cotton in his ears! How thus could he hear all the pleasant, faint voices speaking through the night so close about him? Thoreau, writing from his camp on a sloping bank of the Merrimac, has well described the sounds of the night:

"With our heads so low in the grass, we heard the river whirling and sucking, and lapsing downward, kissing the shore as it went, sometimes rippling louder than usual, and again its mighty current making only a slight, limpid, trickling sound, as if our water-pail had sprung aleak and the water were flowing into the grass by our side. The wind, rustling the oaks and hazels, impressed us like a wakeful and inconsiderate person up at midnight, moving about, and putting things to rights, occasionally stirring up whole drawers full of leaves at a puff. There seemed to be a great haste and preparation throughout Nature, as for a distinguished visitor; all her aisles had to be swept in a night by a thousand hand-maidens, and a thousand pots to be boiled for the next day's feasting—such a whispering bustle, as if ten thousand fairies made their fingers fly, silently sewing at the new carpet with which the earth was to be clothed, and the new drapery which was to adorn the trees. And the wind would lull and die away, and we, like it, fell asleep again."

But I am dwelling too long upon this rare wakefulness in camp, rather than the ordinary and business-like repose of the night. One's sleep in the crisp air, after the fatigues of the hard day, is sound and serene. But the morning! Ah, that is the time that tries men's souls! In *this* land one would find it very unpleasantly cold to be with her when

"Jocund Day
Stands tiptoe on the misty mountain-top."

You awake at daylight a little chilly, re-adjust your blankets, and want again to sleep. The sun may pour forth from the "golden window of the east" and flood the world with limpid light; the stars may pale and the jet of the midnight sky be diluted to that deep and perfect morning blue into which you gaze to unmeasured depths; the air may become a pervading champagne, dry and delicate, every draught of which tingles the lungs and spurs the blood along the veins with joyous speed; the landscape may woo the eyes with airy undulations of prairie or snow-pointed pinnacles lifted sharply against the azure— yet sleep chains you. That very quality of the atmosphere which contributes to all this beauty and makes it so delicious to be awake makes it equally blessed to slumber. Lying there in the utterly open air,

15

breathing the pure elixir of the untainted mountains, you come to think even the confinement of a flapping tent oppressive, and the ventilation of a sheltering spruce-bough bad.

ICY ABLUTIONS.

This was practically the end of the trip.   There were several days of marching and work later than that before we reached Fort Hall and the Agency of the Bannock Indians, in Southern Idaho.   Thence, having separated from my companions, I went northward by stage to Montana, visiting Virginia City, Bozeman, Helena, and Fort Benton.   At the latter place a steamer was obtained by which I descended, in a seven days' voyage, the Upper Missouri to Bismarck, Dakota.   This was then the terminus of the Northern Pacific Railway, by which I journey to St. Paul, and so on along the magnificent route of the Chicago, Milwaukee, and St. Paul Railway to New York, and home.

INDEX.

INTERESTING BOOKS
FOR
HOME READING.

Carleton's Farm Ballads.
Farm Ballads. By WILL CARLETON. Illustrated. Square 8vo, Ornamental Cloth, $2 00; Gilt Edges, $2 50.

Carleton's Farm Legends.
Farm Legends. By WILL CARLETON. Illustrated. Square 8vo, Ornamental Cloth, $2 00; Gilt Edges, $2 50.

Carleton's Young Folks' Centennial Rhymes.
Young Folks' Centennial Rhymes. By WILL CARLETON. Illustrated. Post 8vo, Cloth, $1 50.

Harper's Cyclopædia of British and American Poetry.
Harper's Cyclopædia of British and American Poetry. Edited by EPES SARGENT. Large 8vo, nearly one thousand pages, $4 50.

Tennyson's Poetical Works.
The Poetical Works of ALFRED TENNYSON, Poet-Laureate. Complete Edition, with *The Idyls of the King* arranged in order. With numerous Illustrations and Three Characteristic Portraits. 8vo, Paper, $1 00; Cloth, $1 50.

Tennyson's Songs, with Music.
Songs from the Published Writings of Alfred Tennyson. Set to Music by various Composers. Edited by W. G. CUSINS. With Portrait and Original Illustrations by Winslow Homer, C. S. Reinhart, A. Fredericks, and Jessie Curtis. Royal 4to, Cloth, Gilt Edges, $5 00.

Tennyson's Lover's Tale.
The Lover's Tale. A Poem. By ALFRED TENNYSON, Poet-Laureate. 32mo, Paper, 10 cents; Cloth, 25 cents.

Shakspere: A Critical Study of his Mind and Art.
By EDWARD DOWDEN, LL.D., Professor of English Literature in the University of Dublin, Vice-President of "The New Shakspere Society." 12mo, Cloth, $1 75.

Coleridge's Ancient Mariner. Illustrated by Doré.
The Rime of the Ancient Mariner. By SAMUEL TAYLOR COLERIDGE. Illustrated by GUSTAVE DORÉ. A Large and Sumptuous Volume. Folio, Cloth, $10 00.

Mahaffy's Greek Literature.
A History of Classical Greek Literature. By J. P. MAHAFFY. 2 vols., 12mo, Cloth, $4 00.

Rolfe's English Classics.

English Classics. Edited, with Notes, by W. J. ROLFE, A.M. Ill'd. Small 4to, Flexible Cloth, 56 cents per volume; Paper, 40 cents per volume.

SELECT POEMS OF GOLDSMITH.—SELECT POEMS OF THOMAS GRAY. SHAKESPEARE'S MERCHANT OF VENICE.—THE TEMPEST.—HENRY VIII.—JULIUS CÆSAR.—RICHARD II.—MACBETH.—MIDSUMMER NIGHT'S DREAM.—HENRY V.— KING JOHN.—AS YOU LIKE IT.—HENRY IV. Part I.—HENRY IV. Part II.— HAMLET.— MUCH ADO ABOUT NOTHING. — ROMEO AND JULIET. — OTHELLO.— TWELFTH NIGHT.—THE WINTER'S TALE.—RICHARD III.—KING LEAR.—TAMING OF THE SHREW.—CORIOLANUS.—ANTONY AND CLEOPATRA.—COMEDY OF ERRORS. —CYMBELINE.—MERRY WIVES OF WINDSOR.—ALL'S WELL THAT ENDS WELL.— MEASURE FOR MEASURE.—TWO GENTLEMEN OF VERONA.—LOVE'S LABOUR'S LOST. —TIMON OF ATHENS.—TROILUS AND CRESSIDA.

Cowper's Task.

The Task. A Poem in Six Books. By WILLIAM COWPER. 32mo, Paper, 20 cents; Cloth, 35 cents.

English's American Ballads.

American Ballads. By THOMAS DUNN ENGLISH, LL.D. 32mo, Paper, 25 cents; Cloth, 40 cents.

Our Children's Songs.

Our Children's Songs. Illustrated. 8vo, Ornamental Cover, $1 00.

Poets of the Nineteenth Century.

Poets of the Nineteenth Century. Selected and Edited by the Rev. ROBERT ARIS WILLMOTT. With English and American Additions, arranged by EVERT A. DUYCKINCK, Editor of "Cyclopædia of American Literature." Comprising Selections from the Greatest Authors of the Age. New and Enlarged Edition. Superbly Illustrated with 141 Engravings from Designs by the most Eminent Artists. In elegant small 4to form, printed on Superfine Tinted Paper, richly bound in Extra Cloth, Bevelled, Gilt Edges, $5 00; Half Calf, $5 50; Full Turkey Morocco, $9 00.

Shakspeare's Dramatic Works.

The Dramatic Works of William Shakspeare, with the Corrections and Illustrations of Dr. JOHNSON, G. STEEVENS, and others. Revised by ISAAC REED. Illustrated. 6 vols., Royal 12mo, Cloth, $9 00; Sheep, $11 40.

Shakspeare's Dramatic Works and Poems.

The Dramatic Works and Poems of William Shakspeare. With Notes, Original and Selected, and Introductory Remarks to each Play, by SAMUEL WELLER SINGER, F.S.A., and a Life of the Poet, by CHARLES SYMMONS, D.D. Illustrated. 1 vol., 8vo, Sheep, $4 00; 2 vols., 8vo, Cloth, $4 00; Sheep, $5 00; Half Calf, $8 50.

Ballads of Battle and Bravery.

Ballads of Battle and Bravery. Selected by W. G. M'CABE. 32mo, Paper, 25 cents; Cloth, 40 cents.

Halpine's (Miles O'Reilly) Poems.

The Poetical Works of CHARLES G. HALPINE (Miles O'Reilly). Consisting of Odes, Poems, Sonnets, Epics, and Lyrical Effusions which have not heretofore been collected together. With a Biographical Sketch and Explanatory Notes. Edited by ROBERT B. ROOSEVELT. Portrait on Steel. Post 8vo, Cloth, $2 50.

Bayne's Lessons from My Masters.

Lessons from My Masters: Carlyle, Tennyson, and Ruskin. By PETER BAYNE, M.A., LL.D. 12mo, Cloth, $1 75.

Osgood's American Leaves.

American Leaves: Familiar Notes of Thought and Life. By Rev. SAMUEL OSGOOD, D.D. 12mo, Cloth, $1 75.

Sir Walter Scott's Poems.

The Lay of the Last Minstrel.

32mo, Paper, 20 cents; Cloth, 35 cents.

The Lady of the Lake.

32mo, Paper, 25 cents; Cloth, 40 cents.

Marmion.

A Tale of Flodden Field. 32mo, Paper, 25 cents; Cloth, 40 cents.

Sheridan's Plays.

The Rivals and The School for Scandal. Comedies. By RICHARD BRINSLEY SHERIDAN. 32mo, Paper, 25 cents; Cloth, 40 cents.

The Book of Gold, and other Poems.

By J. T. TROWBRIDGE. Ill'd. 8vo, Ornamental Covers, Gilt Edges, $2 50.

The Poets and Poetry of Scotland:

From the Earliest to the Present Time. Comprising Characteristic Selections from the Works of the more Noteworthy Scottish Poets, with Biographical and Critical Notices. By JAMES GRANT WILSON. With Portraits on Steel. 2 vols., 8vo, Cloth, $10 00; Cloth, Gilt Edges, $11 00; Half Calf, $14 50; Full Morocco, $18 00.

Deshler's Afternoons with the Poets.

Afternoons with the Poets. By C. D. DESHLER. 16mo, Cloth, $1 75.

Songs of Our Youth.

Set to Music. By Miss MULOCK. Square 4to, Cloth, $2 50.

Sermons Out of Church.

By Miss MULOCK. 12mo, Cloth, $1 25.

King Arthur.

A Poem. By LORD LYTTON. 12mo, Cloth, $1 75.

English Men of Letters. Edited by John Morley.

(12mo, Cloth, 75 cents a volume.)

JOHNSON. By Leslie Stephen. —GIBBON. By J. C. Morison. —SCOTT. R. H. Hutton.—SHELLEY. By John Addington Symonds.—HUME. By Professor Huxley. —GOLDSMITH. By William Black—DEFOE. By William Minto. —BURNS. By Principal Shairp.—SPENSER. By Dean Church.—THACKERAY. By Anthony Trollope.—BURKE. By John Morley.—MILTON. By Mark Pattison.—SOUTHEY. By Edward Dowden.—CHAUCER. By Adolphus William Ward.—BUNYAN. By James Anthony Froude. — COWPER. By Goldwin Smith. — POPE. By Leslie Stephen.— BYRON. By John Nichol. — LOCKE. By Thomas Fowler. — WORDSWORTH. By F. W. H. Myers.—DRYDEN. By G. Saintsbury.—HAWTHORNE. By Henry James, Jr.—LANDOR. By Sidney Colvin.—DE QUINCEY. By David Masson.—LAMB. By Alfred Ainger.—BENTLEY. By R. C. Jebb.—DICKENS. By A. W. Ward.—GRAY By E. W. Gosse.—SWIFT. By Leslie Stephen.—STERNE. By H. D. Traill.

Cox's Why We Laugh.

Why We Laugh. By SAMUEL S. COX. 12mo, Cloth, $1 50.

Mason's Samuel Johnson.

Samuel Johnson: His Words and His Ways; What He said, What He did, and What Men Thought and Spoke Concerning Him. Edited by E. T. MASON. 12mo, Cloth, $1 50.

Bigelow's Bench and Bar.

Bench and Bar: a Complete Digest of the Wit, Humor, Asperities, and Amenities of the Law. New Edition, greatly Enlarged. By L. J. BIGELOW. Crown 8vo, Cloth, $2 00.

Egleston's Villages and Village Life.

Villages and Village Life, with Hints for their Improvement. By NATHANIEL HILLYER EGLESTON. Post 8vo, Cloth, $1 75.

Goldsmith's Poetical Works.

Poetical Works of Oliver Goldsmith. With Illustrations by C. W. Cope, A.R.A., Thomas Creswick, J. C. Horsley, R. Redgrave, A.R.A., and Frederick Tayler, Members of the Etching Club. With a Biographical Memoir, and Notes on the Poems. Edited by BOLTON CORNEY. 8vo, Cloth, Bevelled Boards, $3 00; Cloth, Gilt Edges, $3 75; Turkey Morocco, Gilt Edges, $7 50.

Goldsmith's Plays.

Goldsmith's Plays. 32mo, Paper, 25 cents; Cloth, 40 cents.

Goldsmith's Poems.

Goldsmith's Poems. 32mo, Paper, 20 cents; Cloth, 35 cents.

Friends Worth Knowing.

Glimpses of American Natural History. By ERNEST INGERSOLL. Illustrated. Square 16mo, Cloth, $1 00.

Symonds's Studies of the Greek Poets.

Studies of the Greek Poets. By JOHN ADDINGTON SYMONDS. Revised and Enlarged by the Author. In Two Volumes. Square 16mo, Cloth, $3 50.

Symonds's Sketches and Studies in Southern Europe.

Sketches and Studies in Southern Europe. By JOHN ADDINGTON SYMONDS. In Two Volumes. Post 8vo, Cloth, $4 00.

The Old House by the River.

The Old House by the River. By WILLIAM C. PRIME. 12mo, Cloth, $1 50.

Later Years.

Later Years. By WILLIAM C. PRIME. 12mo, Cloth, $1 50; Half Calf, $3 25.

I Go a-Fishing.

I Go a-Fishing. By WILLIAM C. PRIME. Crown 8vo, Cloth, $2 50; Half Calf, $4 50.

Under the Trees.

Under the Trees. By Rev. SAMUEL IRENÆUS PRIME, D.D. Crown 8vo, Cloth, $2 00.

Benjamin's Contemporary Art in Europe.

Contemporary Art in Europe. By S. G. W. BENJAMIN. Copiously Illustrated. 8vo, Cloth, Illuminated and Gilt, $3 50; Half Calf, $5 75.

Benjamin's Art in America.

Art in America. By S. G. W. BENJAMIN. Illustrated. 8vo, Cloth, Illuminated and Gilt, $4 00.

Benjamin's Atlantic Islands.

The Atlantic Islands as Resorts for Health and Pleasure. By S. G. W. BENJAMIN. Illustrated. 8vo, Cloth, $3 00.

Spofford's Art Decoration Applied to Furniture.

Art Decoration Applied to Furniture. By HARRIET PRESCOTT SPOFFORD. Illustrated. 8vo, Cloth, Illuminated and Gilt, $4 00; Half Calf, $6 25.

Art Education Applied to Industry.

Art Education Applied to Industry. By GEORGE WARD NICHOLS. Illustrated. Square 8vo, Cloth, Illuminated and Gilt, $4 00.

Pottery and Porcelain.

Pottery and Porcelain of All Times and Nations. With Tables of Factory and Artists' Marks, for the Use of Collectors. By WILLIAM C. PRIME, LL.D. Illustrated. 8vo, Cloth, Uncut Edges and Gilt Tops, $7 00; Half Calf, $9 25. (In a Box.)

Miss Young's Ceramic Art.

The Ceramic Art: a Compendium of the History and Manufacture of Pottery and Porcelain. By JENNIE J. YOUNG. 646 Illustrations. 8vo, Cloth, $5 00.

Swinton's Studies in English Literature.

Studies in English Literature: being Typical Selections of British and American Authorship, from Shakspeare to the Present Time; together with Definitions, Notes, Analyses, and Glossary, as an Aid to Systematic Literary Study. By WILLIAM SWINTON. With Portraits. Crown 8vo, Cloth, $1 75.

Gibson's Pastoral Days.

Pastoral Days; or, Memories of a New England Year. By W. HAMILTON GIBSON. Superbly Illustrated. 4to, Cloth, $7 50.

Reclus's History of a Mountain.

The History of a Mountain. By ELISÉE RECLUS. Illustrated. 12mo, Cloth, $1 25.

Reclus's Earth.

The Earth. A Descriptive History of the Phenomena of the Life of the Globe. By ELISÉE RECLUS. With 234 Maps and Illustrations, and 23 Page Maps printed in Colors. 8vo, Cloth, $5 00; Half Calf, $7 25.

Reclus's Ocean.

The Ocean, Atmosphere, and Life: being the Second Series of a Descriptive History of the Life of the Globe. By ELISÉE RECLUS. Profusely Illustrated. 8vo, Cloth, $6 00; Half Calf, $8 25.

Flammarion's Atmosphere.

The Atmosphere. By CAMILLE FLAMMARION. With 10 Chromo-Lithographs and 86 Woodcuts. 8vo, Cloth, $6 00; Half Calf, $8 25.

Homes Without Hands.

Homes without Hands: being a Description of the Habitations of Animals. By the Rev. J. G. WOOD, M.A., F.L.S. With about 140 Illustrations. 8vo, Cloth, $4 50; Sheep, $5 00; Roan, $5 00; Half Calf, $6 75.

Man and Beast, Here and Hereafter.

Man and Beast, Here and Hereafter. Illustrated by more than Three Hundred Original Anecdotes. By the Rev. J. G. WOOD, M.A., F.L.S. 8vo, Cloth, $1 50.

The Illustrated Natural History.

The Illustrated Natural History. By the Rev. J. G. WOOD, M.A., F.L.S. With 450 Engravings. 12mo, Cloth, $1 25.

Published by **HARPER & BROTHERS**, New York.

☞ HARPER & BROTHERS *will send any of the above works by mail, postage prepaid, to any part of the United States, on receipt of the price.*

2 —

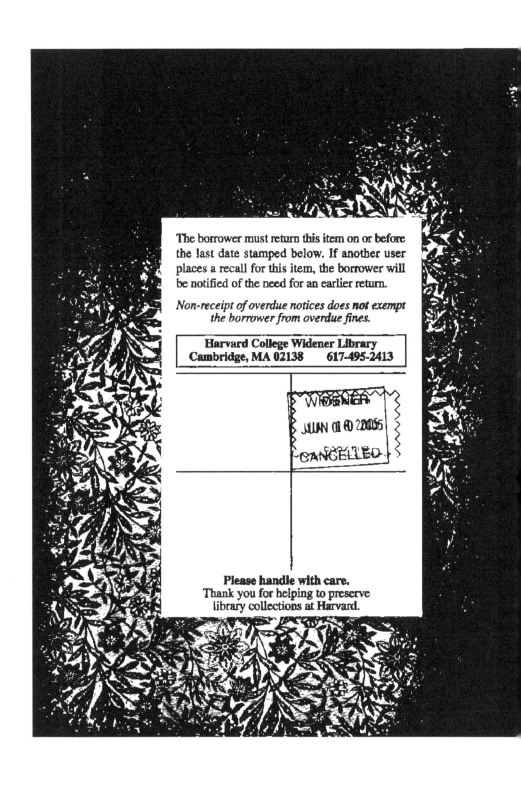

CPSIA information can be obtained
at www.ICGtesting.com
Printed in the USA
BVHW042012060820
585567BV00003B/109

9 780342 066179